Red Tree,
Faeries and Huma

Wendy Berg

SKYLIGHT PRESS

First published in Great Britain by Skylight Press,
210 Brooklyn Road, Cheltenham, Glos GL51 8EA

Designed and typeset by Rebsie Fairholm
Printed and bound in Great Britain

www.skylightpress.co.uk

ISBN 978-1-908011-06-0

CONTENTS

Foreword by Gareth Knight   5

Introduction
Of Elves and Men   7

Chapter One
Faeries at the Bottom of the Garden   16

Chapter Two
The Two Trees   31

Chapter Three
The Ship of Solomon: From Jerusalem to Avalon   38

Chapter Four
The PenDragon Dynasty: Faeries of the Stars and the Stones   45

Chapter Five
The Work of the Faery Priesthood   56

Chapter Six
Ygrainne, Merlin and Uther PenDragon   66

Chapter Seven
Gwenevere's Ancestry   73

Chapter Eight
Gwenevere's Abductions   85

Chapter Nine
The Ritual of the Knight of the Cart   99

Chapter Ten
Why Faeries marry Humans   115

Chapter Eleven
The Dolorous Blow: the Sword and the Stone   134

Chapter Twelve
The Dolorous Blow: the Blood and the Spear   147

Chapter Thirteen
Qui l'on en Sert?   164

Chapter Fourteen
A Guided Journey to the Ship of Solomon   185

Bibliography and Index   189

Contents

FOREWORD

As a life long student of the Arthurian tradition in its many aspects, scales fell from my eyes when I first came upon Wendy Berg's *Red Tree, White Tree* with its fascinating new light on the faery tradition. So much so, that I prevailed upon her to contribute the gist of her ideas as a long appendix to my edition of *The Arthurian Formula* by Dion Fortune and Margaret Lumley Brown (Thoth Publications, 2006) for I felt her contribution was at least on a par with the original material of these two great leaders of esoteric thought, and indeed in some respects a considerable advance on them.

So much, indeed, that it led to a new stimulus and direction to my own researches, resulting in *The Faery Gates of Avalon* (RJ Stewart Books, 2008) testing out some of her suggestions. This led me to conclude that certain of the ladies in the early Arthurian romances were no mere damsels in distress, but faery beings initiating knights into the mysteries of Faeryland.

All this stems from Wendy's startling conclusion that Queen Gwenevere herself was a faery. The suggestion has indeed been put forward by some respected academic scholars, in *Guinevere, A Study of her Abductions* (Turtle Press, 1951) by Professor K. G. T. Webster, and in *Lancelot and Guenevere* (Phaeton Press, 1970) by Professors T. P. Cross and W. A. Nitze. They attracted little notice in academic circles, but Wendy Berg throws the whole matter into high relief by her informed esoteric insight.

For she is not afraid to ask fundamental questions or to challenge facile assumptions. And many contradictions that we have come to take for granted about Gwenevere are rendered crystal clear when we realise that "her purpose within these stories is very simple: she is a Faery amongst humans, and the entire corpus of Arthurian legend revolves around this, and around her marriage to the human King Arthur. The relationship between human and Faery lies at the very core of the Arthurian stories. … Once this premise is accepted then so much else falls into place."

Nor does elucidation end here, for it leads on to an investigation of the real nature of the 'Grail question' and the origin, nature and destiny of the Grail Hallows themselves. "The Grail question is no longer the right question," she says, "and we need to move on. … The Grail Question no longer serves us, neither are we served by the answer: 'It serves the servants of creation', which serves only to send us round in circles upon a treadmill that sounds full of esoteric promise but gets us nowhere." There must be something more to be discovered.

This may well be found if we can answer the question *Why was the Faery race entrusted with the guardianship of the Grail Hallows?* for the Grail Castle to which all seekers of the Grail are led has all the hallmarks of a faery castle. And then, later, *Why were the Grail Hallows removed from Jerusalem?* – the answer being that they, with all other Faery weapons such as Arthur's sword Excalibur, were being returned from whence they came, once their cycle of use had been accomplished.

I leave it to Wendy to draw further startling but convincing conclusions that stem from all this, embracing the nature of the red blood and the white, and the identity of the mysterious brother of the Grail King. And advise you to tarry with me no longer but to embark upon the illuminating quest that the rest of this book represents.

Gareth Knight

INTRODUCTION
Of Elves and Men

I began to write this book after I had been handed a glass of red wine and a voice in my head said: "If you drink that, you'll die."

I do not usually hear voices in my head, nor was there anything wrong with the wine. But on this particular occasion I took serious note of what was happening since I was not at a party but in the middle of a magical ritual performance of something which lies at the very heart of the Western Mysteries: the story of Arthur and Gwenevere. It was Gwenevere who had spoken to me.

Any student of magic will know that to mediate these roles in a ritual setting is not something to be taken lightly. When something unexpected happens in the performance of a ritual, it must be noted carefully and dealt with in an appropriate manner. The forces which flow through any mythological characters are considerable, and especially so when they are deliberately invoked and enhanced in a ritual setting. But such forces are not necessarily well balanced, and indeed the very nature of the Arthurian mythology is such that the characters are *not* balanced, they are *not* perfect archetypes but embrace the totality of humankind with its weaknesses and failings as well as its strengths and triumphs. The characters of the Arthurian stories are very far removed from the Gods and Goddesses of ancient myth and legend, although there is inevitably a temptation to regard them as such.

The purpose behind this particular ritual was one which is referred to as 'the redemption of the archetypes.' Those responsible for writing and performing it were aware of the inherent imbalances within the Arthurian mythology and, within the carefully controlled dynamics of a ritual magic setting, were endeavouring to take a small step towards setting some of those matters straight by aligning them with the perfect pattern contained within the mind of God.

Although King Arthur and Queen Gwenevere together form the central axis around which much of our mythology revolves, there is a great deal about them, both as individuals, and in their partnership, which is not as it should be. For a start, their marriage is famous not for the manner in which it upholds the virtues of that honourable state but for the fact that Gwenevere, according to most versions of the legend, was having an affair with her husband's best friend Lancelot. The childless state of her marriage with Arthur suggests a possible cause of this unhappy situation, and as Gwenevere seems to have lacked authority as a Queen and to have been altogether a rather pale and characterless individual, perhaps it was not surprising that they ran into difficulties. At any rate, according to the legends, as time went on the originally powerful Court of Camelot with its noble company of the Knights of the Round Table became dispersed and weakened as one by one its knights disappeared in search of the Holy Grail, most of whom then spectacularly failed to find it. So far as Arthur himself is concerned, it seems that once he had fought his initial battles and established his kingdom he then tended to lose direction and fade from the story. His life and purpose lack any real climax, and this inevitably seems to originate from his unfulfilled relationship with Gwenevere. He dies ignominiously at the hand of Mordred who was probably his own ill-conceived son.

This puts things somewhat bluntly, but there can be no doubt that as a model of perfection Arthur and Gwenevere fall short. Whatever Merlin's grand designs had been when he brought about the conception of Arthur through magical means at Tintagel, and then so carefully guided him through his early days of his kingship, these do not seem to have been achieved.

Why should this matter? Well, it matters very much indeed, because it is through such characters as Arthur and Gwenevere and the Knights of the Round Table that the divinely inspired impulses from the spiritual worlds above us, and the foundation of the inner, deeper worlds which lie in the earth beneath us, are brought together. These forces are channelled into the collective unconsciousness of those who live and breathe upon this earth and who work out these spiritual impulses through their daily lives. This process happens whether we like it or not and whether we believe in it or not. It happens whether we regard Arthur and Gwenevere as fact or fiction, as historical or mythological, or even if we never think about them at all.

If the status and power of King Arthur appears to diminish towards the end of his reign, he nonetheless still shines beside his wife Gwenevere who appears to have been ineffectual right from the start. It would seem that the only noteworthy things she achieved as Queen were to have an affair with Lancelot and to get herself abducted by a variety of characters and with extraordinary frequency. Apart from these indiscretions, she is otherwise described in the conventional terms of the literature of the Middle Ages which heaps praise upon her as the fairest woman of the

British Isles but cannot disguise the fact that she didn't seem to have a tongue in her head or a purpose to her life.

It has always struck me, and, I think, many other readers and commentators of the Arthurian legends, how altogether unsatisfactory Gwenevere is. She just doesn't seem to be up to the job. Even allowing for the conventions of the time in which the majority of these legends were written in their present form (the late 12th and early 13th centuries) she remains a pale shadow. But why should this be so? The stories are full of well characterised women whose authority and purpose is supported by real strength of personality. One has only to bring to mind those such as Morgan le Fey, Kundrie, Luned, or the Lady of the Lake in her many manifestations, all of whom are strong females of distinct and consistent personality, each with a task to accomplish and seemingly beholden to no-one in the pursuit of their purpose. As the head of the kingdom alongside her husband King Arthur, Gwenevere should have been the most powerful, wise and eloquent of all these women. Yet we can form little impression of her as a distinct or consistent character and are left with the odd situation that the Ladies of the Lake are far more powerful: that it is they, rather than Gwenevere, who are the power behind the throne.

Another odd fact about Gwenevere is that her ancestry is virtually unknown. Who, for example, is Gwenevere's mother? Although the origins of the Arthurian mythology lie far beyond the mundane world, it is the way of every myth that it will attach, at various times and places, to actual and historical characters. It can be interesting and useful to link mythological characters with known historical places and persons, and the process can lead to many new insights. (Though there is always the danger that each researcher inevitably believes that the 'Arthur' he or she has discovered is the one and only Arthur and that all others are, by inference, not real.) But this makes it all the more curious that while potential King Arthurs have been found in abundance and shown to have been living simultaneously in Cornwall, Wales, Scotland and the Midlands during a period which spans several centuries, there is virtually no evidence of any link between Gwenevere and an actual physical location or historically recorded character.

There is no doubt that it would have benefited King Arthur, as with any King, to have married into the nobility in order to cement his claim to the throne. According to historians and mythographers such as Geoffrey of Monmouth and Thomas Malory he had to fight for his throne, and it would have been helpful to his cause if he could have married a bride who was well-endowed with land or who would have brought about an alliance with a neighbouring King. There was surely no dearth of contenders. But Gwenevere has a tenuous ancestry to say the least, and she brought with her neither land nor allegiance. In fact, her dowry seems to have consisted of a single piece of furniture – the Round Table.

Later versions of the story such as the Vulgate Cycle[1] suggest that her father was Leodegrance, King of a land called Cameliard or Lyonesse, although such a country will not be found on any map. Earlier versions make no mention at all of Gwenevere's origins. Yet the Celtic belief was that the right of succession was traced through the female line, and certainly Arthur's sister (or half-sister) Morgawse was not only a powerful Queen in her own right but her four sons, Gawain, Gareth, Gaheris and Agravaine each play a prominent role in the stories and were obviously possessed of considerable status and power.

It makes no sense, therefore, that Gwenevere apparently comes from nowhere. In the process by which myth earths itself into historical reality, the Arthurian stories are abundant with eligible women, and the consensus of silence on Gwenevere's ancestry is all the more puzzling.

Struggling to come to grips with the process of 'the redemption of the archetypes', I was puzzled as to what archetype Gwenevere actually represented. None of the conventional roles which she would be most likely to represent actually fit her at all comfortably. There is clearly a need to make her into something, and many have attempted to do so, but the process of matching Gwenevere with standard feminine roles is often little more than wishful thinking. We would like Gwenevere to be an archetypal Queen so we try to find ways in which the cloak of Sovereignty can be hung upon her, but we succeed only in mistaking the cloak for the figure beneath it. Gwenevere is no Sophia, nor is she a Goddess, nor a mother, and she is not even a very convincing human being.

But to attribute her with an archetypal weight which she doesn't have, or to assume that she has some sort of problem which needs to be solved, or to ignore her altogether, are all approaches which to my mind rather miss the point. If something of the real purpose and meaning of her presence within the stories can be discovered then surely a much fuller understanding of the Arthurian stories would result.

It is often said, particularly in regard to the stories of the quest for the Holy Grail, that it is essential to ask the right question. The results of Percivale's failure to ask the right question after he had witnessed the Procession of the Grail were extreme: the Grail Castle and all its inhabitants disappeared and it was a long time before he found them again. Once I had asked *who* Gwenevere was, the answer came very rapidly. She is neither an archetype, nor a Goddess, nor an ineffectual human being. *She is a Faery.*

That is to say, she has an objective reality of her own, Faery kind. She exists within that Faery reality and she comes from a Faery Kingdom which also has its own, objective reality. She has a real, Faery family. She cannot conform to human expectations of Queenliness because she is not human. The concept and expression of what is meant by 'Queen' in her own land is very different to our own. Her purpose within these stories is very simple: she is a Faery amongst humans, and a great deal of the entire corpus of the Arthurian and Grail legends is an exploration of the relationship between human and Faery. At the centre of this is Gwenevere's marriage with King Arthur.

Once this basic principle is accepted, so much else falls into place. To take but one example, the usual translation of the name Gwenevere is "White Shadow." This name does not, as is often assumed, indicate a pale or ineffectual or weak human but a *shining Faery*. It is an accurate description of her physical appearance to human eyes, and of how the white light of the Faery world shines bright and clear through the physical form which she and others of her kind must adopt if they are to exist within the human world.

The implications for the evolution of both the Faery and human races in the marriage between Arthur and Gwenevere are at once profound and disturbing. If we accept that Arthur, that manly symbol of heroic leadership within the world, was married to someone who was from a different and non-physical race of beings, then our concept of reality is severely threatened. While we can explain Gwenevere in human terms or confine her, along with the other representatives of her race in these stories to that vague never-never-land to which we tend to dispatch everything we cannot otherwise explain, 'the realm of the archetypes', then we have denied her reality and effectively side-stepped the challenge which she poses. If we believe that Arthur has objective reality then we must also believe the same of Gwenevere. And if we believe this, then we are challenged to take a new and very different look at the stories in which this couple are King and Queen, because their marriage bridges two different worlds of reality in a way which affects all those of both their worlds, human and Faery.

In the light of all this, the message of these stories becomes different indeed. The Faery world cannot be explained or understood in human terms, and to do so has been the source of much of the misunderstanding of Gwenevere's purpose. But if it is accepted that the Arthurian legends are the written record of an attempt to explore and heal the relationship between the two races which inhabit the earth, Faery and human, then a way forward from their apparent failure is revealed.

To look at the Arthurian legends from the Faery point of view is illuminating, if not always very comfortable. Humans in general and, it has to be said, King Arthur in particular, have a limited understanding of the Faery race who are often much closer to us than we might care to believe. But Gwenevere has made herself known to me as a loveable, endearing, characterful, curious and wonderful friend. The relationship between us has become one of mutual exploration in which boundaries are tested, realities probed and pomposities laughed at. We have reached an understanding of our differences that has developed into an acceptance which in turn has become creative and life-enhancing. The relationship between Faery and human, whether this is between the same or opposite sex (although the concept of 'sex' has limited relevance to the Faery world) has to be one of mutual trust and respect. The Faery partner can learn many things from humankind, not least a sense of boundary, but the human partner should beware of becoming entranced by Faery glamour. Nor must the human partner blunder heavy-footed into the fragile constructs of the Faery world, trailing clouds of worldly garbage. The Arthurian and Grail legends are littered with examples of just such inter-world pollution which bears only too close a resemblance to the junk-littered state of the planet Earth.

But the over-riding message, first from Gwenevere and then from others of her race who approached me as I began to write, was that something must be done to heal the division, misunderstanding and downright denial which presently exists between Faery and human, and it must be done urgently. One of the greatest fears of the Faery race is they will be forgotten. Their destiny in the progress of evolution depends to a considerable extent on the human race and, conversely, without the Faery race the human race will fall far short of all that it might be.

The gradual building of any one relationship between human and Faery, particularly when they are King and Queen, serves a much wider purpose than the purely personal. Any bridge of understanding is built in order that the path is easier for others to follow. It is my belief that this is what was intended in Gwenevere's period of stay within the human world as Arthur's wife, even though they achieved only a limited success. Yet the foundations which prepared the way for their union had been painstakingly laid through many centuries of magical endeavour, and much of that magical work is recorded, albeit in a disguised form, in the Arthurian and Grail legends. Within these legends is the record of the work of an Inner Priesthood who frequently appear as characters in the stories. Their actions are often inexplicable in terms of everyday behaviour, but are the memory of an ancient magic which so often was designed specifically to explore and heal the relationship between human and Faery.

If the stories of Arthur and Gwenevere, and of the Grail, were the only evidence available to us of the attempt to unite the races of human and Faery then we could easily overlook or dismiss them. But there are many other sources. A thread which runs through many early Irish, Welsh and Breton stories is that of the problems and the blessings of the relationship between the human race and the Faery race. Early descriptions of the Faery race can be found in the pages of the Irish tales of the Children of the Goddess Danu, the Faery race of the Tuatha dé Danaan. The Tuatha dé Danaan gave way to the human race of Milesians, and as the years passed the Faery race became less real to human perception. The process of their 'fading' was reflected in the gradually changing stories which continued to remember and record the events, but forgot their true origin. The Faeries became seen on the one hand as the imaginative invention of storytellers, or on the other hand were elevated to the status of Gods and Goddesses, neither of which is a realistic approach.

Another surprising source of material concerning the Faery race is the Bible, in particular the first two chapters of Genesis. Even more may be discovered in the Gnostic tracts and the works of the Apocrypha which, although contemporary to much that found its way into the Bible, were for various reasons excluded from the official version.

Another source of the earliest Faery history can be found in the writings of J.R.R. Tolkien. His work has always attracted an enthusiastic readership, and the recent film of his trilogy *The Lord of the Rings*[2] has attracted many millions. It is often said by enthusiasts of his work that part of its attraction is that it somehow seems to be real; it appears to be working at a deeper level than pure fantasy. And this is perfectly true: Tolkien's *Elves* are not creatures of the imagination but Faeries by another name. They are not tiny creatures who live under toadstools but tall and shining beings of great beauty, intelligence and wisdom who, it has to be said, often compare favourably with their human counterparts.[3] And so it is also with the Faery race. The power of Tolkien's work lies in the fact that he has not invented a fantastic or unreal story but that he used his imagination as the means by which he could remember some of the ancient history of our world when the human and Elven/Faery races walked the land together. *The Lord of the Rings* and its fore-runner *The Silmarillion*[4] describe their shared history, charting the relationship between them, and showing how the human race gradually gained supremacy.

The Arthurian and Grail legends continue that story. The names of the characters have changed but the story-matter remains the same, and although our natural tendency is to place Tolkien and the Arthurian legends into separate mental compartments, the very act of realisation that the same Faery race is described in both can in itself be illuminating. At the root of all this, both symbolically and actually, is the matter of blood. The blood of the human race is red, but the blood of the Faery race is white. It was for this reason that the Faery Gwenevere believed that if I, in my ritual representation of her character, drank red wine, she would die. At that actual moment the wine so strongly symbolised red, human blood that she believed that if she, through me, ritually consumed it then she would no longer be able to sustain her existence as a white-blooded Faery. It would have been like receiving a blood transfusion but of the wrong blood-group. Faeries' blood is of white star-fire, but humans have the red blood of Earth in their veins.

The story of the relationship between Faeries and humans reaches back almost beyond memory, but sufficient traces may be discovered to enable us to piece this history together. The Arthurian story as it has been written so far culminates in the relationship between Arthur and Gwenevere, but while this attempt to bridge the worlds may now be realised as only a partial success, it is for the present and future generations to understand and build upon their work. In order to look towards our future with the Faery race, and understand the implications that this has for the future of the planet we share with them, we must first understand our shared history.

One of the most striking symbols of Tolkien's Elven race is that of the White Tree, whose many offshoots reappear throughout his epic story as an enduring sign of hope and survival against the odds for the Elven race. The Red Tree of humanity is less well-documented, but it can be found in the legend of the Ship of Solomon that is explored later in this book. In the story of the Ship of Solomon, the joining of the Red and White Trees is brought about by the mediation of a third tree, the Green Tree of the Way of the Heart. The following pages are an exploration of how this Way can be followed by all who would like to understand more of the Faery race, and work with them towards a shared future.

1   The version used is *The Lancelot Grail Reader,* ed. Norris J. Lacy (New York: Garland Publishing, Inc. 2000)

2   J.R.R. Tolkien, *The Lord of the Rings* (London: George Allen and Unwin Ltd, 1954)

3   I am indebted to Gareth Knight, who first put forward this thesis in *The Magical World of the Inklings* (Shaftesbury: Element Books, 1990; reprinted in a revised edition by Skylight Press, 2010)

4   J.R.R. Tolkien, *The Silmarillion* (London: George Allen and Unwin Ltd, 1977)

CHAPTER ONE
Faeries at the Bottom of the Garden

Who are the Faeries?

I use the spelling 'Faery' rather than 'fairy' not because the former has any particular merit over the latter but to reflect the recent tendency to recognise a difference in meaning between the two words. When I refer to Faery, I am not referring to fairy stories in the sense of the imaginative tales often written for children about the tiny creatures of the natural world. Nor do I mean something that exists only in the imagination, although the imagination is one of the best means by which the Faery world can be contacted. By Faery I mean the race of beings, very like humans in some ways but in other ways very unlike, which inhabited the earth before the human race and which now exists in parallel with, but mostly invisible to, the human race.

This is not to say that Faeries are real and fairies are make-believe. Both are real, but it is important to understand the difference. The fairies' existence is closely linked to the natural, living, vegetable world. Flower-fairies, for example, have forms which are an almost inseparable part of the plant with which they are associated, and their shape, colour and distinctive vibration is closely attached to the life and form of that particular plant. By way of example one may quite easily, in a dreamy mood in the garden on a hot summer's afternoon, tune in to the fairy forms which can be found dancing about the nearby flowers. The sunflower fairy will be seen in golden yellow, not in larkspur blue or carnation pink. A lily-of-the-valley fairy will be perceived to be wearing the delicate whites and the fresh greens of spring, not the rich crimson of an autumnal chrysanthemum. The lives of the flower fairies are very much an extension and expression of the plant, and their life-energy is linked to the life of the flower. They are dancing, moving expressions of the spirit of the flower. A flower fairy cannot live for long when its flower has died.

Many other fairy creatures can be placed under the broad category of pixies or goblins, or any of the numerous other local names for these small beings. Like fairies, they are generally much smaller than humans and are associated with the living vegetation of the earth. Their lives are also closely linked with the natural, vegetative forms upon the planet although they are less ephemeral than the flower fairies. They are part of the planet's consciousness, an expression of the infinite varieties and moods and facets of the planetary being, and they have been upon the earth since it was created. Their evolution is therefore intrinsically linked to the planet's rhythms and any changes or development in them is as slow as that of the rocks themselves. A 21st century pixie is much the same a pixie of ten thousand years ago. There were goblins on the earth at the time when the dinosaurs were lumbering about. They are part of the fullness of expression of the planetary being and their purpose is fulfilled simply through their existence. Understandably, they hold little truck for the human race which to them is but a brief passing phase, a blink of the planetary eye in the cosmic year. They sometimes like to mimic humans, but generally speaking their attitude towards the human race is one of indifference.

There is a world of truth in the adage "I'll believe in you if you believe in me." Our everyday human perception, struggling to find something tangible which the concrete mind can latch on to, tends to invent or impose a definitive shape, form, or colour when these are lacking. When tiny beings such as fairies or goblins are closely associated with natural objects then a suitable form is readily suggested by that object. Fairies are not so fixed into form as are humans; their shape is fluid and changeable and they will appear differently to different people and at different times.

Nevertheless, fairies are an integral part of the Green World which is inhabited by elementals, fairies and Faeries. Another important point is that the Green World is inhabited by the birds and animals which are also a part of our human world, and because these creatures are visible to normal human sight they form the vital function of linking between the two worlds. The appearance of a white hart, or a black dog, or a raven, will often indicate the opening of the ways between the human and Green World, and those whose awareness is drawn to these creatures are alerted to the fact that the veil between the worlds is about to be lifted and may allow the seeker to pass through.

But by 'Faery' I refer to those beings of a form which is very close to human form and who lived on earth before humans emerged as a separate race. They are generally rather taller than human beings and their bodies shine with light and are fluid with colours not of the physical world or the visible spectrum. There are male Faeries and female Faeries, although the difference between the genders is not so pronounced as in humans and their method of reproduction is not linked to sexual organs. Their form is moderately fixed, in that they tend to adopt one expression of form throughout their very long lifetimes. This is partly a matter of our perception, but partly their own choice. They have great intelligence, deep wisdom, humour, and a well-developed understanding of the earth. They have an understanding of Deity and of the angelic and archangelic hierarchies which they share with humans. In fact it may be said that in their joy and harmonious sharing in creation they are much nearer to the angels than are we.

Faeries do not use speech in the same way as humans although their appreciation of the nature of sound and vibration is so much more developed than ours that their communication, through this means, is subtle and refined. Their speech is nearer to song, although their use of sound bears no similarity to the foursquare harmonies of Western music, but relies on infinite subtleties of tone and tiny shifts in vibration. And they do not need to use audible sound perceptible to human ears, but respond to far more subtle changes in vibration.

Their mode of living is closely attuned to the shifting qualities of light. They are not elemental creatures as such: their bodies contain air, fire and water but these elements are not the same as their earthly equivalents and it is more useful to think of them in terms of light: the light of air, the light of fire, and the light of water. They use and experience light much as we use and experience the physical elements. Colour, light and sound to the Faery race are all facets of one substance, so they will for instance experience the colour violet as one vibrating sound and the colour blue as another vibrating sound.

These concepts are better experienced rather than described, and the best way to do so is through the raised state of consciousness attained through meditation. Another approach to experiencing the state of being of the Faery race is to try to develop an awareness of synaesthesia: the ability to 'hear colour' or to 'see sound'. Those who naturally possess this ability find that without conscious effort their senses make unusual connections, and they will see a piece of music as a series of shapes, colours or physical sensations, or hear different colours as different sounds. But it is possible for many people to develop synaesthesia to a certain extent, particularly when meditating or day-dreaming, and to practice the technique is a sure way of approaching the state of being of the Faeries, for whom sound *is* colour and colour *is* sensation.

Faeries are intimately connected with the rhythms of the planet in ways that are beyond our perception, and they are much closer to the processes of creation than are humans. The earth is very much their concern, and they are intimately connected to it. Yet their approach to it and their relationship with it is very different to ours, and they see its changes in a way that is far less rooted in physical reality. Their consciousness is closely linked to earth but at the same time is attuned to the vast movements of the universe. If one imagines the changes in energy which are manifested when the tides of the great oceans rise and fall, then the Faeries are in like manner attuned to the inner tides: those of the planets, the sun, the moon and especially the stars. Because of their great age, Faeries hold within their consciousness the expression of many of the ages of the earth, and although they appreciate the broad differences between, say, the present Piscean Age and the former Age of Aries, the quality of each Age forms an equal part of their consciousness and is not lost to memory. Whereas humans tend to see things from a worm's eye view, and in small chunks, Faeries experience the much longer rhythms of the cosmic tides and the cyclic movements which take thousands of years to manifest their effect on earth.

One of the most important differences between the Faery and human races is that Faeries do not experience desire in any way that humans would generally recognise. They do not have the physical, sexual desire of humans, nor do they experience desire for anything but that which is an expression of the fullness of the light of God. The full spectrum of light contains qualities which, when unpolluted by any shadow of any kind, will only bring about the best possible good. One might say that God, light and love are three facets of the same thing, so that the fullest possible light is an expression of the fullest possible love, and this is God. Faeries' understanding of light is as far beyond our understanding as is their appreciation of colour and sound. There is as much distinction, to them, between violet and lavender as we would experience between the sound of a rock band and the sound of a harp. Vibration is the key to all.

It is not always appreciated that there is as much variety among the Faery kind as there is among human kind, and the same span of human consciousness and endeavour which produces priests, scientists, teachers and poets is also found within the Faery race, though they do not display any of the human tendency for abuse, whether of self, others or the planet.

An important point to bear in mind is that they are not as fond of humans as we would like to believe! Their attitude towards the human race is mixture of indifference, ignorance, dislike, curiosity and, from a minority, a genuine desire for understanding and synthesis born of an appreciation of our shared destinies upon earth. In fact much the same as our attitude towards them. The feelings humans may experience at the thought that we share our planet with another race of beings are also experienced by many of the Faeries, particularly as they got here first! But this book is concerned with the individuals of both races who are ready and willing to communicate with each other.

There are many ways in which the two races of Faery and human can interact, and there are a small number of Faeries who deliberately step down their rate of vibration in order to come closer to our world and to form a partnership with humans. It is with those who have found their way into recorded history such as Gwenevere, Arwen, Melusine and Étaín that we are particularly interested, because their actions were deliberately designed to bring about a closer relationship between the two races, and because we have recorded accounts of some of their work.

The major hurdle we must overcome when looking for ways in which to work co-operatively with the Faery race is always the hurdle of disbelief. Myth and legend suggest that the Faery race gradually disappeared underground or to another, remoter place after the arrival of humans, but this is not really so. It is the Earth, not the Faeries, that has changed in its rate of vibration. The Earth which we now inhabit and regard as the basis of our reality is not the same as the Earth which the Faeries originally inhabited.

The other important difference between the Faery race and the human race is that Faeries are immortal while the humans are born, die and (according to one's belief) are re-born. This is not to say that Faeries never die, for they do undergo a sort of 'fading' which comes through the stresses which any near-physical body in an imperfect world will experience. Although they are far purer in 'body' than the human race they are not perfect beings, and any less than perfect being will, in time, decay. In fact there are many signs that the Faery race is nearing the end of its viable form and that some sort of change is imminent, although this may well be in terms of many human life spans. There would appear to be a growing urgency for change amongst some of the Faeries, and to this end they are a good deal more forthcoming in their attempts to contact and work with the human race than has been the case for some time. Faeries may be immortal but they can't go on for ever! Because their existence is so closely bound up with that of the planet earth, the (relative) imminence of such changes is of great importance, and is also inextricably bound up with the current extreme and potentially catastrophic changes to the planet.

In order to understand these changes more fully it may be helpful to look at what happened when the earth underwent its last great change, usually referred to in Christian cultures as the Fall.[1]

The Fall is usually interpreted with the corollary 'from Grace'. The implication is that before the Fall there was no sin whereas after the Fall there was hardly anything else. But the term can better be understood in a more literal and un-emotive manner: it simply describes the time when the level of vibration of the Earth changed. The Fall has no direct connection with a departure from innocence into the ways of evil, but is a factual account of what happened at the point in the earth's evolution when it descended into a more dense state of physicality, which is when the Faery race gave way to the human race. This was not a fall from the grace and love of God but the process by which it descended from what is now its etheric level into the level of its present physicality.

Esoteric tradition gives a name to the Age which preceded the Fall, calling it the Age of Lemuria, which is said to have lasted from c.18,000–14,000 BC. The Age of Lemuria was the original Age of the Faeries; it was they, not humans, who inhabited the earth at that time.

However, it is not especially helpful to think of any of this purely in terms of linear time, because this makes Lemuria seem so long ago that the mind boggles when trying to get a grasp of its meaning. It is more helpful, and more accurate, to think of Lemuria as still existing but on the level of a less dense reality than that which we now inhabit, as if our present earth is rather like a ball which has dropped down out of the sunlight and landed with a thud. Something akin to the nature of this can be experienced when we lift our consciousness in meditation to the higher levels of the astral plane or beyond and are disturbed by the telephone: we return with a bump to the level of our normal physical reality. Another example can sometimes be experienced in the period between waking and sleeping when we begin to drift out of our bodies but suddenly fall back into them with a disconcerting jolt. This jolt is the equivalent of the Falling of the Earth from its previous state into its present condition. And like ourselves, it can also be raised up again, although this will take a little more effort. But it means that the condition of Lemuria, and of the Faery, Lemurian beings, is still accessible to us.

The gradual unfolding of the hierarchy and families of Faeries covers many thousands of years, although such divisions of time have only limited meaning in this context. Towards the end of the period of establishment of the Faery race the first human beings started to appear. The Age which succeeded the Faery Age of Lemuria was the Age of Atlantis, and it was during this Age that the Faeries gradually gave way to the human race, although the humans of this Age were not quite as they are now, and were very long-lived. As well as being more recent in terms of linear time, Atlantis is also nearer to us in vibration because it is denser than Lemuria. Because of the problems which faced the Atlanteans such as those of power, control over the planetary resources and the unfettered expression of human desires for that power and control which are only too familiar to us, the Age of Atlantis came to an abrupt and cataclysmic end.

The Faeries' state of being is sometimes thought to be synonymous with Paradise and the Garden of Eden, and a discussion of these very concepts, albeit in brief and somewhat obscure form, is found within the opening chapters of Genesis. Far from being a simple story of disobedience and punishment, the early chapters of Genesis deal with many of these topics, not least that of the Faery race.

Adam and Eve's initial state of existence within the Garden of Eden is pre-human *and* pre-Faery, although the account of what happened in the Garden is as compressed as the description of the seven days of creation. Up until the moment that Eve ate of the fruit of the Tree of Knowledge they were still in a pre-Lemurian state of existence, neither human nor Faery, but with the potential to become either. They represent the root race from which humans and Faeries evolved. At the moment at which they 'ate the fruit' and discovered that they had sexual organs they became human. Thus the Faery Age of Lemuria plays almost no part in Genesis which jumps straight from pre-Lemuria into the late Atlantean period not long before the Flood. Until that precise moment it was still possible for Adam and Eve to become either human or Faery. And there were certainly Faeries in the Garden of Eden, as the authors of Genesis well knew.

Genesis describes the precise time when the earth Fell in deceptively simple terms: "Unto Adam also, and to his wife, did the Lord God make coats of skins, and clothed them."[2] Our imagination readily conjures a picture of the hand of God reaching down and threading a needle with which to cobble together some pieces of leather that conveniently happened to be lying around, although this does raise the awkward question of how there could be dead animals in the Garden!

However, these coats of skins were not leather jerkins of the type popularly sported by Robin Hood, and Adam and Eve had in any case already made themselves aprons of fig leaves to cover their nakedness so there was little need for the Lord God to exercise his needlework skills. Nor can we really imagine that the Almighty was so concerned to save the embarrassment of Adam and Eve that he directly intervened in their lives to provide them with tunic and trousers. It has to be said that the Lord God of Genesis speaks and acts in a way that is far removed from any normal concept we have of the Supreme Deity. Whatever qualities one might bring to mind to describe God, qualities such as omnipotent, loving, transcendent, the almighty, the creator of the cosmos, then the God of Genesis (and indeed most of the Old Testament) does not possess any of them. If we take this verse of Genesis literally it becomes nonsense, yet clearly something of great significance is occurring at this moment.

The phrase "coats of skins" does not refer to clothes but to that moment in creation when the binding limitation of the physical body within its containing skin was first made real. It is this coat of skin which marks the essential difference between human and Faery. The edge of our human, physical body is defined by our skin. We know where we stop and where something else starts. Our skin forms the dividing line between 'in here' and 'out there'. Faeries do not have this definitive limitation to their form, and the creation of the limiting skin marked the first moment of the physicality of Adam and Eve. Up until this moment they, and the earth, were as the Faeries and their energy was closely intertwined with the fluid, elemental energies of their natural surroundings. But this first event upon the physical body of the Earth also denoted the first moment of linear time: the ticking of the clock of mortality of the human world which began when Eve picked the fruit of the tree of the knowledge of good and evil.

The Bible has more to say about this moment, although it is told so briefly that it is easily missed. We are familiar with the first tree, the so-called tree of good and evil. This is the tree referred to by the wise serpent when it suggested to Eve that she should take and eat its fruit. But we know that serpents don't talk, and must therefore ask who was this second presence in the Garden that so vehemently disagreed with 'God'. There was clearly a disagreement in high places as to the future state of the earth and its inhabitants, with God coming down on the side of the status quo and the serpent advocating change. Whatever final interpretation may be placed on these dissenting voices they are in essence the voices of the two opposing energies of change and stasis. The only problem is that the voice of stasis has habitually been ascribed to God and is therefore popularly assumed to be 'good', and the voice of change has been ascribed to the serpent who must therefore be 'evil'. In evolutionary terms, which is what this section of Genesis is all about, this is the wrong way round.

According to Genesis II, 16-18, God commands Adam (for Eve has not yet been created) "Of every tree of the garden thou mayest freely eat; But of the tree of the knowledge of good and evil, thou shalt not eat of it; for in the day that thou eatest thereof thou shalt surely die."

But this is not the whole truth, and the serpent makes sure to tell Adam and Eve what will really happen, not missing the opportunity to point out that God also knew what would really happen but had been economical with the truth. "And the serpent said unto the woman, Ye shall not surely die; For God doth know, that, in the day ye eat thereof, then your eyes shall be opened; and ye shall be as gods, knowing good and evil."[3] That is to say, at that moment they will know the difference between stasis and change, life and death, mortality and immortality, whereas up until that moment they had assumed that their condition was the only state of existence. As we know, Eve ate the fruit because she saw that it was "a tree to be desired to make one wise"[4] and she also gave some fruit to Adam, who ate what she gave him.

Genesis offers us several conflicting pieces of information about this tree, and inevitably each party interprets it according to their own ends. The Lord God says that if they so much as touch the tree they're dead. The serpent contradicts this, telling them that they won't die if they touch it, but they will undergo a change of state, and as a result they will understand the difference between 'good' and 'evil'. We tend to assume that before they ate the fruit they did not understand the difference, but Eve intuits that this change of state or consciousness will bring *wisdom*, and the possession of the quality of wisdom certainly brings the ability to distinguish between good and evil.

However, the essence of the situation is that the Earth has *already* changed: the seed of change has already long been planted, taken root, grown to maturity and borne fruit within the Garden. Even if Eve had not picked the fruit it would soon have fallen, died, and been reborn. Having picked it, Eve's next step has to be to eat it in order to 'take in' or understand the concept of Death for herself: the act of consuming the fruit becomes a consummation. Eating the fruit starts the clock of mortality ticking, and time, physical limitation and death begin at that moment. Adam and Eve descended into matter and, their bodies having acquired density and fixed form such that they must be contained in skin, they stepped out of Eden and down into the physical world which was waiting for them.

So much for the first tree, the Tree of Knowledge of Good and Evil which perhaps might more accurately be called the "tree which makes you human". It is often assumed that this is the end of the story, but God now makes reference to a *second tree*. His concern is that Adam, in his present human state of mortality, should not now experience the state of immortality that would be his if he ate the fruit of this second tree. "And the Lord God said, Behold, the man is become as one of us, to know good and evil: and now, *lest he put forth his hand, and take also of the tree of life, and eat, and live for ever*" ...[5] (My italics.) The sentence is incomplete; some vital words seem to have been omitted, but we have been told enough. God cannot be referring here to the first tree (the Tree of Knowledge) because Adam has already eaten from it. What, then, are the properties of this second Tree?

The second Tree in the Garden is fundamentally different to the first, but has equal relevance to these two first beings upon earth and indeed to all those who come after them. The first tree brings death, but the second tree brings immortality. The first tree symbolises the condition of humankind and the second tree symbolises the condition of Faery. There are two trees in the Garden of Eden: human, and Faery, and the symbolism is of vital importance. The problem that the Lord God was so anxious to avoid, and with good reason, was that Adam should have simultaneous access to two states of being, human *and* Faery. He could be one or the other, but not both at the same time.

Eating the fruit of the first tree means that Adam and Eve now have physical bodies, self-awareness and self-consciousness. In spite of their apparent fall they also have the knowledge and understanding that provides the potential for them to lift themselves upwards from their apparent fallen position. By knowing themselves, they also know the created world, and their 'below' has opened up into 'above'. They know who they are, what has happened to them, and what to do about it – except that it would appear that they do not know of the second tree, and not even the serpent points it out to them. As it is, the second tree is not mentioned again within the pages of the Bible, and if this were our only record of its existence it might well have been forgotten.

So far as the account offered by Genesis is concerned, there was no going back. The Lord God hastily removes Adam from the garden and makes sure that he can't ever return by setting Cherubim and a flaming sword at its entrance,[6] although this is not the punishment of popular belief but is simply to prevent him getting back in to eat from the Tree of Life. From now on Adam can only go forwards and take his first steps along the path of humanity.

But one more detail catches our eye just as we are about to leave the Garden of Eden. The Biblical account makes it quite clear that when God banishes Adam from the garden he does not banish Eve. Genesis III: 24 states, rather baldly but matter-of-factly: "So he drove out the man ..." We would expect to read: "So he drove *them* out ..." And we find the same words again in the next verse: "So he drove out the man ..."

Given the wholesale disappearance of the female from the early Biblical account of humankind, a censorship which may be attributed initially to Hebrew scribes but was thereafter universally adopted, one would have thought that there would have been an eagerness to record beyond any doubt whatsoever that Eve was driven from the Garden alongside her hapless husband. It had already been made clear enough that the ensuing woes of the world were all her fault in the first place for listening to the serpent and leading Adam astray. Yet we are told twice that only Adam was driven from the Garden, and while the Lord God expressed concern that Adam should be prevented from eating from the Tree of Life he did not seem to have had any such concerns about Eve; in fact he seems to have completely forgotten about her. The omission of Eve's name is very odd, and without wishing to tread in the mire of gender issues, it cannot just be dismissed as an oversight.

Can we assume that there was potential or actual difference between Adam and Eve's state of being within the physical world? The Faery Tree of Life was now denied to Adam, but the curious omission of Eve's name at this point hints that it may still have been available to her. If she was not banished from the garden nor even prevented from eating from the Faery Tree of Immortality, then in effect she was now also able to experience the Faery state of existence and to walk freely between the worlds. It is interesting to note that the great majority of Faeries who enter the human world are female Faeries. However, suffice it to say that from this moment on Adam, at least, is firmly and surely human, and the gate of return into the Immortal Clan of Faery is closed to him. The Bible makes no further mention of the Tree of Immortality and the Faery beings it represented.

However, the Tree of Immortality grew vigorously and persistently, and pushed through into the light and air in many unexpected places, and would not be forgotten. Those such as J.R.R. Tolkien, and the many authors of the Arthurian and Grail legends, and those who espoused the Gnostic or esoteric aspects of Christianity, all held the memory of this tree. These memories of the Faery Tree of Immortality and of what it represents express our yearning for something which seems to be lost forever. Not just for the state of innocence, but for a whole race of beings whose tree also grew in the Garden of Eden. Humankind turns its face to the stars and wonders what meaning lies there. This is not the same as a yearning for God; it is a yearning for the knowledge of our remote forebears. When we have found them then we know where we came from, and when we know where we came from we are better able to understand what we may become. Many mythologies offer an answer to the question "where do I come from?" Or if not an answer, at least an attempt at a definition of what we struggle to put into words.

One such attempt, in words which ring clear and true, is found in the few surviving lines of the Orphic tablets which date from many centuries BC. These tablets were small, thin sheets of gold which were placed in a tiny cylinder and hung upon a golden chain about the neck of the newly deceased. They were inscribed with instructions for the after-life which were expressly designed to help the discarnate souls to *remember* certain things which, in incarnation, had been erased from their memory. The soul at this point is stepping into an unknown region and needs a map and some clear directions in order to find its way back to the source.

The tablets indicate that once it had passed through the gates of death, the soul would encounter two Well-springs. The first of these should not be approached ...

> "Thou shalt find on the left of the House of Hades a Well-spring,
> And by the side thereof standing a white cypress.
> To this Well-spring approach not near."

But the second would offer the questing soul what it needed for its journey:

> "But thou shalt find another by the Lake of Memory,
> Cold water flowing forth, and there are Guardians before it.
> Say: "I am a child of Earth and of Starry Heaven;
> But my race is of Heaven (alone). This ye know yourselves.
> And lo I am parched with thirst and I perish. Give me quickly
> The cold water flowing forth from the Lake of Memory."
> And of themselves they will give thee to drink from the holy Well spring,
> And thereafter among the other Heroes thou shalt have Lordship...."[7]

The forbidden well is the Well of Forgetfulness. Incarnation in earth represents the state of Forgetfulness, and it is not appropriate for the soul to go that way. In incarnation, the veil between the worlds is closed, often mercifully, and we are not granted the memory of where we came from; it is often much better that we should not know of these things. But after dying to this world, many souls are ready to move on. Having encountered the Lake of Memory the soul is offered the chance to drink from its Well although, as always, it must first ask the right question. The question is prefaced by the statement that the soul has now come to realise what it might have forgotten whilst on earth: that it is not, after all, a child of earth. The soul that has reached this far knows that although it may for many life-times have been a child of earth and the starry heaven (i.e. it has passed through several periods of incarnation on earth separated by periods in the 'heaven' of the discarnate state), the race to which it belongs is that *of heaven alone.*[8] Having reached this place of understanding, it is then able to demand the information which it needs. The realisation that it lacks this information is felt with urgency, much as those parched with thirst desire a draught of cold water. The guardians of the well grant the request, and the soul is now free to move on and, ultimately, take its place among the heroes, those who have been previously known only through myth and legend as the race of the Gods.

This Inner-world landscape with its two Well-Springs is the Garden of Eden by another name, and the choice which confronts the questing soul is that which confronts all humans who retain some trace of memory of the Tree of Immortality. But let us take warning from the Guardians of the Well of Memory that these are not matters to be taken lightly, nor to be entered into in a spirit of mere speculation. These same concepts were the well-spring of visionary inspiration and creativity but also of profound discontent, to another who remembered the Faery Tree of Immortality, the poet William Sharp, who wrote at the turn of the 19th into the 20th century under the name of Fiona Macleod.

Amongst his many volumes of poetry and prose, perhaps his most well-known work is the prose-drama *The Immortal Hour*[9] which was later used by Rutland Boughton as the libretto for an opera of the same name. The story describes how Étaín, a Faery woman, finds herself within the human world. Although she knows she has come from a fairer place than that which now surrounds her, she has lost her memory and, unable to remember where she came from, becomes the unwilling partner in a human/Faery marriage.

William Sharp possessed strong memories of the Faery world, whose inhabitants he describes so clearly and so passionately that one cannot but conclude that he was not imagining but remembering. His work is infused with a spirit of Faery which rings clear and true, often to the extent that he appears to perceive the human world through the eyes of Faery and to experience its forms and colours with Faery sight. It may well be that 'Fiona Macleod' was his Faery partner, with whom he was living in as close contact as one may while in incarnation in a human body. If this is so, then it puts her alongside other Faery women such as

Gwenevere, Arwen and Melusine who each in their various ways found the means to enter and co-operate with the human world.

To read William Sharp's work can bring about real changes in consciousness and perception of those of the Faery race who share the planet with us. His desire to re-unite with his Faery origins fuelled an immense creativity but this was always tempered with a profound and relentless sense of loss and severance which could not be resolved while he was in incarnation.

In *The Secret Gate*[10] he describes his desire to return to the Faery world; not the Faery world of the imagination but the actual, real, pre-human Faery world. He can only return to this former state of existence by re-entering the Garden of Eden, and to do this he must pass through the barrier of the flaming sword wielded by the Cherubim, identified here as the Master of Hidden Fire.

> From out the dark of sleep I rose, on the wings of desire:
> "Give me the joy of sight," I cried, "O Master of Hidden Fire!"
> And a Voice said: *Wait*
> *Till you pass the Gate.*

The strength of his desire to regain what he knows he once had, but lost, speaks for itself. But we must remember that this is not the same as the desire to return to a 'Paradisal innocence' of some happy land where everything is sweetness and light and all problems disappear. This is the desire to return to a state of existence which was once his reality, the world of Faery which he knows can be found somewhere in the Garden of Eden. Perhaps the Lord God of Genesis may after all have had the welfare of the sons of Adam at heart when he attempted to make this return impossible. We can walk between the worlds if we are able, but it is not easy or comfortable to be in both worlds at once.

1   Looking towards the future, the anticipated change which is sometimes referred to as 'Ascension' will reverse the process of the Fall and the present physical body of the Earth will be taken up into the etheric.
2   *King James Bible*, Genesis III, 21
3   ibid, III, 4-5
4   ibid, III, 6
5   ibid, III, 22-24
6   ibid, III, 24

7   Quoted from Jane Harrison, *Prolegomena* (Cambridge University Press, 1903,
    reprinted USA Princetown University Press 1991) page 574
8   Tolkien suggests the same idea when he refers to the race of Men as the 'Guests',
    or 'Strangers', whose ultimate fate extends beyond the 'Circles of the World
    That Is'.
9   Fiona Macleod, *Poems and Dramas, Collected Works Vol VII*, arranged by Mrs
    William Sharp (London: William Heinemann, 1901)
10 ibid, page 289

CHAPTER TWO
The Two Trees

The Biblical account of the events in the Garden of Eden, rather than describing a fall from innocence into sin, describes the process by which the single pre-human, pre-Faery race separated into the two strains of human and Faery. Once this separation had occurred, the Bible records only the history of the human race. The Faery race and the Faery Tree of Immortality are not referred to again. Where, then, may we find the written history of the White Tree of Faery?

As we mentioned in the Introduction, its history may chiefly be found in the work of J.R.R. Tolkien, who drank freely at the Well of Memory. The Elves of Middle Earth are none other than the Faery race, and the term 'Elven' can be freely interchanged with 'Faery'. In fact the words Elf and Elven derive from a root that indicates 'shining' which is a perfect description of these light-filled beings.

When Tolkien describes how the race of Elves were born on earth long before the race of Men appeared he does not use the word Lemuria to describe their world, but there can be little doubt that his age of Elves is one and the same as the Lemurian age. Tolkien's first race of Men are of the age he calls Númenor, or Atalantë, which name, by accident or design corresponds to the age we generally refer to as Atlantean. His account of how the two races developed and intermingled over many thousands of years is astonishing for its detail, but over and above the fascination and enjoyment of reading his work is the message he offers us: that the destiny of the earth depends ultimately on the combined efforts of the Elven/Faery and human races to work together in harmony and understanding. This message tends to have become obscured by the more immediate concerns of the story of *The Lord of the Rings*, for although *The Fellowship of the Ring* saw Elves and Men working together to achieve the destruction of the One Ring this is but a small part of the larger picture as told in *The Silmarillion*.[1]

Briefly, Tolkien's history of the earliest days of Elves and Men is thus...

Tolkien calls the first Deity 'Ilúvatar', and describes how the world was brought into being through the medium of sound; the three 'great themes' sung by Ilúvatar. Tolkien's cosmology gives particular emphasis to the order of creation which corresponds to what we would now call the

Archangels, but which he calls the Valar. Excluding the evil Valar Melkor there are fourteen Valar, seven male and seven female, who between them govern the basic principles of the created universe. In the metaphor of the song of creation Ilúvatar's first theme is marred by a second, discordant theme which is not of his own making but introduced by the greatest of all the Valar, Melkor. Melkor creates a music designed purely for his own ends rather than as an harmonious contribution to Ilúvatar's song. After unsuccessfully attempting to include Melkor's discordant theme within the harmony of the greater music, Ilúvatar temporarily brings the entire song of creation to silence.

Eventually he creates a third great theme which is designed to reconcile the disharmony. The product of this third great theme is his creation of a race whose combined destiny and ultimate purpose will be to bring the discordant theme of Melkor into harmony with the greater harmony of creation. This race, collectively known as the Children of Ilúvatar, consists of Elves *and* Men.

Yet within this one race there are significant differences, and the difference between the two musics of Elves and Men is described with heart-breaking perception. The music of the Elves is beautiful, soft and deep, although tempered with a great sorrow which nevertheless is an intrinsic part of its beauty. The music of Men is loud and harsh, lacking in depth, lacking in harmony, and endlessly trumpeting upon the same limited tunes. Moreover, the music made by Men tries to drown out the music of the Elves by its violence. Eventually though, the best sounds that men are capable of producing are taken up into the music of the Elves and become part of its harmony.

Here in a nutshell is the history of the relationship between the Elves/Faeries and Men/humankind, and it is clear that Tolkien was under no illusions as to the comparative characters of the two races, nor to the aggressive ways in which Men would react to the Elves. Yet the problems which exist between them are clearly but a reflection of the conflict brought about by Melkor at a higher level, and which they have been specifically created to resolve. Optimistically, Tolkien predicts that at an unspecified time in the future some humans will find a way in which to lead the process by which the human race will become united with the Elven race. The inference is that when this has been achieved, the discordant and evil theme of Melkor will also thus become resolved into the harmony of one great theme.

Tolkien's vision is not at variance with the Biblical version of these earliest days of earth's history. Like the writers of Genesis, he suggests that Elves and Men are of the same root race, although according to *The Silmarillion* their appearance on earth is separated by many thousands of years. When the Earth was ready, Ilúvatar created the Elves, although the Earth they awoke to was not in its present form and was lit only by starlight. The Elves were especially loved by the Valar, and indeed some of them were so close in spirit to these Archangelic beings that soon after their creation they retreated into the heavenly worlds to live amongst the Valar. Of those who remained, it is the group of Elves known as the Silvan Elves who came closest to the human world, and the human perception of Faeries is for the most part based on our perception of the Silvan Elves. Those familiar with the films of *The Lord of the Rings* will probably be aware that Legolas, who features prominently in them, is one of the Silvan Elves.

While Ilúvatar describes the Earth as being created for both Elves and Men, he also says that he will give Men something new, a gift of freedom which is not possessed by the Elves. The nature of the gift is complex, and carries several important implications. The first is that Men will have free-will, whereas the Elves do not, and they will be able to create or direct their own lives and that of those about them even beyond even the bounds foreseen by Ilúvatar when he sang the three great themes. This partakes of the actions of Melkor, whose theme was born of his own wilfulness.

The second part of the gift given to men is that their destiny will ultimately have effect not only upon earth but far beyond it, that is to say beyond the confines of our solar system. This gift will often appear to be misused but, at the end, all that Men do will become absorbed into the greater harmony and to the glory of the One God Ilúvatar.

The third implication of the gift is that because of this freedom Men will only stay on earth for a short while before they depart, and as a result they will be known as the 'Guests' or 'Strangers'. This suggests that the Elves/Faeries, who have not been given the mixed blessing of the benefits of this especial gift, do not have free-will, nor will they ever be capable of creating anything which takes them outside the original plan of creation in the song of Ilúvatar. In addition, they will not be able to die or leave the Earth unless they are killed or die through sorrow. Thus it becomes clear that the Elves are almost entirely dependent on Men for the final working out of their destiny. They cannot leave the earth until Men, through the exercise of their free-will, bring about such changes to the Earth that the Elves are free to leave.

It is perhaps worth mentioning again here that the Faeries (or Elves) are still tied to the earth's etheric and astral body, though not its physical body. The Elves will be unable to leave the astral earth of their Lemurian world until even that has been taken up into the light of God. Although he does not use such terms as etheric or astral, Tolkien's vision of what constitutes the earth includes these higher and more subtle levels of reality. The ending of the earth he refers to is not, one hopes, the cataclysm of nuclear war or other manifestation of Armageddon but the happier possibility of the raising up of the earth from its present physicality into the status of an Ascended or Sacred planet.

While Tolkien makes it very clear that the role of the Elves is to bring great beauty into the world, and that they will experience a great bliss because of this ability, they are passive in their destiny. They rely on Men to achieve it on their behalf because Men have the gift of Death, and it is only this which will bring about the lasting change which will permit them to leave.

As was observed in Chapter One, there is a clear correlation between the condition of Men and the first tree of Eden, and between the Elves and the second tree of Eden. The first tree is the tree of mortality and death, the second is the tree of immortality. But whereas the Bible makes only brief mention of the second tree it is of great consequence in Tolkien's work and he gives it considerable attention. He attaches major importance to the whole concept of the Two Trees, elaborating on their symbolism and tracing their development down through the ages. In fact he presents the reader with their history from the moment of their creation, through the time in which they appeared in his interpretation of the Garden of Eden, then into the Lemurian and Atlantean ages and beyond. Tolkien's trees contain the living root of the Faery and human races from the very earliest of times. One is the Elven or Faery tree, and the other is the human tree, and each is intimately connected with the life and evolution of the race of beings they represent.

Tolkien names the Two Trees 'Telperion' and 'Laurelin'. Telperion was the elder, just as the Elves are the elder race. Its leaves were dark green above and shining silver beneath, and it bore silver flowers that deposited a dew of silver light. Laurelin was the younger tree, just as the race of Men is the younger. It had leaves of a brighter green which were edged with gold, and clusters of flame-yellow, horn-shaped flowers which deposited a golden rain on the ground. Its flowers gave warmth and light. Laurelin represents the Sun, the Solar Logos of the human race. Telperion represents the Moon and the stars, and was the White Tree, the Faery Tree of Immortality, the second tree of the Garden of Eden.

Elven destiny is intimately linked with the line of descent of trees from Telperion which, as a continuing symbol of what once had been, provides them with an enduring connection with the starlight into which they were born. Telperion was killed by Melkor, but the Valar Yavanna created another tree in its place. This second White Tree was called Galathilion, and it grew in the white-walled, crystal-staired city of Tirion in the stellar world of the Valar, at the foot of the tallest tower in the city.

In time, as this heavenly, stellar world inhabited by the Valar became further removed from the earthly world and because of their fear of Melkor, the Valar raised a barrier of high mountains to guard it, and set a string of enchanted islands, like a net, in the astral seas which lay to the East. Between the enchanted islands and the withdrawn world of the Valar lay a solitary island named Tol Eressëa. And this island, the 'Lonely Island', is the equivalent of the time and place we now call Lemuria. Like Tol Eressëa, it moves with the cycle of cosmic tides and according to our own perception and understanding. Sometimes near and sometimes far, its remoteness is not fixed in time or space, and we must pass through the protecting veil of the enchanted islands in order to reach it. Tol Eressëa is where the remotest promontory of physical land dissolves into the astral seas and where the furthest reaches of remembered time may still be touched upon in dream and meditation. It was on Tol Eressëa that Celeborn, the seedling of Galathilion, was planted. It symbolised the essence of the white walls and crystal stairways of the starry world of Tirion. To the Elves, born under the starlight before the sun and moon were created, this was home.

At the end of the Lemurian Age, a seedling of Celeborn took root, and this seedling was called Nimloth, the White Tree of Númenor or Atlantis. The early Númenóreans looked back to Tol Eressëa as a time and place of great beauty and inspiration, and the connection between Elves and Men was at that time still close, and for the most part one of respect and harmony. However, like the age of Atlantis which it symbolised, in later years Nimloth was neglected. Its death was caused by the "Lord of the Rings", Sauron, who was thus instrumental in causing the final severance between the human inhabitants of Númenor and the Elves of Tol Eressëa. Happily, one of the Númenórians, Isildur, managed to take a fruit, which later bore a shoot and in its turn became another White Tree. Isildur was one of the few to survive the Flood which soon afterwards overtook Atlantean Númenor, and he and a few others escaped from its sinking lands upon a ship which took them into the world of Men: Middle Earth. He planted the White Tree in these mortal lands, where it and its descendants were known simply as the White Tree of Gondor. Even this White Tree of Gondor was also destroyed by Sauron, and others which stemmed from it also perished, such that at one point it was believed that the line of White Trees had come to an end and a dead stem known as The Withered Tree was all that remained.

With perfect symbolism, it was Aragorn and Gandalf who, when the Wars of the Rings had been brought to a close and Aragorn was crowned King, discovered that a previously unknown sapling had survived. It is this White Tree which symbolises the continuing, tenuous, presence of the Elves into our own time. Through contact with this tree we are able to reach back to their time and place of birth beneath the starlight and through doing so, find our own source of being.

But Tolkien has more to say concerning the early relationship between humans and Elves which is of great significance. We have seen that he avers, like the writers of the Genesis, that although Elves and Men were originally of the same 'theme' or root race, at some very early point in their development their paths separated. But he describes how, at times, the races of Elves and Men not only came together through marriage but that some members of both races who had for many years intermingled through mixed marriages were eventually *given the choice* as to whether they would incarnate as Elves or humans. He calls those who lived in such close harmony with each other the 'Peredhil', a word which means 'Half-Elven'.

Tolkien particularly associates the term Peredhil with two Elves, Elros and Elrond. Elros chose to be human, and his heirs were the first Kings of Númenor or Atalantë. But the better known Elrond chose to be Elven, and played a more prominent role in Middle Earth where he was the guardian of one of the greatest Elven havens, Rivendell. He married Celebrian, the daughter of the Elven Galadriel, and it is their daughter, Arwen, who brings us very close to the heart of the matter of the union between the two races.

Arwen, as the daughter of two Elves, was of pure Elven blood. But her love for Aragorn prompted her to choose to remain in Middle Earth when the rest of her Elven kindred took to their ships and sailed West to the Undying Lands. The dilemma which faced Arwen is therefore the same dilemma that was posed to Adam and Eve. Although Arwen did not choose to be mortal she had to take on physicality in order to continue to live upon the physical earth. Mortality was the inescapable result of her decision to remain in Middle Earth: she had to change just as the Earth changed. It is very likely that there are still those of the Elven/Faery race who choose to 'miss the boat' which sails towards the Undying Lands of the West, aware of what they have left behind but mercifully able to die at the end of their allotted span. We are now very firmly in Tolkien's Fourth Age, the age of Men, but the option is still given to Elves to incarnate within the human world, and those who have chosen to do so will be acutely aware of the implications of their choice.

Tolkien's intuitively inspired re-membering of the early history of Elves and Men forms a vital background to the Arthurian and Grail legends. Let us now return to these legends in the light of what we have learnt from his vision.

1   J.R.R. Tolkien, *The Silmarillion* (London: Allen and Unwin, 1977)

CHAPTER THREE
From Jerusalem to Avalon: The Ship of Solomon

At the heart of the Arthurian and Grail legends lies an Inner Plane Temple devoted to the Mysteries of the unity of the Faery and human races. This Temple no longer exists on the physical plane, but the work of its Priesthood informs and inspires the stories of Arthur, Gwenevere, the Court of the Round Table and the Quest for the Holy Grail.

It is described in detail in the legend of *The Ship of Solomon*, a story which can be found in Malory's *Morte D'Arthur*[1] and in the Vulgate Cycle.[2] It is not well-known, and its symbolism remains obscure until it is properly understood as the description of a Temple of the Western Mysteries devoted to furthering the unity of Faery and human. It is not a real ship made out of wood, nor an imaginary fantasy, but the memory of a Temple which now only exists on the Inner Planes of creation even though it may well once have had a physical counterpart. This is a Ship of the Priesthood, an Inner Temple inhabited by the initiates of men, women and Faeries who work between the worlds. The Bible makes no mention of its existence, but its survival within the Grail literature bears witness to a line of tradition which although excluded from Holy Writ, has like the White Tree survived against all odds.

The metaphor of a ship which travels through space and time is found in many mythologies, and it is certainly central to Tolkien's vision of the Westward journey of the Elves from Middle Earth into the Undying Lands. In essence, any such ship is a containing vessel which moves through the astral waters of the Inner worlds and safely carries its cargo of beings from one level of existence into another. It represents the 'egg' of the human or Faery aura in which the body, detached from its physical, earthly location, voyages out in perception and travels through the planes of creation. Usually some treasure is sought, and brought back home by the successful adventurer, although such bounty will consist of spiritual riches rather than actual gold. The purpose of the Ship of Solomon is to carry a vital treasure of the Western Mysteries from Jerusalem to the Inner island of Britain that we call Avalon, where it will be discovered by those who seek the Grail.

The Ship of Solomon was made by King Solomon and his Queen, Sheba, for one born of a different land: Galahad of the islands of Britain.

Yet its meaning is not reserved for this one man but has relevance for the whole of human and Faery kind, and the ship may be sailed in by all those who genuinely seek the meaning of these Mysteries of Faery and human. The objects placed within it are the keys to its Mystery.[3]

The story tells how King Solomon was troubled by a series of dreams and visions concerning the identity of the last man in his line of descent, and he was concerned to discover not only who that man would be, but how certain important secrets could be communicated to him. As a means to this end he therefore built the Ship, as a Temple, with particular care given to the manner and materials of its construction and to the choice of sacred artefacts placed within it. One might almost think of it as an Inner Plane time capsule. He was advised in this great undertaking by his Queen, Sheba, and the Ship was created largely through the direction and promptings of her inner vision. Although she is enshrined in tradition as the Queen of Ethiopia and mother of Menelik the first King of Ethiopia, her short marriage to Solomon was directed towards the achievement of certain important magical tasks. The time she spent with him ensured that a particular strand of his wisdom would be kept safe for future generations, but this wisdom was entirely different to that enshrined within the Temple of Jerusalem. The ancient tradition housed within the Temple of Jerusalem is espoused by many esoteric fraternities who still actively and ritually work within its symbolic framework of meaning. Much has been written upon the esoteric wisdom which was literally enshrined within its stones. But the Temple of the Ship of Solomon is devoted to the thread of Inner wisdom that belongs to the Faeries, from their genesis in the Garden of Eden to their future redeemer, Galahad.

Sheba's advice to Solomon was to build a ship out of wood which would not rot, even through the 2000 years which Solomon estimated to be the period of time before his last descendent would discover it. We should not take this instruction literally: it is not a boat in the normal ocean-going sense but a Temple whose form exists upon the astral planes and which can only be sailed through the means of the imagination.

She then told Solomon to remove the sword of his father David from the Jerusalem Temple and place it in the ship! In terms of esoteric symbolism the sword is of special significance and represents the true spiritual direction of the person who owns it. We have only to think of the significance attached to King Arthur's sword Excalibur to begin to understand what the sword of David might symbolise to the Hebrew race whose religious traditions and beliefs were enshrined in the very fabric of the Jerusalem Temple of King Solomon, where the Ark of the Covenant was permanently housed. Within the Temple, King David's sword was the symbol of that very spiritual impulse and of the hopes and aspirations of the nation to whom it belonged. To take it from the Temple and put it somewhere else can only be an indication that some of the working out of this particular spiritual impulse had to take place elsewhere.

More precisely, the Queen told Solomon to take the *blade* of the sword only, that is, to separate it from the pommel, hilt and scabbard which were presumably to be left in the Temple. It is the blade which represents the spiritual impulse; the pommel and hilt are the means by which the bearer of the sword 'gets a grip' on it in order to wield and express that destiny within the physical world.

But what can be the meaning of all this? If Solomon wanted to place his father David's sword in his Temple Ship, why break it in two? Why not just put the whole sword in? Comparison with another symbolically broken sword in *The Silmarillion* may be useful here. "The sword that was broken" in *The Silmarillion* was the sword Narsil, which translates from the Elven language as "sun and moon", and with an implied meaning of "red and white."[4] Its shards were kept at Rivendell, the Middle Earth Garden of Eden, until such time as it would be re-forged for Aragorn at the end of the Wars of the Ring. In its new form it was inscribed with signs which indicated the coming together of the Elven and human races: seven stars to represent the Elves, and the Sun and Moon to represent humankind. Thus Narsil originated in the Elven or Faery world but passed down into the human world where it became instrumental in the re-union of the two races. Solomon's actions suggest that the same might also hold true for King David's sword.

Solomon constructed a new pommel, using his knowledge of the properties of precious stones and the inherent properties of the mineral kingdom. He did so in such a way that although the new pommel was made of many different gemstones they were so finely joined together that they looked like one single stone which contained all the colours of earth. In the language of Qabala this stone represents the Kingdom, the physical earth, with all its properties and 'colours' melded into one complete wholeness. Magic indeed! But behind the symbolism is the sense that the blade was now joined to a representation of the *whole* earth and therefore the spiritual destiny of the complete sword was now linked to a greater purpose than before.

After Solomon and the Queen of Sheba had joined the naked blade of the sword to its new pommel and hilt, the Queen made a new belt for the sword. She made the belt from hemp, and King Solomon asked her why she had made it from such unworthy material. She replied that they had done as much as they were able at that time, and prophesied that the real belt would be made in the future by another. Her meaning seems to be that the final connection between the sword and its future owner could not be made at the present time, and in fact it was Dindrane, the sister of the Grail Knight Percivale, who would make the new belt. She called it "Memory of Blood."

When the work was completed, the sword was laid at the foot of a bed that had been constructed in the middle of the ship. Many other such 'beds' appear in Arthurian and Grail literature. They are not for sleeping in but are comparable to the sarcophagi of ancient Egyptian tradition upon which the initiate in the Mysteries would lie down and enter into meditation or trance. Such sarcophagi were an important part of the final stages of the initiate's training and many inner visions and tests would be set by this means. Any seeker of the Mysteries who discovers the Ship of Solomon upon the Inner Planes may lie upon this bed and receive the wisdom and challenges that will be offered to them.

Finally, King Solomon laid his own crown at the head of the bed to indicate the Innerworld line of Kingship. The crown was veiled in white silk to indicate that the future owner of the crown had not yet passed through the veil and descended into the world.

So the Ship of Solomon took shape as a Temple, though not built in bricks and mortar. It is a vessel that contains a Mystery; it houses precious artefacts that make a connection between our earliest times and the end of our present era. The newly made sword of David which will eventually be taken up by Galahad, contains the whole of human experience. Its pommel represents the physical earth, its hilt contains the memories of the earliest, pre-human times, and its blade represents a line of Inner wisdom that had passed down through the Hebrews but which would now take a very different path.

The Temple Ship having been prepared, the Queen then attached three spindles of wood to the bed. One spindle was white, and was joined to the middle of one side of the bed so that it stood upright. Opposite it, on the other side of the bed, was a red spindle. A third spindle was placed across the top of the first two so that it joined them together, and this spindle was green. These three pieces of wood had not been painted but displayed their inherent colour.

The story continues by describing the same events in the Garden of Eden that are found in the Book of Genesis, but with a number of significant differences. In the legend, as in Genesis, the serpent suggests to Eve that she should pick the fruit of the Tree. She does so, but some of the branch remained attached to the fruit. She offered the fruit to Adam, who took it and ate it, but the branch remained in Eve's hand. Up until that moment Adam and Eve were spiritual beings who could have lived for ever, but as a result of Eve's action they were expelled from the Garden. The branch that Eve still held, was green. Thinking that it would be a perpetual reminder of their loss, she stuck the branch into the ground. It took root and flourished, and in a short while grew into a large tree, but although the original branch had been green, the trunk, branches and leaves of its offspring were all *white.*

This White Tree became a sign to all Eve's descendants that their inheritance was not lost forever but would one day be recovered. They called it The Tree of Life, and it gave them such joy that they grew many more trees from this first tree by breaking off twigs and planting them in the ground. Each sapling retained the white colour of its parent. But when one day Adam and Eve "engaged in carnal union" as the story puts it, beneath the first White Tree, the human race was born. At this moment of the birth of the human race the White Tree turned green, and started to produce flowers and fruit. In fact all the saplings which came from the White Tree from that time on were green, although all those which had come into life before the physical union of Adam and Eve remained white.

Later, as also told in Genesis, Cain killed his brother Abel. At this moment the White Tree turned red, and from that time on none of the shoots taken from it survived. This is perhaps symbolic of the fact that brother had killed brother, but over and above this it represents the red blood of the new-born race of humankind which is spilt upon the earth in sacrifice, and of the death which is the 'gift' of humankind. Wounding, suffering and death are the human experience, whether this is through murder or accident, or through sacrifice either real or representational. The motif of blood, of drops of blood and the sacrificial and healing power which blood contains is one of the most persistent themes throughout the Arthurian and Grail legends.

The story of the Ship of Solomon contains considerably more detail about the Garden of Eden than that offered by Genesis. But in this version, there is only one Tree in the garden, which indicates that the writer was aware that human and Faery were both of one root race. The suggestion in Genesis that Eve was not banished from the Garden and was able to retain her link with the Faery Tree of Immortality is repeated, and much more strongly, in the story of the Ship of Solomon. Here, the White Tree and its descendants spring directly from the branch which Eve breaks from the First Tree and takes with her out of the Garden.

The three changes of colour displayed by the tree taken by Eve from the Garden provide a simple but memorable symbol. This tree was originally green, the colour of nature, to symbolise the verdant planet upon which these two races would live. The firstborn offspring of this tree was white, this being the colour of the Faery race, the Firstborn upon earth. In this story, the moment of Adam and Eve's first act of physical union is given far greater significance than in Genesis because it is this moment, rather than when they simply became aware of their nakedness, which marks the time when the human race came into being.

The offshoots of the White Tree remained white as a symbol that the Faery race now formed a separate line of growth. Each detached shoot contained life from the moment of its separation and survived and reproduced without the process of death or rebirth taking place, as does the Faery race. But the green tree generated by reproduction through flowers and fruit, death and rebirth, as does the human race.

When the White Tree turned red, no further shoots taken from it survived, in token of the fact that no new races or life-forms would come into being from then on. In fact the tree itself bore no flower or fruit from the moment of Abel's death. Yet all three trees survived and were still alive in the reign of King Solomon. When his Queen took cuttings from them in order to fashion the spindles that would be set in the bed, the red tree spilt drops of blood upon the ground.

The Ship of Solomon encapsulates, upon the Inner Planes, the vitality of the Mysteries of the Red and White blood conjoined by the green. It is the cross-piece of the green spindle which makes this a living Mystery, for although the two distinct blood-lines of Faery and human are represented it is the tree of green, the colour of the heart, which provides the continuing link between them. As Tolkien so clearly tells us, it is only when the two themes of the Faery and human races join together in harmony that the evil discordance brought into the world will be resolved. The Ship provides a vital link between the earliest Mysteries of the Faery and human races within the Garden, and the later development of these Mysteries within Avalon, for it takes them westwards out of the ancient cradle of civilisation and into the fertile ground of the Faery tradition of the British Isles.

But as with many such Innerworld Temples, a guard is set upon the entrance such that while the genuine seeker can gain entry the treasure hunter finds only what he or she deserves. The Vulgate Cycle[5] describes how, when it reached Avalon, the Ship was discovered by one named Varlan, a neighbouring King to Lambor, who was one of the early Grail Kings and father to the Grail King Pellehan. Varlan and Lambor fight a battle in which Varlan is defeated and all his men are killed. He flees to the coast, where he discovers the Ship of Solomon moored at the shore. He boards it, but ignores the Mystery of the bed and the spindles of wood and is attracted only by the Sword of David. He removes the sword from its scabbard and takes it back to land, where he uses it to strike Lambor on the helmet. The sword is so sharp that it not only cuts through the helmet but passes straight through Lambor and his horse in a single blow. As a result, two kingdoms are laid to waste. Varlan, having failed to take heed of the sword's supernatural powers, is so pleased with it that he decides that he might as well have the scabbard as well, and returns to the ship. He takes up the scabbard and re-sheathes the sword, but instantly falls down dead.

1   Thomas Malory, *Le Morte d'Arthur,* ed. Janet Cowen (London: Penguin Books, 1969)

2   ed. Norris J. Lacy, *The Lancelot-Grail Reader* (New York: Garland Publishing Inc, 2000) pages 335-351

3   We cannot help but note the similarity between the names of Galahad of the Arthurian legends and Tolkien's Gil-Galad who was one of the most famous of the Elven Kings and also the last of his line of descent. He was the last Elven King upon Middle Earth and he led the "Last Alliance" of Elves and Men. So too will it be with Galahad.

4   All translations from Elvish are from Robert Foster, *The Complete Guide to Middle Earth* (London: Unwin Paperbacks, 1978)

5   ed. Norris J. Lacy, *The Lancelot-Grail Reader* (New York: Garland Publishing Inc, 2000) pages 46-47

CHAPTER FOUR
The PenDragons:
Faeries of the Stars and the Stones

As we watch the Ship of Solomon sailing into the heart of British mythology with its precious cargo of the Mysteries of the White and Red Trees, a number of questions arise. What *are* the native myths and legends of the British Isles and why would King Solomon direct his Ship of the Mysteries towards them? These tiny islands at the Western edge of the European land mass have functioned for thousands of years as a bubbling cauldron of mythological ingredients thrown in by an endless succession of invaders. Unlike the ancient Egyptians, whose powerfully charged conservatism preserved the essence of their magic almost unchanged for thousands of years, the islands of Britain have been influenced in every which way, and in this rich and complex brew many of the original ingredients have sunk almost without trace.

Our monotheistic religion looks to Christ as the focus of our worship but we can search the Bible in vain for any clues as to the stories of our heroic ancestors who might have lain down the foundations of our Mysteries. Our magical and mythological yearnings might prompt us to search for memories of our Faery kindred immortalised in the starry constellations, but there would seem to be little record of our remote forebears amongst the Greek heroes and heroines who shine out in the night skies. The peoples of the Book (Christians, Hebrews and Muslims) share the same spiritual forefather in Abraham, but Abraham came down out of the mountainous regions of the Middle East, and these lie a very long way from our own lands. We possess only the faintest of memories of our first parents, our land's first mother and father, and their first offspring. The British Isles are peculiarly lacking in Gods and Goddesses!

There are several reasons for this. It may in part be attributed to the unfortunate habit of the Druids, those priests of early Celtic times, to avoid writing anything down. There can be no doubt that they possessed immense knowledge and wisdom and were heirs to a long and mighty tradition of esoteric practice. But for the most part we can only make inspired guesses as to what they actually knew or did. It may also be true to say that the British are not very good at being reverential. The concept of native Gods and Goddesses is treated with something akin to embarrassment even though we happily adopt those from other pantheons, whether Native American, Egyptian, Greek or Hebrew.

The problem with this is that it has had the effect of severing two of the important links between Faery and human. The first of these is the link is between the Gods and the earthly Temples which hold the incoming spiritual energies in a stable and lasting form. The Priesthood of these Temples construct forms and patterns, through the liturgy and ritual actions of religious and occult practice, in order to receive these energies and utilise them to inspire and inform humanity – patterns such as are found in the Ship of Solomon. Some of these ancient Temples are based on the Temples of Atlantis: the Temple of the Sun, and the earlier Temple of the Sea and the Stars that looks back to the work of the Temples of Lemuria. But the link between them and the starry Gods and Goddesses whom they once served is now tenuous indeed as far as the native tradition of the British Isles is concerned.

The second link is between these archetypal Temples and our own everyday lives and spiritual endeavours, and this link is also broken because we neither remember how these Temples worked nor recall the form of their rituals; we have forgotten the identity and nature of those who served within them. Yet it is within such Temples that our links with the Faery Priesthood were once maintained, particularly during the time when the race of Faeries was beginning to give way to the race of men. It is important that we rediscover the essence of these ancient Temples so that we may begin to align ourselves more closely with their work and remember their Faery Priesthood. And part of that remembering is to realise just how much of their work lies at the basis of the native tradition of the British Isles that is the foundation of the Arthurian and Grail mythology.

A good place to start is the body of literature which was recorded by the early Celtic scribes. Much of what they wrote was later to merge smoothly into the Arthurian legends and the stories which have come to be called The Matter of Britain, but much of it originates in a far earlier period of history. The legends of Arthur and Gwenevere, of Merlin the Magician and of the Round Table and its Knights are the record of our most ancient mythology even though at first sight they would appear to be too recent to have anything useful to say about what was happening in the Faery Temples of Atlantis or Lemuria. But, for example, in *The Mabinogion*,[1] a collection of early Brythonic Celtic tales, we can find much information that fills in the gaps of the early accounts of the relationship between human and Faery. In *The Mabinogion* we can trace some of the developing relationship, through the ages, of the Faery or Elven race of Lemuria, the Faery priesthood and the sacred Kings of Atlantis, and of the early human race. More importantly, we can also find faint traces of our first, stellar, father and mother, the lost God and Goddess of our islands. Once we have discovered them, we can come to a better understanding of the true purpose and roles of Arthur and Gwenevere, for their marriage was the culmination of long centuries of previous endeavour.

One of the earliest tales in *The Mabinogion* is the story of *Culhwch and Olwen*. The story opens with an account of an important and symbolic marriage which occurred long before Arthur and Gwenevere appeared upon the scene. The names of the couple in question are Cilydd and Goleuddydd. Goleuddydd is the daughter of Amlawdd Wledig, and Amlawdd Wledig was married to a woman whose name reveals the essence of the Faery race as revealed in Celtic mythology: she was called "Gwen", which means "White." Here, in Amlawdd and Gwen, are the very beginnings of the remote family whose progeny formed the stuff of our mythology. Here are the celestial mother and father of native British legend and our connection with the Faeries and with the stars.

The name Gwen or Wen which is so often used as a prefix in Celtic and Faery names is indicative of the pure white power of inspiration and creativity which surges up through any who are open to its energy, whatever their race or origin. This fountain of inspiration is that which empowers the creativity of poets and artists such as William Sharp and Tolkien. It is through its outpouring energy that the white fire of the stars can be contacted by the act of remembering which reconnects every spirit to its stellar origins, human or Faery.

This first, archetypal Gwen may be equated with the remote and ancient figure of the same name who appears in the Welsh Triads.[2] Triad 52 describes the mysterious Goddess Gwen PenDragon. "And one ... was three nights in prison in Caer Oeth and Anoeth, and three nights imprisoned by Gwen Pendragon, and three nights in an enchanted prison under the Stone of Echymeint. This Exalted Prisoner was Arthur."[3]

In this tantalisingly brief description is mapped out the same initiatory progression back to shared ancestral memory of the Faery race that we found in the Orphic Tablets. First, the 'imprisonment' of the soul within the confines of the physical world and the physical body. Then, the first step back towards the stars immediately following the death of the physical body, and the first recollection of stellar origins after drinking from the Well of Memory. Finally, the reconnection of the two, earthly body and stellar body, within the consciousness of the questing soul.

However, Triad 52 is not simply a description of what happens to the soul after death, but explains how the journey undertaken by an Initiate of the Mysteries to the stars and back again can be made *while still in incarnation*. This was, and still is, one of the most important initiatory processes of all Temples of the Mysteries, ancient and modern, and is therefore a vital record of the work of the Faery Priesthood that can be brought through into our current magical work.

The Triad begins by describing the first stage of the experience of ease and dis-ease which is found within the earthly prison of the Castles of Oeth and Anoeth. The names of these Castles may be translated as "Ease" and "Hardship" respectively, and it is said that they were composed of human bones. The prison is therefore the prison of the physical body, where the descriptions of "ease and hardship" or "joy and suffering" offer a pretty fair summing-up of the human experience of living on earth.

There follows a stage in which the questing soul begins to recollect something of its Faery/stellar origins, and in this instance the contact with the stars is made through the mediation of the stellar goddess Gwen PenDragon who acts as Initiator. While her name Gwen indicates that she is a stellar Goddess, 'PenDragon' narrows down the field of stars to one particular constellation, that of Draco the Dragon. More specifically, this Lady of the Stars can be found in the head of the Dragon, because "Pen" means "head." Her full title therefore is "White Head of the Dragon" and in the night sky she can be seen clearly in the three bright stars that form a triangle at the head of Draco: Eltanim, Juza and Alwaid. She represents the pure, stellar inspiration which empowered a race of Priest-Kings, the PenDragons, of whom the best remembered is Uther PenDragon the father of King Arthur. As the work of the PenDragons was seminal to the unfolding of the Arthurian mythos it comes as no surprise to learn at the end of the Triad that the "prisoner," the questing soul who undertakes this initiatory journey, is none other than King Arthur.

The empowerment by an inner, feminine source lies at the basis of the Celtic belief. Gwen PenDragon is not an Earth Goddess; she is not the Sovereignty or Innerworld Queen of the land such as the Queen of Avalon or the Lady of the Fountain (both of whom also appear in *The Mabinogion*) but a Star Goddess; the white, shining Mother of Faery who watches over the islands of Britain.

In his book *The Star Mirror*,[4] Mark Vidler describes the intimate and often literally mapped out connection between the earth and the stars. He demonstrates a series of isosceles triangles which proliferate in both the stellar constellations and in their corresponding terrestrial formations in prominent hills and mountains on the surface of the earth, world-wide. These patterns are delineated upon the imaginary grid formed by the lines of latitude and longitude which divide up the celestial and terrestrial spheres. Having noted that the three brightest stars of the head of the Dragon (the PenDragon) form an isosceles triangle in the celestial sphere, Vidler finds "... a marked correspondence between the head of Draco on the celestial sphere in AD 2000 and the position of the British Isles on the terrestrial sphere. When the dragon is bought down to Earth, the head sits neatly over these islands."

The correspondence is more than neat, it is positively astounding, for he demonstrates that the first of the three stars is now (c.AD 2000) passing vertically over Ben Nevis which is the highest point in Scotland and Great Britain; the second of the three stars is passing vertically over Mount Brandon which is the second highest point in the Irish Republic and the most extreme westerly mountain in Europe, and the third and brightest of the three stars, Eltanim, the eye of the dragon, is passing vertically over the unique and very distinctive man-made Silbury Hill near Avebury. Here are the white, Faery dragon of the stars and the corresponding red dragon of the earth literally marked out upon the land.

This same connection between stellar and terrestrial energy was manifested and utilised by the PenDragon Dynasty, sired by Amlawdd Wledig and Gwen PenDragon in the era preceding King Arthur. This dynasty of Priest-Kings was seminal to the unfolding destiny of the races of Faeries and humans, and the Arthurian mythos developed in large part from the patterns they laid down.

The third part of the initiatory sequence outlined in the Triad takes place under the Stone of Echymeint. We no longer know where or what this stone was, but the enchantment which it brought upon those who had reached this stage of the journey would have been brought about by the power which is produced when a terrestrial stone structure is deliberately built to mirror, collect and focus the energy of selected stars or constellations. Examples can be found in the numerous Bronze Age stone circles dotted about the land, many of which are aligned to particular stars. It would be reasonable to suggest that the Stone of Echymeint was deliberately built to harness the energy of Draco. The huge and complex structure of the Avebury stone circles (probably built around 2400 BC) with their long, serpent-like processional avenues and the mound of nearby Silbury Hill would certainly fit the bill.

This third stage of initiation can be described as the descent to the Innerworld. It is this stage which forges a true connection with the stars *and* necessitates the absorption of that experience within the consciousness of the initiate on earth. It is one thing to journey to the stars but quite another to bring them back to earth. The experience is of little use if it is not brought back down and made real in the physicality of the body and the conscious awareness of the initiate. The descent to the land's underworld also represents the descent to the experience and realisation of the stars *inside* the body, leading to the ultimate realisation that, at root, Faery and human are one. This realisation that the uttermost reaches of space are not only 'out there' but also 'in here' leads to the full experience of the human world *and* the simultaneous initiation into the world of Faery. When human and Faery beings are reunited in spirit, the way of return to the stars is made open to those who seek to follow. Little wonder that having experienced this triple initiation the prisoner is said to be Exalted!

But Gwen PenDragon is only one half of the cosmic equation. She is married to Amlawdd Wledig, although concepts such as husband and wife are rather misleading in this instance as they suggest something on the level of a modern marriage between two humans rather than the mating of two cosmic beings. "Amlawdd" may have the same root as the name "Hamlet"[5] who in other mythologies and most notably in his later appearance as the eponymous hero of Shakespeare's play, was traditionally associated with the mill-wheel of the turning Earth.[6]

In the marriage between the light of the stars and the mill-stone of the earth which forms the cosmic background to any union between Faery and human, the essential dynamic is that one is fixed and the other is moving. In astrological terms the result of this marriage is the precession of the equinoxes, so called because every two thousand six hundred years or so the Sun rises at the Spring equinox against the background of a new zodiacal sign. The phenomenon is caused by the tilt in the earth's axis which causes it to wobble in its slow spin about the sun. Each change in sign produces a subtle but profound effect upon the nature and quality of life on earth. The sun appears to be moving backwards through the twelve segments of the sky marked by the zodiacal constellations, hence our present 'backwards' movement from Pisces to Aquarius.

The paradox is that while it seems to us from our subjective and worm's eye view here on earth that we are standing upon the fixed point while the stars are moving backwards, the truth is that it is we who are moving away. We must remember that we can also, within our consciousness or imagination, swing the other way. Our perception of the Atlantean and Lemurian/Faery races and their 'time' is that they are moving ever further away and, convinced of this fallacy, we make it the more so by our belief.

"The time is out of joint. O cursed spite That ever I was born to set it right," says Hamlet in some despair at the seeming impossibility of his task. The rotten-ness which he detected in the state of Denmark was not, as he eventually realised, because his mother was behaving badly but because the turning of the mill appeared inexorably to be disjointing his conception of time. Our habitual perception of things from the perspective of linear time results in the gradual apparent removal of human kind from our stellar partners, our brothers and sisters of the Atlantean and Lemurian ages.

The problem is not Hamlet's alone: finding a way to re-connect with our forgotten ancestry is something which concerns more and more souls as the Earth hurtles forward into the New Age. But Hamlet's achievement was to find the way in which to re-align the dis-jointed time *within himself* by stepping out of the restrictive illusion of linear time symbolised by the turning wheel of the precession of the equinoxes. When he returns from his period of exile in Britain he has found a serenity in which these paradoxes are resolved. "If it be not now, it is to come – the readiness is all." He has passed through the stellar initiation, in which the nature of linear time is understood and its restrictions transcended; he now holds within himself the knowledge and understanding of the wholeness of all things.

At root we are all human *and* Faery: we are of the same root race and we hold the imprint of the Faery race within our own energy systems just as the Faeries hold the human blueprint within themselves. Faeries, like humans, also have seven major centres of energy, but these are not the same centres as the human centres. The Atlantean's root chakra, in the early days of their development, was the equivalent of our Sacral Chakra, which later moved down into what now forms our Root Chakra. This chakra did not become fully integrated in the Atlantean age, and the resulting increase in sexual energy and its typical manifestation in the polarised aspects of male and female was, quite literally, the root of their problems. This energy not only over-stimulated their Solar centre but also resulted in the neglect of their heart centre. These inner changes were externalised in the rift between the increasingly ego-driven Sun Temple and the deeper wisdom of their oceanic and stellar worship in the Temple of the Sea and Stars.

Faeries find the light of the physical Sun hard to tolerate and their primary connection is with the stars (of which the Sun is but one) although they are linked to our sun at an energetic level. They retain a very close connection with the stars, especially constellations such as Sirius, Lyra, Corona Borealis, Orion, and Cygnus.

So far as the sparse written records show, the title of PenDragon was taken only by Uther and his elder brother Ambrosius Aurelianus. Although King Arthur was Uther PenDragon's son, he was born many hundred years later. The answer to this apparent conundrum is revealed in the stars. The reign of the PenDragon Dynasty coincided with the era in which the Pole Star was not the present Polaris at the tip of the tail of the Little Bear, but Thuban, which lies in the constellation of Draco. The period in which the constellation of Draco contained the Pole Star spanned the 3rd Millennium BC, and it is to this period that the PenDragon Dynasty can therefore be ascribed. The constellation of the Little Bear with which Arthur is particularly associated was at one time considered to have been part of Draco, which originally had two wings. Draco now only has one wing: it has given birth to the Bear just as Uther PenDragon gave birth to Arthur. (It is interesting to note that the 3rd Millennium BC was also the time of the great pyramid builders of Egypt: Djoser, Khufu, Khafre and Menkaure; and, in the British Isles, was when the great megalithic structures such as Stonehenge and Avebury were built.)

During the era of the PenDragons in Britain the red and white blood of human and Faery was symbolised, quite naturally, by red and white dragons. The title PenDragon has an unquestionable ring of power to it and brings to mind many manifestations of dragon energy: the deep currents of the Earth's energy, the kundalini fire within the body and the white celestial fire of the constellation Draco. But it was the white blood of their starry PenDragon mother which ran in their veins, and if history has since relegated them to that time of mud and muddle called the Dark Ages, the truth is that these Priest-Kings were of a very different era.

During Uther PenDragon's reign, the Kingship was briefly snatched by a usurper of the name of Vortigern. Vortigern was not of the royal blood-line of the PenDragons and he was not fit to carry the burden of the spiritual impulse of that time. This is explained in Geoffrey of Monmouth's well-known account of Vortigern's tower and the two dragons which lay beneath its foundations, and offers an interesting description of the existing state of the relationship between human and Faery at that time.

Pressed on all sides by dissenters within the kingdom which he had recently usurped, Vortigern retreated to Snowdonia where he attempted to build a strong tower that would provide him with a place of refuge. The tower repeatedly fell down. Merlin, who was as alive and influential in the PenDragon era as in the later days of Arthur, advised him as to what lay at the root of his problem. He saw that the tower had been built over a pool, and that at the bottom of the pool were two great stones. Within each of the stones lay a sleeping dragon, one red, one white. When Vortigern dug beneath the crumbled ruins of his latest tower he found a deep pool of water just as Merlin had predicted. He had it drained, and the two stones, the dormant dragons, were revealed.

Dragons are energy. Their energy is the earth energy expressed in the ley lines which curve through the surface of the land, the kundalini energy of the human and Faery body, the DNA of the human and Faery body and the stellar energy of the sea of space. As with any energetic manifestation they will be perceived in various forms according to the needs and perceptions of the time, and the usual interpretation of these red and white dragons beneath the tower is that they symbolised the opposing factions of Celt and Saxon.

But the tower built by Vortigern represents his own attempt to forge a link between the earth and the stars, human and Faery. If he had been successful in his attempt he would have proved his ability to take on the spiritual destiny of that age. He would have achieved the balanced intertwining of the red and white dragon energies, human and Faery, like the intertwining of the strands of DNA, up and down through all the levels of his own body and the tower of his endeavours. The pool which lay beneath the tower was the mirror which, if this balance is achieved, exists between the terrestrial and earthly worlds. The Stone of Echymeint and the Castles of Oeth and Anoeth were both properly constructed Temples which correctly aligned the energies of earth and stars, but Vortigern was not successful. Having failed to achieve this balance and connection within himself, his tower fell.

Each of the two PenDragon brothers, Uther and the elder Ambrosius Aurelianus, were ascribed their own distinct part in bringing through the work of that era. The Norman writer Wace[7] describes the magical events which took place at the moment of Ambrosius's death. At the evening of his passing, a star, or perhaps a comet, appeared in the sky. Only one ray of light issued from this stellar body, which was very bright. From the ray of light came a flame which was shaped like a dragon, and from the dragon's mouth two rays of light shone. This makes an obvious link with the constellation of Draco and the Head of the Dragon. One ray of light was directed towards France where it reached as far as Mount St. Bernard in the South. The other shone to Ireland where it divided into seven distinct beams of light.

This prophetic sign is at the core of these Mysteries of red and white, human and Faery, earth and stars. These two countries have each kept alive the dragon's flame which elsewhere has become dim: the Faery race of the Tuatha dé Danaan in Ireland, and in France (more specifically the South of France) the priesthood of Christ and Mary Magdalene.

Immediately following the death of Ambrosius, Merlin asked for stones to be brought from Ireland to build a PenDragon 'cemetery': Stonehenge. He promised that it would last until the end of the world, and what he had in mind was of the same nature and function as the Stone of Echymeint, a construction which would become an earthly vessel of communication between the earth and the stars, human and Faery. Merlin moved the chosen stones by magical means, and they became the Temple in which the soul of Ambrosius Aurelianus could mediate in perpetuity the encircling dragon energies between the stars and the land. This King and his land are one, and the spirit of the King within his stone chamber remains as guardian, initiator, and holder of the pattern between the stars, vital to the earth, and those who inhabit the earth. The work of Aurelius PenDragon is of such importance, and it is a pity it is now barely remembered.

The passing of the era of the PenDragons marked the time of the final disappearance of the Faery/Elven race from the physical land. Many stories describe how the Faeries can now be found within the Earth, in the world inhabited by Ambrosius Aurelianus. Similar stories are told of various members of the Faery Tuatha dé Danaan who each retreated into their own designated Brugh following the appearance and gradual supremacy of the human race. Newgrange for example (*Brugh na Boyne*) houses the spirit of Oengus Óg who may be contacted at this place. The expression 'underworld' can be misleading because it gives the impression that the Faery race now literally lives beneath the surface of the earth. There is no doubt that the Earth's natural formations such as rounded hills, or its rocks and crystals, or the wells and springs which bubble up from its depths readily form *gateways* which access the Inner worlds now inhabited by Faeries, but they should not be confused with the Faeries' actual location, which is all around us but not upon the physical plane. 'Deeper' is really 'higher' in the sense of being less dense, less physical, vibrating at a higher level. 'Within the earth' refers to the stone temples which were constructed to maintain the connection on earth between Faery and human through our shared link with the stars. Thus Merlin's construction of Stonehenge as a tomb for Ambrosius Aurelianus functions as a gateway to the stars in just the same way as the Stone of Echymeint.

The building of these stellar-aligned temples coincided with the final separation between the Faery race and our present physical earth. Their purpose is to maintain the spirit of the Faery race within the earth and to enable us to communicate with them. Those who inhabit and empower these structures through their extended consciousness are members of the Faery Priesthood, and their work continues to this day in order to provide an opportunity for any who seek this initiation.

1   Trans. Lady Charlotte Guest, *The Mabinogion* (London: J.M. Dent and Sons Ltd, 1906)
2   Trans. R. Bromich, *Trioedd Ynys Prydein* (Cardiff: University of Wales Press, 1961)
3   Quoted from Caitlín Matthews, *Mabon and the Mysteries of Britain* (London: Arkana, 1987)
4   Mark Vidler, *The Star Mirror* (London: Thorsons, 1998) page 117ff
5   See Caitlín Matthews, *Arthur and the Sovereignty of Britain* (London: Arkana, 1989) page 263
6   For a discussion of this, see Giorgio de Santillana and Hertha von Dechend, *Hamlet's Mill* (Boston: Godine, 1977)
7   Wace and Lawman, *The Life of King Arthur,* trans. Judith Weiss and Rosamund Allen (London: J.M. Dent, Everyman Paperbacks, 1997)

CHAPTER FIVE
The work of the Faery Priesthood

Table 1 shows a family of fourteen siblings, the offspring of Gwen PenDragon and Amlawdd Wledig.

There is a great deal of underlying symbolism in the story of this 'family' of fourteen which has remained hidden for many years within the pages of early British mythology. It can only loosely be compared to a family in the modern sense of the word, but represents an Inner Plane group, a magical Order, whose essential purpose and identity remained intact throughout the PenDragon era which preceded the Arthurian era. It displays all the qualities of a true Inner Priesthood and the strength of its spiritual purpose and identity overrides its outward appearance.

The work of this Order stems from its stellar parents, Amlawdd and Gwen. Their fourteen children comprise the PenDragon Dynasty, Priest-Kings who looked back to the star-lit world of their ancestors and forward to the human age of Arthur, and whose task was to remember the patterns of Faery and bring them forward into the coming age. They were guided throughout their long period of rulership by the Atlantean priest Merlin, and they in turn guided the construction of ancient temples which would literally preserve in stone the link with the Faery race which was now fading fast from human memory.

In the order in which they appear in Table 1, the names of this family are Rhienlwydd, Ygrainne the mother of King Arthur, an un-named daughter, and Goleuddydd. Then there is another un-named daughter who married Custennin, the brother of Ysbaddaden the giant. Then comes Cynwal Hundred-Hogs who must surely have been a man! The significance of the hogs, or swine, will be explored later. Cynwal was the father of the beautiful Gwen Alarch whose name means White Swan. Next is Gwrfoddw Hen (Old Gwrfoddw) who was male, Tywanwedd who was female, and Gwyar, also female; then Llygadrudd Emys whose name means Red-Eyed Stallion. Finally there is a group of four Elves or Faeries whose identity is revealed by their Faery names: Gweir White-Spear-Shaft, Gweir Brave-Wicked, Gweir Servant-of-Birds and Gweir Silver-Brow. True to all Faery families their individual identity is less distinct than in humankind. The same phenomenon can be found, for example, in the stories of the 'true and false Gweneveres' which we shall look at more closely in a later chapter.

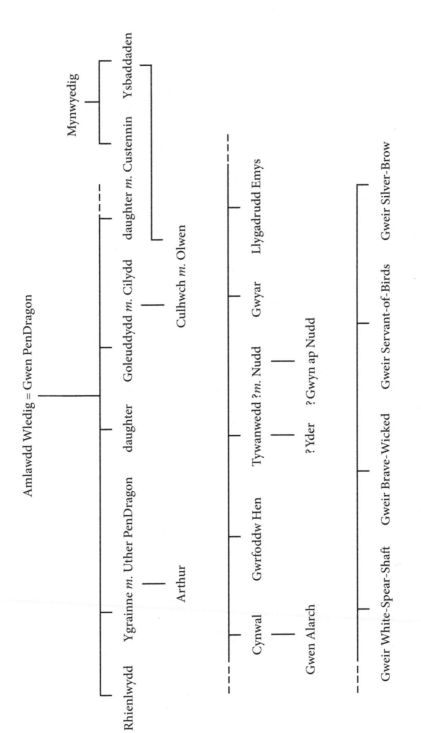

Table 1: The Children of Amlawdd Wledig and Gwen PenDragon

All told, here are seven females (of whom at least two as we shall discuss later are Atlantean Priestesses), three human males and four male Faeries! Here is a group of disparate beings who nevertheless existed as a united Faery and human Priesthood which provides us with some vital insights into the foundation upon which the later Arthurian impetus was built. Some of these figures are well-known, others less so, and some will probably always remain unknown. The names Cynwal and Gwrfoddw Hen tell us very little. For Llygadrudd Emys the Red-Eyed Stallion we can use our imagination to visualise the thundering hooves of such a creature, perhaps man, perhaps wild white horse, perhaps an animal akin to the red-eared white hounds belonging to the Faery King Gwyn ap Nudd that can sometimes be glimpsed through the mists on Glastonbury Tor.

A real clue to the nature of the work of this combined Priesthood of Faery, human and animal can be found in the story of Goleuddydd, one of the women of the family. She has more recently become overshadowed by her sister-Priestess Ygrainne the mother of King Arthur, but her work was very similar to that of her sister. Like Ygrainne, Goleuddydd incarnated within the physical world at this seminal time of change between Faery and human in order to bring about a successful mating between the two races. Her name translates as "Bright Day". Like Ygrainne, she functions upon many levels and reaches back into an age far beyond the early Celtic story in which her tale is briefly told. She appears only in the first few pages of *Culhwch and Olwen*, but this brief episode suggests something of her true status, for she is referred to as a Queen. She is married to a man named Cilydd, the son of Cyleddon Wledig.

We are told nothing more of her husband, but his name and his father's name 'Cyleddon' show that they were both of the area of Scotland once known as the Forest of Celidon, now better known as the Caledonian Forest. The geographical location of the Caledonian Forest is in the centre of the Southern Uplands of Scotland around the peak called Hart Fell. This is one of those magical locations which, like an iceberg, reveals some small manifestation within the physical world, yet much more remains hidden in the astral waters beneath the surface of reality. Many of the magical locations within the British Isles – as indeed of all lands – are the outer manifestations of ancient Inner-world temples, and the work of this Priesthood was especially linked with this physical location, along with the better-known sites of Stonehenge and Tintagel.

Although these temples may have some physical counterpart it is the Priesthood attached to them which gives them their particular identity, and the particular work of each group of the Priesthood will influence the especial atmosphere of that site. This is something that can be picked up by anyone who has a little psychic intuition or the willingness to still the conscious mind and tune in. Tintagel, physical location of the conception of Arthur through Merlin's magic, is still very much a place where things are initiated. The Forest of Celidon was also closely linked with the work of the arch-mage of Britain, but at an earlier stage of development of these Mysteries. It was in this forest that Merlin lived during his period of madness and isolation and where he was eventually joined by his sister Gwenddydd who built him a Star Temple.[1] It is to this same forest Temple that Tristan and Isolde eloped in order to escape the attentions of King Mark of Cornwall.[2]

The mating of Goleuddydd and Cilydd attracted great attention and held no little significance for the population at large, for, as the story tells us, the whole country prayed that they should have a child. But once Goleuddydd was pregnant she became 'mad' and, refusing to go indoors, wandered in Celyddon forest just as had Merlin before her. Indeed her madness may well be a metaphor for an Innerworld journey initiated by Merlin himself. "From the time of her pregnancy Goleuddydd became wild, and wandered about, without habitation; but when her delivery was at hand, her reason came back to her. Then she went to a mountain where there was a swineherd, keeping a herd of swine. And through fear of the swine the queen was delivered. And the swineherd took the boy, and brought him to the palace …"[3]

Merlin appears to us in several distinct forms. He is the High Priest of Atlantis who inspires the folk soul of these islands from the Inner Planes, but he is also the *Merlin Silvestris* who incarnated within the world and experienced the initiation of the nadir. As we have seen, his influence was of major importance in the setting down of the patterns of energy between the stars and the stones during the PenDragon era in order that the memory of the stars and the Faery races remained within the land long after its human inhabitants had forgotten them. But in this later period he spent much time in Celyddon Forest talking to his pet pig!

There is rather more to this than meets the eye of course, just as there is also to Goleuddydd's experience immediately preceding the birth of her child, for the pig is the totem animal of the Celtic White Goddess, Ceridwen. Ceridwen's bubbling cauldron symbolises the vessel of the cosmos, and its depths contain the primal matter of creation. Through her totem of the sow she provides the spiritual nourishment of the milk of the stars to all those who come under her aegis. The presence of the Swineherd at the birth of Goleuddydd's son is therefore not an indication that she chose to give birth in a pigsty although of course this event is not without its parallel. The term 'Swineherd' indicates the presence of a Priest of the Great White Goddess, and reveals that Goleuddydd was attended at the birth of her son by a Priest of these Mysteries who may well have been Merlin himself.

Having safely given birth under the proper magical conditions, Goleuddydd was then free to return to her normal life. In fact, soon after the birth of her son she died to this world. But this is not the end of her story because shortly before her death she told her husband that he should not marry again until a two-headed thorn tree grew upon her grave. This odd stricture or *geasa* tells us more about Goleuddydd, because the Faery hawthorn tree is a marker of places where the veil between the worlds is thin, and where an entrance to the Faery world is likely to be found. As the hawthorn tree has two distinct varieties that flower red and white, this then becomes an evocative symbol of the Priestess who lay beneath it. Here again is the distinction between the white Faery blood of the stars and the red human blood of the earth, and we can readily see the hawthorn tree as a descendant of the Red and White Trees of Edenic mythology. Goleuddydd is a Priestess of the Faery race who adopts human form in order to bring about the birth of one who will lead others in the quest to unite those two worlds. Like her sister Ygrainne, her work is achieved by bringing about the birth of a child who is half Faery, half human. And although it was Ygrainne's child Arthur who achieved the greater fame it might be argued that it was Goleuddydd's child Culhwch who was the more successful in achieving his destined task.

Seven years elapsed before Cilydd found the two-headed thorn growing on Goleuddydd's grave, at which time he was free to re-marry according to Goleuddydd's *geasa*. But as soon as his future wife learnt of Culhwch's existence she put a new *geasa* on him to the effect that he would never find a wife until he won Olwen, the daughter of Ysbaddaden the giant. When it is the will of the gods that one person alone must achieve a certain task at a certain time then a stricture or binding must be put in place upon others to ensure that only the required outcome takes place. Culhwch is the child of a marriage between human and Faery, and has been raised by the Priesthood in a Temple of the Mysteries in order to undertake certain magical tasks that will bring about changes in the faltering relationship between Faery and human.

The story of how Culhwch wins the hand of Olwen offers a wonderful example of a close working relationship between human, Faery, Atlantean and giant, all part of the family of Amlawdd Wledig and Gwen PenDragon. Although the word 'giant' popularly tends to conjure up an image of a blundering and slow-witted ape, this is not a helpful approach. Giants like Ysbaddaden serve as guardians of the Faery race, many of them retaining close links with their stellar counterparts, such as Boötes the Bearkeeper, or Ophiuchus the Serpent Bearer. Their sometimes obstructive nature is demonstrative of their role as protector. Ysbaddaden's name means "hawthorn" and it is his connection with this sacred Faery tree which reveals his role as Faery guardian.

On one level, the story of how Culhwch finally wins the hand of Olwen can be read as a conventional tale of how a man proves his valour and wins his lady, but a deeper reading reveals how it also sets out the many challenges which can be encountered by anyone who attempts to bridge the worlds between human and Faery. Olwen's name, which means White Track, is an evocative description of the shining paths of the Faery folk as seen through human eyes. Wherever she walked, white trefoils sprang up behind her. These can be likened to the white tracks of the stars imprinted upon the surface of the land, the impression that is caused by the white stellar energy that runs through the Faery veins.

After his period of apprenticeship in the Mysteries is completed, Culhwch rides out from the sanctuary of Temple of Celyddon to the outer world of King Arthur and the Court.

> "And in the youth's hand were two spears of silver, sharp, well-tempered, headed with steel, three ells in length, of an edge to wound the wind, and cause blood to flow, and swifter than the fall of the dewdrop from the blade of reed-grass upon the earth when the dew of June is at the heaviest. A gold-hilted sword was upon his thigh, the blade of which was of gold, bearing a cross of inlaid gold of the hue of the lightning of heaven; his war-horn was of ivory ...About him was a four-cornered cloth of purple, and an apple of gold was at each corner ..." [4]

This wonderful description makes his appearance shine out from the pages. He is an ambassador between the worlds of Faery and human, emerging from his obscure origins like the sun appearing from behind a cloud. But there is much in this description which goes deeper than the convention of the times which demanded that every maiden was the most beautiful in the world and every knight was the best attired. None of Culhwch's weapons could have been intended for physical battle: a silver spear and a golden sword will not carry a cutting edge. These are the weapons of light, the weapons of Faery. They form a bridge between the Faery world and the human world, at one and the same time symbolic of the separation of human and Faery, and of the means by which they will be reunited.

Earlier descriptions of such Faery weapons can be found in the Irish counterpart of *The Mabinogion*, the *Lebor Gabála Érenn* which tells how the Faery race of the Tuatha dé Danaan emerged from four cities: Falias, Gorias, Finias and Murias. They brought with them four magical weapons: from Falias came the stone which is now sometimes called the Stone of Destiny *La Fial*; from Finias came a spear, from Murias came a cup or cauldron, and from Gorias came the sword.

These four magical weapons will be studied in greater detail later, but it is well worth bearing them in mind throughout the following chapters. From these earliest appearances they have passed into legend and esoteric lore, and along the way acquired a formidable weight of human history and significance, but it is essential to remember that they were originally *gifts from Faery*, brought from the world of Faery as magical and talismanic symbols of immeasurable power and significance for the future of both races.

Current esoteric practice recognises the power of the four-fold symbolism contained within these weapons but often fails to acknowledge their original significance, preferring to interpret them from a purely human point of view. They can be equated, for example, with the four Jungian functions of consciousness: sword/intellect; wand/intuition; cup/ emotion and stone/sensation. This approach can be a useful psychological tool and will often lead to worthwhile realisations of the comparative strengths and weaknesses of an individual's psychic make-up. But to use them primarily within the parameter of human endeavour in the world, even when that endeavour is allied to the spiritual world, is to neglect their intended meaning and purpose. Our forgetting of their original and greater meaning lies alongside the more general forgetting which has occurred with regard to our Faery companions who share the land.

Culhwch is not riding out to make battle with cuts and blows, but comes as vanguard to the magical work between the worlds, and his Faery weapons are symbolic of that work. The silver spears are the symbol of the stellar world of the Faeries; the sword of gold is the blade of the sun's light. The third magical weapon is the cup, though Culhwch carries an ivory horn. In later times the fourth weapon, the shield, carried a symbol of the identity of its owner and this custom eventually developed into the intricate heraldic designs familiar to us in mediaeval art. Culhwch's shield is a purple mantle which has an apple of red-gold at each corner. The same mantle also appears in another story in the Mabinogion, *The Dream of Rhonabwy*, where it has passed to King Arthur – who in many ways is the successor to Culhwch.

The name of the mantle was *Gwen*! One of its properties was that whoever wore it would be invisible to those about him, yet the wearer would be able to see everything. Another mysterious property of this mantle was that it "would retain no colour but its own".[5]

This is the well-known cloak of invisibility, the stock-in-trade of every wizard from Merlin to Harry Potter, but its nature is more subtle than is popularly assumed. It is a Faery gift offered to those who travel between the worlds in order to ease their passage. Indeed it might be more accurate to say that the cloak is a technique rather than an actual object, because when it is worn it indicates that the wearer is functioning at a higher level than that of the physical world. We would now call this technique "rising in the spirit vision" or "entering a higher state of consciousness", although these terms are not those used by the early storytellers. When it is said that the cloak would not allow any colour on it but its own this is a matter of physics, not poetic hyperbole. The purple colour of the cloak indicates the indigo of the astral levels, the rate of vibration which must be touched upon in order to enter into the inner world of Faery. If the wearer of the cloak has not achieved that level of vibration then he has not entered those worlds. Once that level of vibration has been achieved then the wearer will not be seen by those of the physical world because he is vibrating at a higher level, although he will be able to perceive the physical world.

The four red-gold apples, one at each corner, are symbolic of the four cities of Faery: Finias, Gorias, Falias and Murias. Thus the cloak becomes more than a means of entering the Faery worlds, it also becomes a map of the territory, so that wearer can orient him or herself at the centre of the four Innerworld directions.

Having been invested with the Faery weapons and gifted with the Faery cloak, Culhwch sets out upon his tasks within the world of humanity. At the end of his quest he successfully gains the hand in marriage of Olwen, although we must remember that this is not the object of his task so much as his reward once he has accomplished it. He has a job to do, and the happy marriage simply is the icing on the cake. His task is to build bridges between the races of human and Faery which others may then follow.

When he arrived at the Court of King Arthur, Culhwch asked King Arthur for help in his quest. Often blind to the world of Faery, Arthur denied any knowledge of Olwen or her parents but he did agree to allow some of his men to accompany Culhwch on his search. Culhwch wasted no time searching the physical world but immediately returned to the borders of Faery. We know this is so, because the story describes how the landscape about them begins to conform to rules which are not of this world: the normal parameters of time and space no longer apply. Culhwch and Arthur's men come to a wide open plain, upon which stands a great castle. They travel towards it all day, and a second and third day, but get no nearer to it.

When after great difficulty they finally reach the castle, they encounter the shepherd Custennin who is in the employ of the giant Ysbaddaden, Olwen's father. The figure of the shepherd or herdsman, a Faery guardian, is frequently met at the threshold of the worlds and this particular shepherd is of especial interest to us because he is also closely related to Ygrainne, having married one of the un-named daughters of the PenDragon family. It is unfortunate that little record remains of this woman as there is no doubt that she was as remarkable as the rest of her kindred. When she hears Culhwch and his warriors coming, she runs towards them. Cei (often spelt as Kay), who is one of Culhwch's party, seems to know her already because when he sees her approaching he snatches a log from a nearby pile of wood. As she tries to embrace him, Cei thrusts the log between her hands and she squeezes it so strongly that it becomes like a twisted withy. Her super-human powers conjure images of the ancient Serpent-Goddess, and her primal origins are revealed when we are told that she and Custennin have had twenty-four children. (Ysbaddaden killed twenty three of them, but that is another story.)

Ysbaddaden sets Culhwch thirty-nine tasks which he must accomplish before he can win the hand of Olwen. Many previous suitors had tried their hand at these challenges, but none had succeeded. The greatest task is to snatch the comb and shears which can be found between the ears of the boar Twrch Trwyth. This boar is no mere tusker: any group of Arthur's knights could have subdued such a boar without much difficulty, but the threat it posed to the kingdom displayed all the characteristics of a psychic attack and was therefore not something that Arthur could easily deal with.

In fact the boar is no more an actual boar than the swineherd who attended Culhwch's birth was an actual swineherd, and the challenge it symbolises is not something that can be matched by physical strength. The problem is the Inner Plane imbalance that needs to be restored. Twrch Trwyth is the name of the son of another ruler of ancient Britain, Taredd

Wledig, and just as the denomination 'swineherd' indicates one order of the Priesthood so the denomination 'boar' indicates another. Twrch Trwyth and his seven sons have misused the power of their position and are now posing a threat to the stability of Arthur's kingdom. Culhwch's quest is to track down and eliminate the source of imbalance which exists within the Priesthood, and because of his ancestry he is the best man for the job. Misuse of power at such a level of responsibility causes very real problems, and dealing with them is more difficult than actually killing a wild boar.

The chase is on. Twrch Trwyth rampages like a dark storm through Ireland, then Wales, and finally through Cornwall and beyond, into the drowned lands of Lyonesse. Although the tale reads like an exciting hunt, the quarry is not of this world. And we should take note that at the end of the story Twrch Trwyth has not been killed: it was not possible to eradicate the order of Priesthood which he had abused, only to push it back into the pre-physical levels. But in the greater story of the Mysteries of Faery and human, Culhwch had achieved good and lasting work.

1   A fuller discussion of this can be found in: Wendy Berg and Mike Harris, *Polarity Magic* (St Paul, Minnesota: Llewellyn Publications, 2003)
2   In a purely geographical sense Scotland is a long way to travel in order to hide from the King of Cornwall! But the nature of the Temple of the Mysteries which had been established there provided an attractive refuge for this couple, who must have known of its existence.
3   Trans. Lady Charlotte Guest, *The Mabinogion* (London: Dent and Sons Ltd, 1906)
4   Trans. Lady Charlotte Guest, *The Mabinogion: Kilhwch and Olwen* (London: J.M.Dent and Sons Ltd, 1906) page 97
5   Trans. Lady Charlotte Guest, *The Mabinogion: The Dream of Rhonabwy* (London: J.M.Dent and Sons Ltd, 1906) page 143

CHAPTER SIX
Ygrainne, Merlin and Uther PenDragon

The most famous member of the Priesthood of Amlawdd and Gwen PenDragon is Ygrainne, whose mating with Uther PenDragon brought King Arthur into physical existence. Ygrainne's name is variously found as Ygrainne, Igerne, Eigr (in the *Parzival* of Wolfram von Eschenbach she is called Arnive),[1] but the root of her name is related to the Irish "Grainne", which indicates "Light of the Sun." All agree that she was Arthur's mother but it is generally assumed that having played her part at Tintagel in conceiving Arthur through Merlin's magic, she had then finished what she came to do. However, unlike her sister Goleuddydd, Ygrainne reappears much later in the Arthurian legends as told by Chrétien de Troyes and Wolfram von Eschenbach, in whose accounts of the Grail legends she reappears as a mature, white-haired Priestess who presides over a Castle of Women. We might perhaps think of this as a Mystery School founded on Atlantean principles.

But we must start with the conception of Arthur, for this was indeed a momentous event which resulted not only in the birth of a son but in the real beginning of the Arthurian legend, and with his birth came also the bursting into life of one of the richest outpourings of story in the western civilisation. However, when these stories are read with the additional level of understanding that they are for the most part a record of the lives and relationships of Faeries and humans working together about the Round Table, they immediately become not only a great deal more interesting, but also acquire a new and vivid relevance for the present day.

The story of Arthur's conception has passed into popular legend. The gist of it is that Ygrainne was married to a Cornish nobleman named Gorlois, although we are told nothing of his early life or of Ygrainne's life with Gorlois except that, presumably, they lived together at Tintagel Castle on the north coast of Cornwall. Gorlois, of whom it is recorded that he served Uther PenDragon in battle, was invited with Ygrainne to an Easter-day feast at Uther PenDragon's court in London. Uther was immediately attracted to Ygrainne, and made his intentions perfectly clear to her. When Gorlois was alerted to what was happening he immediately returned to his castle at Tintagel and took Ygrainne with him. Uther demanded that they should return to London, but Gorlois refused. His refusal so angered Uther that he travelled West with an army of men and began to ravage Cornwall. Gorlois, for reasons which make little sense in terms of battle logistics, left Ygrainne in Tintagel Castle because it was well-defended and went off to stay at nearby Dimilioc, explaining this strange decision by saying that if the worst came to the worst they would not *both* be in immediate danger.

This odd reasoning on the part of Gorlois is the first hint we get that, as is so often the case in the Arthurian legends, all is not what it seems. Gorlois knew that Uther's real target was not himself, or even Cornwall, but Ygrainne, so his obvious move would have been to have stayed with her rather than taking himself out of the way. It may well be that Gorlois understood more than history has given him credit for, and if he knew of his wife's origin and purpose (and we have no reason to assume that he did not), removing himself from the scene when it became evident that the time had come for great magic to take place, puts him in a different light.

On hearing that Gorlois was no longer at Tintagel with his wife, Uther's swift reaction was to surround and cut off Dimilioc, thus leaving Gorlois isolated. He then consulted Merlin, who told Uther that he would change Uther's appearance so that he looked like Gorlois, and change his own appearance into that of a man called Britaelis in order that he could accompany Uther into Tintagel Castle.

Uther spent the night with Ygrainne and Arthur was conceived. Meanwhile, at Dimilioc, Uther's men stormed the stronghold and Gorlois was killed. Uther lost no time in taking Tintagel as his castle and Ygrainne as his wife. And thus a sea-change in the destiny of the islands of Britain was achieved within the space of a few hours. Gorlois lost his life so that the intended act could take place and, in addition, the honour of the mother of the future king was spared as it could now be said that Arthur was conceived *after* the death of her husband.

As we have seen, the blood of Uther was infused with the white star-blood of Gwen PenDragon, so this marriage reached back into the age of the ancient PenDragon dynasty of Priest-Kings. Interestingly, Wolfram von Eschenbach, another recorder of Arthurian legend, furnishes Uther with a different genealogy to the one given in the previous chapter, but he also confirms that Uther is of Faery origin. His grandfather, according to Wolfram, was one Mazadan, who was abducted to the Faery kingdom which Wolfram calls Faimurgen. (Faimurgen or Morgan le Fey is found in many of the Arthurian legends, although the name is normally given to a Faery rather than a country.) Once there, he married his abductor,

a Faery called Terdelaschoye, which can be translated as "Land of Joy."
Their children were Lazaliez and Brickus, the former said by Wolfram to
be responsible for founding the Angevin dynasty in France, and the latter
being the father of Uther PenDragon.

Rather than bearing Uther any grudge for what had taken place,
Ygrainne was entirely happy with the new arrangement and it can only
be assumed that she foresaw what was to happen and was probably fully
compliant with it. As is often the case, this story is now so familiar to
us that we tend to accept it without much thought. But in magic, as in
all things, if it isn't broken then it doesn't need fixing and if we have any
regard for Merlin's abilities as arch-mage of Britain then we should guess
that he would not readily waste his skills on providing a good night for
his King. Ygrainne was no hapless wife of a local dignitary but a Priestess
who had come to earth for a particular reason. Indeed, presuming that
Ygrainne knew exactly what she was doing and why, there would have
been no need for Merlin to have brought about any shape-shifting upon
himself, his men, or Uther. In the absence of her husband Gorlois,
Ygrainne could simply have opened the back door and let them in. The
shape-shifting is only another device invented by later interpreters who
perhaps do not fully appreciate Ygrainne's part in this. Assuming that she
was both unknowing and unwilling, the only possible excuse they could
offer for her behaviour would be that because of their disguise she didn't
realise what was going on.

We might even ask why Merlin had to be there at all, but the
foundations for the attempt, through Arthur and Gwenevere, to unite the
Faery and human races and to re-align the ruling court and Kingship of
Britain with the Faery Temples and Priesthood of Atlantis had so carefully
been put into place over so long a time that no mistakes could be made.
Merlin had previously overseen much of this, and his presence was
certainly necessary to ensure that this final act was properly carried out.
As we have noted, the birth of Culhwch which in many ways anticipates
that of Arthur, was overseen by an order of the Priesthood which in all
likelihood was led by Merlin himself. But there is one important difference:
Culhwch's main task was to set right a problem which existed within that
very Priesthood.[2] Arthur on the other hand was not a Priest but a King,
and his role lay within the outer world of men, not within the inner orders
of the Mysteries.

As for Merlin himself, far from being the irascible pointy-hatted
wizard of popular conception he was of course also of Atlantean origin.
In her novel *The Sea Priestess*[3] Dion Fortune describes in detail a certain

Priest of the Moon who, as the story unfolds, makes his presence known to a modern-day Priestess of the name of Vivienne le Fay Morgan. The story describes how with the help of the Priest of the Moon, Vivienne le Fay Morgan brings a fresh magical initiative into the contemporary world. Based upon the power and magic of Isis, this initiative is intended to bring through the power of the feminine as a counterbalance to the over-masculine tendencies of western society, and to restore the sanctity and wonder of magical polarity to the marriages of men and women.

Curiously, and perhaps in order to conceal his real identity from all but the genuine seeker, Dion Fortune only names the Priest of the Moon once within the book, when she reveals that he is Merlin. If it had been her intention to place a veil over the real identity of this inner-plane Priest then her attempt certainly worked. But there is another veil here also, for not only does she identify Merlin with the Moon Priest but she reveals that the Moon Priest is a Priest of Isis. Thus we learn that Merlin is a Priest of Isis, and Dion Fortune is probably the first to have made this connection. If we consider Merlin as a Priest of Isis this puts a very different gloss on the events at Tintagel and sets them within one of the most ancient and respected of all magical traditions.

The implications behind this act of magical mating between Uther PenDragon and Ygrainne are of course many-faceted and undoubtedly raise the somewhat heated question of blood-lines, genetic manipulation and the meaning of the sacred blood which is connected with the Holy Grail. The problem with theories of this nature is that the concept of holy blood almost inevitably comes with the attachment of better, or purer blood, concepts which are generally viewed with justifiable distaste. Nevertheless, something of this nature took place at Tintagel and if we reject the whole issue out of hand then we reject the holy baby with the unholy bath water.

It has to be said that esoteric tradition is much to blame in this, according a near deification to the Atlantean Priesthood whose actual aim was to preserve the line of *Faery* blood. Uther and Ygrainne were attempting to create a fully human King whose stellar ancestry would, it was hoped, allow him more easily to bridge the gap between Faery and human, and to set this relationship at the head of the rulership of the islands of Britain. Arthur's main task, after he had finished the preliminary minor skirmishings necessary to conquer the usual uprisings from the petty kings, was to marry one of the Faery race. He therefore had to be someone who, by virtue of his ancestry, was of a suitable background for this challenge. It is not easy to be married to a Faery.

In *The Sea Priestess*, when Merlin becomes aware of the imminent corruption within the Sun Temple he returns to the older and purer precincts of the Temple of the Sea and the Stars to renew his contact with Isis.

> "Now the Priest of the Moon … had seen that the seership had fallen on evil days, and had gone back, as men must, to an older and purer faith, tracing the river to the rill till he came to the pure source; and he worshipped the Great Mother under Her forms of moon and sea, and in this he was wise, for with Her are hidden the secrets of human life, though with the All-father are the keys of the spirit. In his prime he set out to seek a land where life might be lived unsullied by the decay of a dying race, and he travelled with the tin-ships to the Islands of the Sea …"[4]

Here is the key to much. Isis represents the throne of the human Priesthood but also of the Priesthood of the Faery race. In the language of the many peoples who identify the Shining Ones as the precursors of their own race, she is the first of the Shining Ones.[5]

It cannot be emphasised enough that there are many levels within the Faery race. But as time passes, so they have been remembered with less objectivity, and the overall tendency has been to elevate some of them to the status of deity rather than to see and understand them as a parallel race, albeit with much to teach their human counterparts. Within the race of Shining Ones the feminine being whom many cultures know as Isis was one of the foremost of that race, and within the context of the relationship between Faery and human races it is, as Dion Fortune suggests, from Isis that all true and pure initiatives must have their source.

There are several layers of time-scale running concurrently within *The Sea Priestess*, but there is one constant factor: that it is the corruption of the pattern held in Atlantis which drives Merlin and all those who work under his aegis to return to the pure source, whether they are doing so in the present moment, the England of the 1930s, or the age of King Arthur. The point Dion Fortune is making is that this deviation from the pattern is always there in potential, just as Atlantis is always there in potential. Atlantis didn't end with the flood, it separated from our present physical reality. It still exists upon the etheric and astral planes, and the patterns which are held within its Temples upon the Inner Planes do not necessarily now conform to the true pattern of the Will of God any more than they did immediately prior to the so-called Fall. When such deviation becomes particularly noticeable, such as in the time immediately before the flood, or in the pre-Arthurian era of the PenDragons, or in the 1930s of Dion Fortune's Britain, then Priests such as Merlin initiate a new, purer impulse which may be brought through into manifestation.

The mediaeval author Robert de Boron makes a similar point in the language of his time in his chronicle entitled *Merlin*.[6] He states that Merlin's birth has been brought about by Demons who wanted to bring to birth one who would counteract the redeeming power of Christ by telling humankind of everything that had taken place in the past, and to deceive humans. This is somewhat muddled thinking, and overlaid with the worst of mediaeval Christianity, but the grain of truth is there. 'Daemons' (beneficent spirit beings) rather than 'demons' is a more accurate description of the spirits who brought about the birth of Merlin. Boron's suggestion that Merlin was concerned to bring to humankind an awareness of all things past is very near to the truth. Merlin was, and still is, concerned with bringing through a remembrance of our shared past and future destiny, particularly in our relationship with the Faeries. Boron describes how Merlin tells Arthur "Two hundred years before you were born your fate was fixed and prophesied."[7] We might extend that period of time to two thousand years, but the sentiment is surely accurate.

Merlin (and the Priesthood with which he worked) is the lynch-pin in all of this. He knew of the Elves and the Faeries of Lemuria and he knew of the Temples of the Sun and the Stars in Atlantis, and in order to bring them through into the mundane world he incarnated at the time of the PenDragons. It is indeed his knowledge of things past which is at work here, although we would no longer view this as counteracting the redeeming power of Christ. The redeeming power of Christ does not disregard or reject anything which has gone before into some kind of evolutionary dustbin of misfits but embraces and remembers all, bringing it back into the whole. Boron describes how Merlin, even as a child, had knowledge of the past, but it was Christ who gave him knowledge of the future. Although apparently voicing a conventional mediaeval piety, Boron speaks a profound truth, and one which will be taken up again later.

The work of the Faery Priesthood continues to this day; its aims are unchanged and its rituals are still worked. Many of those mentioned in these chapters can still be contacted, and their love and guidance are offered freely to all genuine seekers.

1   Wolfram von Eschenbach, trans. A.T. Hatton, *Parzival* (London: Penguin Books, 1980)
2   Symbolised by his hunting down and killing the disruptive Boar Twrch Trwyth.
3   Dion Fortune, *The Sea Priestess* (London: Aquarian Press, 1957)
4   ibid, Chapter 10
5   Discussed at length by Christian O'Brien and Barbara Joy O'Brien, *The Shining Ones* (Cirencester: Dianthus Publishing Ltd)
6   Robert de Boron, trans. Nigel Bryant, *Merlin and the Grail* (Cambridge: D.S. Brewer, 2001) page 46
7   ibid, page 112

CHAPTER SEVEN
Gwenevere's Ancestry

Now that we have laid the foundations, we can move closer to those at the centre of the story: King Arthur and Queen Gwenevere. As we have seen, Arthur's birth marked the culmination of the work to reunite Faery and human which, under the guidance of Merlin, had been carefully put into place over a very long time. It was certainly the intention of the Faery/human Priesthood that as a result of Arthur's ancestry and the long years of preparation he would be the ideal man for the job of forming a strong and lasting bridge between the human and Faery races.

But where did Gwenevere come from? As was discussed in the Introduction, the inspiration behind this book was the revelation that Gwenevere was not human, but Faery. If we return to the same genealogical tables which are so forthcoming in offering information about Arthur's ancestry we find that they give no information whatsoever as to Gwenevere's predecessors. She appears as if from nowhere and is apparently without lineage. However, this very lack of historical evidence for Gwenevere's human ancestry is meaningful in itself and not simply the result of an oversight. If she had possessed human ancestry it would have been recorded, and if those who told and wrote down these stories believed her to have had a human family but found themselves short of any actual names they would have been perfectly capable of inventing some!

Aside from the genealogical tables there is a small amount of historical evidence of Gwenevere's forebears, albeit somewhat contradictory in nature. Geoffrey of Monmouth[1] says she was born of a noble Roman family but had been brought up in Cornwall in the house of Cador, the Duke of Cornwall. Wace and Layamon agree that she was related to Cador.[2] It has also been suggested that she was the daughter of one Gwrtheyrn Gwrtheneu, advisor to Urien of Rheged, ruler of one of the ancient northern Kingdoms.[3] This Northern connection is given some confirmation through the existence of an intricately carved gravestone, said to be from Gwenevere's grave, which can be seen in the museum at Meigle in the east of Scotland. Urien was certainly a contemporary of Arthur and became closely involved in the stories of the Round Table when he formed a union with Arthur's half-sister Morgan. But although

Urien appears in several of the Arthurian legends and there are a number of possible occasions when the mythographers could easily have mentioned that Gwenevere had been brought up in his court, they do not make anything of this opportunity.

In the early days of Arthur's kingship, during which period, by all accounts, he spent much of his time consolidating his position and conquering other claimants to his land, it would have been an obvious step for him to have married the daughter of one of the lesser kings and thus in theory at least brought about peace and unity between their lands and people. But there is no suggestion in any of the stories that Gwenevere was the daughter of a rival king or that she came with any apparent benefit to him at all, and we must ask *why* Arthur chose her, if indeed he had any choice in the matter. There must have been plenty of other eligible young women in his kingdom. In fact his choice makes no sense at all when judged by the usual criteria. If Gwenevere's ancestry had been human then she would certainly have been expected to have brought something in the way of dowry with her, whether of land, wealth or property. Famously, she was endowed with a single gift: the Round Table.

Given that Gwenevere was a less than obvious choice, it is also curious that there is no recorded comment on Arthur's choice of bride. There is no record that anyone found the match in any way unexpected or strange. There is always uncertainty in interpreting lack of evidence but the silence of those who surrounded Arthur, such as the Knights of the Round Table, does suggest that Arthur's choice was perfectly acceptable at the time. We may now have difficulty in accepting the reality of a marriage between a human and a Faery but it would appear that those of Arthur's time did not find it something that invited comment. After all, as we have seen, it had happened many times before.

We do have other sources of information concerning Gwenevere's ancestry, and all of these confirm her Faery origin. First, a counterpart to Gwenevere appears in Irish mythology: Finnabair, who is of the Faery race of the Tuatha dé Danaan. The name Finnabair has the same meaning as Gwenevere: White Shadow, or White Phantom, and a useful comparison can be made between their lives. Finnabair was the daughter of Medb, the Faery Queen of Connacht. Medb's role in Irish mythology reveals much of the nature of Faery mating: she mated with numerous human males, and in fact this union was a pre-requisite for any man who hoped to share the rulership with her at Tara, the place of the ancient High Kings of Ireland.

The chief sources of information concerning Gwenevere's early life are found in the Arthurian legends themselves, particularly in the version known as the Vulgate Cycle.[4] This long and complex version of the legends clearly identifies Gwenevere's father as King Leodegrance of Carmelide, elsewhere called Lyonesse. (Carmelide is variously spelt, and its similarity to Camelot is noted.) Another of the distinctive Faery Kingdoms such as Sorelois and Listenois, Carmelide lay to the Southwest of Arthur's Kingdom. One of the chief cities of Carmelide was Carohaise, which is the Cornish name for the city of Exeter in the neighbouring county of Devon.[5]

There are several clues as to the close connection between Cornwall and the Faery Kingdoms. A profusion of sites related to King Arthur can be found on Bodmin Moor, an ancient granite moorland towards the eastern border of Cornwall, and such a cluster of sites usually reflects an Inner significance behind the physical location. Esoteric tradition goes further, and correlates Leodegrance's kingdom with the drowned lands of Lyonesse which are said to lie off the south-western tip of Cornwall. The Isles of Scilly are the physical counterpart of Lyonesse and in fact two of these tiny islands are named Great Arthur and Little Arthur. The Isles of Scilly are now the only visible remnants of this drowned land, but a comparatively recent rise in sea-level has separated some of the islands which were clearly once joined together, and this inevitably gives rise to the suggestion that the Isles of Scilly were also once joined to Cornwall.

Any drowned lands rekindle memories of Atlantis, and the Isles of Scilly are no exception to this rule, although as any visitor to the coast of Cornwall will know, they fulfil their Atlantean requirements without the need for a more esoteric explanation. Viewed from Cornwall's south-western tip, they lie tantalisingly upon the extreme horizon, sometimes disappearing in the sea mists for days or weeks at a time only to re-appear not quite where you remembered them.

Carmelide will not be found on any map, but it has its own inner geography. In addition to the main city of Carohaise, another named location in Carmelide is Bendigran. This name has several interesting components, ben meaning "head of", and "gran", a name of some complexity, which seems to imply "giant." It is seen, for instance, in Bran, a giant who ruled Britain in pre-historical times. The same name is found in various mutations as Ogvran, Gogfran, or Ocuran Gawr. Some sources even name Bran as Gwenevere's father, for instance Triad 56,[6] which identifies her as the daughter of Gogfran the Giant.

Three Great Queens of Arthur's Court:
Gwenhwyfar daughter of Cywryd Gwent,
And Gwenhwyfar daughter of Gwythr ap Greidawl,
And Gwenhwyfar daughter of Gogfran the Giant.

There is another interesting name here, Gwythyr ap Greidawl. He was one of those in the group from Arthur's court who helped Culhwch in his quest to win the hand of Olwen. He had been engaged to marry Creiddylad the daughter of Lludd, but she was stolen from him by her brother Gwyn ap Nudd, a Faery King whose Innerworld home is Glastonbury Tor. There are a number of fascinating legends connected with Lludd, not least an episode concerning red and white dragons, but we must not become too sidetracked. Suffice it to say that although their connection with Gwenevere cannot be firmly established, these characters are quite clearly Faery, not human.

The suggestion in this Triad that there was not one but three Gweneveres only fails to make sense if we try to interpret its meaning in human terms. In the Faery world there is not such a clear differentiation between one individual and another so the idea that Gwenevere had three Faery fathers is not a contradiction in terms. The four Gweirs of Ygrainne's family (see Table 1, page 57) are a good example of this. A traditional rhyme still current in Wales at the beginning of the 20th century also suggests that Gogfran was Gwenevere's father:

Gwenhwyfar, the daughter of Gogyrvan the Giant,
Bad when little, worse when great.[7]

Though it has to be said that the rhyme is not entirely clear as to who is bad, and who is little. Perhaps Gogyrvan is not always a giant, but when he is, he's even more intolerable? Or perhaps Gwenevere was naughty when she was a child and even worse as an adult!

These names are all from the earlier Welsh versions of the legends, whereas later versions tend to identify Leodegrance as Gwenevere's father. His connection with Gwenevere is very important, and little has so far been made of the significance of his role in the Arthurian mythos. His name indicates "The Great Lion." He is a figure of considerable presence, of a similar status to the other great pre-Arthurian figures of the PenDragon dynasty. As with the PenDragons, his name indicates a clear link with the stars, but in terms of linear time the age of Leodegrance is more distant even than that of the PenDragons. His name places him firmly within the age of Leo, which spanned the period 10,000–8,000 BC. While the PenDragons represented the period of transition between human and Faery, Leodegrance is of earlier, pure Faery/Elven blood. His later appearance in the stories is no contradiction in terms for we are not dealing with the historical time marked out by human lives and deaths. Leodegrance is of the Immortal Clan, and as alive now as he was 10,000 years ago. His purpose, as a representative of the Age and power of Leo, is to channel the connection between a number of the starry constellations and the Arthurian initiative, and this was achieved primarily through his daughter Gwenevere and the Round Table which she brought to Arthur's court.

For some indication of what was involved in this we must turn again to the religious and magical practice of the ancient Egyptians, whose ancient texts provide some of the detail that is missing in the Arthurian legends. Leonine deities feature strongly in early Egyptian cosmology, most notably in the forms of Shu and Tefnut who are the leonine offspring of the great God Atum. Shu was associated with the principle of visible light and space, and Tefnut with the principle of moisture. The most famous manifestation of the Leonine influence is of course the mysterious Sphinx on the Giza plateau, which is believed to have been constructed in the Age of Leo by those who point to the evidence of the water-erosion upon its sides that might indicate its date of construction.[8]

The sun entered the constellation of Leo at the time of the inundation of the Nile. This was the most important physical and spiritual event in the yearly cycle of the ancient Egyptians and absolutely central to their entire belief-system. The annual rising of the waters of the Nile which flooded the land with rich and fertile silt coincided with the reappearance of the star Sirius above the horizon after its disappearance from the sky for 70 days. But the lion was also regarded as having an equally creative, fecundating power. A memory of this is found to this day in the numerous stone fountains constructed in the shape of a lion's mouth, a common enough sight but whose significance is rarely appreciated. Others make a more direct connection between Sirius and Leo and postulate that the inhabitants of Sirius appeared in Leonine form.[9]

The Age of Leo was known to the ancient Egyptians as 'Zep Tepi', the First Time, the age of a civilisation which they knew had preceded their own, and the time in which Isis and Osiris had ruled over Egypt. This period was also known as the Time of Return. Symbolically, it represented a gateway through which, guided by the appropriate funerary rites, the questing soul could step outside of the bounds of linear time and make straight its way of return to the stars.[10] Once this journey had been achieved, it would become one of the Shining Ones, the *Akhu,* or People of the Stars, just as Osiris had returned to his stellar body of light in Orion. When he had achieved this reunion, Isis, now reunited with her stellar body of light in Sirius, mated with him to bring about the conception of the child Horus. Thus were opened the floodgates of fertility between star and earth.

The star Sirius lies at the centre of the Faery universe. Sirius is sometimes called "the Sun behind the sun", indicating that while the star we call the Sun is related to our physical centre of Self in our Solar Plexus and the expression of our Selves within the physical earth, Sirius represents a more hidden centre. The Sun and Sirius stand in relationship to each other as the human and Faery races stand in relationship to each other. The light of Sirius shone upon earth before the light of the Sun was gathered into its present form of being: it is the Faery Sun. Tolkien calls Sirius Helluin. He describes in *The Silmarillion* how when the star-Goddess Varda Elentári created the constellation of Orion, so also she created the star Sirius, under whose blue fires the Elves first opened their eyes upon the Earth, and within whose eyes the light of that star still shines.

The Egyptian symbol for the stellar gateway which opened within the Age of Leo is the *aker,* a hieroglyph of two lions crouching back to back and forming the gateway of the present which unites yesterday and tomorrow, past and future. A more familiar interpretation of this same concept can be seen in the Tarot card Strength, where a woman is holding open a lion's mouth. The woman is the eternal Virgin, Isis.

If we translate this universal symbolism into the language of the Arthurian mythos, we can realise Leodegrance to be a regent of Sirius, a lion of yesterday and tomorrow, guardian of the gateway to the First Time. This gateway into the First Time is symbolised by the Round Table, which is given by Leodegrance to Gwenevere to become a universal glyph at the heart of Arthur's court.

Leodegrance's task, like that of the PenDragon brothers, was to transmit certain stellar influences into the group soul of the inhabitants of earth. The PenDragon brothers laid down the patterns which would link the earth with its starry serpent counterpart of Draco, initially through Ambrosius Aurelianus and the Round Table of Stonehenge, and then through the actual body of Uther PenDragon after he had mated with Ygrainne. Once this preparation had been achieved, Leodegrance was responsible for putting the final piece of the pattern in place, through the glyph of the Round Table which was brought into the human world by his daughter Gwenevere.

The principles at work here are fundamental to all true magical endeavour. First, the connection between earth and stars is made through an enduring symbol, a properly aligned and dedicated Temple built on earth but constructed to universal principles. Next, the principles established within that Temple are literally embodied by those who work within it. On one level the Round Table is a meeting place for a group of like-minded souls who have been brought together by their commitment to the achievement of a common and higher purpose. After the dissolution of Arthur's kingdom the Table returned into Merlin's keeping until such time as it should again be made manifest.

The Round Table symbolises many things. It is the wheel of the precession of the Equinoxes: the rising of the spring Sun against the moving backdrop of the stars and the associated cycle of the movement of the Pole Star. The ultimate journey of the Solar hero is to find the way in which to travel backwards through the cycle of the Ages, to overcome the illusion of linear time, and to find the way of return. This is the archetype embodied by Amlawdd Wledig, the owner of the mill of earth, and his star-white Goddess, Gwen.

Merlin is the interpreter of the Round Table, and will reveal its Mysteries in the appropriate manner to those who seek to understand its significance. Standing between the earth and the starry heavens, Merlin mediates the patterns of the cosmic table and transmutes them into forms which may be more easily perceived upon earth.

The final gifting of the Round Table from Faery to human is described in some detail in the Vulgate Cycle.[11] The story tells how Leodegrance and Gwenevere (this is before her marriage to King Arthur) are invited to a celebration held by King Arthur to mark his defeat of the Saxon marauders. Leodegrance attended with a group of representatives from his own land, but on his arrival at Arthur's court he had so little understanding of what was happening that he had to enquire which noble lord was holding the celebration, and for what purpose.

At face value this story makes little sense. As the ruler of a kingdom apparently near to Arthur's own, how could Leodegrance not know who Arthur was or to what occasion he had been invited? Although the meeting is presented as a description of a simple celebration of Arthur's success in battle it is of course far more than that, and the apparently odd events of the story disguise the much deeper meaning hidden within it: it is a description of a magical ritual in which the many layers of symbolism held within the Round Table are brought together, once and for all. In Leodegrance and Arthur, two great archetypal forces meet for the first time. They are each a representative of different ages and different races, and the story tells us as much when it describes how Leodegrance did not recognise Arthur.

The real purpose of this meeting is that these patterns and influences from different ages can be brought together, and new patterns set in place. The gateway to the First Time of the Shining Ones in the Age of Leo is transmitted through the glyph of the Round Table into the new order represented by King Arthur. On a mundane level this union was finally earthed by the bringing together of Arthur and Gwenevere in marriage, but not before the greater plan held within the Round Table had been established. Gwenevere's part in this was to bring to effect upon the physical level the marriage of her stellar background with Arthur's Solar background. Leodegrance could not himself bring this about: on an energetic level the Stellar pattern must be held by a female in order that the union can properly be made with the Solar pattern held by a male.

It is possible that the author of this story understood the real significance of this meeting, but it was not appropriate for him to present such weighty symbolism in a romance intended for the general reader. Leodegrance and Arthur are not war-lords rubbing shoulders somewhere in the middle of the Dark Ages but represent their own time and place. Their first meeting, thus described, takes place in circumstances which reach through the boundaries of space and time to bring about a change in the patterns which lie at the foundations of the destiny of the land and its people. If this is kept in mind, the rest of the episode now makes much more sense …

The story describes how, at first, the Knights of the Round Table sit separately from the rest of those there gathered. An important point to remember is that these Knights of the Round Table are of course *Leodegrance's* knights. The Round Table has not yet passed to King Arthur, and the Knights of the Round Table are therefore of an earlier, stellar Order. It is only when the marriage between Gwenevere and Arthur occurs on the physical plane that the changes in the universal patterns can be fully brought through, and it is only then that the ancient order of the Knights of the Round Table can be passed into Arthur's safe-keeping and the knights begin to take on the names and characters that have become familiar to us.

But before we attend their wedding, we must retrace the story back to the moment of Gwenevere's entry into the physical world.

It is not often realised that Gwenevere shares with Arthur the distinction of a magical conception. Merlin, whose presence was so much in evidence during the ritual of Arthur's conception is not normally associated with Gwenevere's birth, but he was most certainly involved in the strange events which occurred at that time. Much of the pattern of her later life was put into place during this time, just as with Arthur.

The Prose Lancelot describes how Leodegrance, as yet unmarried, falls in love with a mysterious and un-named woman who arrives at his court. We are told nothing of this woman. If a correlation can be made between Finnabair's mother and Gwenevere's mother then she is the Queen of Faery, but if this is so her identity is heavily veiled.

All seems well until Leodegrance has desire for the woman's maid. One night, after having lain with his wife, his wife gets up out of bed and goes to Mass, during which time Leodegrance uses her absence as an opportunity to lie with her maid, whose husband Cleodalis we must assume also happened to be out for the evening.

It quickly becomes evident that magic and mystery is afoot, and the story now reminds us of the events at Tintagel. Not only does Leodegrance's wife become pregnant that night, so also does her maid. In due course both women give birth to girls, and on the same day. Things rapidly become even more bizarre when not only are the girls discovered to be identical in appearance but they are both given the same name: Gwenevere. In fact, says the storyteller, there was only one way to tell them apart, which was that the 'real' Gwenevere had a tiny birth-mark of a crown upon the small of her back.

What are we to make of all this? The story is couched within a semblance of credibility: a King takes a fancy to a young girl in his court, and the obviously concocted detail of his innocent wife getting out of bed to go to Mass lends her a certain respectability just as the death of Gorlois preserved Ygrainne's honour. An event has occurred which has a power to shape history, yet which does not appear to provoke comment either from Leodegrance or his wife. Leodegrance, in the accepted behaviour of the time in which the story was written, might have been expected to do all he could either to deny that the 'false' Gwenevere was his daughter or at least to have brought her up under a different name and in a different place out of respect for his wife. But in fact not only does he *not* deny that the other baby is his but he makes an odd situation quite incomprehensible to our understanding by deciding to call both girls Gwenevere.

Several layers of reality are uncomfortably rubbing shoulders in this episode. Underpinning them is the unavoidable fact that Leodegrance has two identical daughters both called Gwenevere, one of whom was accepted as 'real' in the sense that she was recognised to be of royal status, while the other was not.

But we must remember that these are Faery children, and the story-teller's version of the events which surrounded their birth cannot be interpreted in human terms. The story bears some similarity to the many accounts of Faery substitution in which the Faeries, desirous either of the possible advantages afforded by a human upbringing for one of their offspring or wanting a human child to rear as their own, substitute a Faery babe for a human babe. The two Gweneveres are two manifestations of the same incarnatory impulse: they are indeed both Gwenevere. Humans have one single spark of spiritual identity which manifests in only one physical body at any one place and time, but this is not so for the Faery race. What in human terms might be thought of as a 'clone' is not so in Faery terms, and while the concept of the individual spark of spirit is common to both human and Faery, the latter race is much more flexible and varied in its manifestation. What would seem inconceivable to us, something we would interpret as loss of our essential, spiritual one-ness, is not so to the Faeries. It is possible for one Faery spirit to manifest in one, or two, or many different places at the same time. It is still in essence one spirit, but it is not confined to one physical place and time as we are. The only real challenge is that because the story is remembered and recorded in later human times and in such a way that insufficient distinction is made between the human and Faery characters, we are tempted to interpret it purely in human terms. The impulse behind this and numerous other episodes of the Arthurian and Grail legends was from the Faery world, and it is only when we look at events from a Faery perspective that we begin to understand them.

However, it has to be said that this dual manifestation was not altogether helpful in the greater plan to which Merlin was working. Although almost identical in appearance, one of the Gweneveres holds a destiny which the other does not, and they are not identical in power or purpose, or even in consciousness. Or, perhaps, one of them was Faery and the other human? Although they were apparently brought up side by side at the court of Leodegrance with little difficulty, things began to go seriously awry when the time came for Gwenevere to enter fully into the human world in order to be married to Arthur.

Geoffrey of Monmouth, and Wace and Lawman all appear to touch upon something of the same memory of the two Gweneveres when they give an account of the strange circumstances of the coronation ceremony of Arthur and Gwenevere. Geoffrey tells how the king and queen are each crowned in separate churches.[12] Arthur is accompanied by men, and Gwenevere by women. From these separate ceremonies each proceeds to their own palace where they sit down to their own separate feast: Arthur with his men, and Gwenevere with her women. Wace tells much the same story but adds that the women who accompanied Gwenevere were the great ladies of the country and also the ladies of her own kind. These can be no other than her Faery kindred who attended this ceremony in their own identity.

But the problems start in earnest on the night before the wedding, when kinsmen of the false Gwenevere plot to exchange her for the real Gwenevere in order to inflict hurt upon Leodegrance. This seems to be an early example of something that recurs many times over in Gwenevere's marriage, the attempts by her Faery family to remove her from Arthur and take her back to her Faery kindred. Here, they bribe Gwenevere's nurse into agreeing to substitute the false Gwenevere into Arthur's bed, and to take the real Gwenevere into the garden just before Arthur is about to lie with her for the first time. Their aim is to capture her and take her to a place far away where she will not be recognised, allowing the substitution of the false Gwenevere to continue undetected.

This is a seminal moment, and again involves a magical mating. Merlin, who has been present at the court for some time, now steps forward into the action and takes control of events before it is too late. Having learnt of the planned substitution and realising that this would put all his plans in jeopardy, he enlists the help of the same Ulfin and Bretel who had assisted him when he brought Uther to Ygrainne at Tintagel. With their help the plot is uncovered, the false Gwenevere exposed, and the real Gwenevere rescued from the hands of the traitors and returned to Arthur's bed in order that their relationship could be consummated.

It would seem that all is now well, and the union between the two races of human and Faery which had been worked towards for so long was about to take place. Yet, as we know, this was not what happened; there is absolutely no indication that Gwenevere had any children. And although Merlin had stepped in to prevent disaster on this occasion, the false Gwenevere continued to live in close proximity to the court where she became the focus for unrest and at least one further attempt at abduction and substitution at a vital moment. Clearly there were those who made the most of their opportunities to disrupt Merlin's work. Whether this was prompted by pure malice or from a genuine objection to the principles behind the marriage between Arthur and Gwenevere it is hard to say, but the attempts on the part of the Faery race to take Gwenevere back to her own Faery kindred continued unabated throughout her marriage. Some of these will be looked at more closely in the next chapter.

1   Geoffrey of Monmouth, *The History of the Kings of Britain,* trans. Lewis Thorpe (Middlesex: Penguin, 1966)
2   Wace and Lawman, *The Life of King Arthur,* trans. Judith Weiss and Rosamund Allen (London: Everyman Paperbacks, 1997)
3   Alexander and William McCall, *The Historic Artur, Gwenhwyvawr and Myrddin, Ancient Brythons of the North* (Durham: The Pentland Press Ltd, 1997)
4   ed. Norris J. Lacy, *The Lancelot-Grail Reader* (New York: Garland Publishing Inc., 2000)
5   There is also a Carhaix in Normandy.
6   trans. R.Bromich, *Trioedd Ynys Prydein,* (Cardiff: University of Wales Press, 1961)
7   Quoted in Lady Charlotte Guest's translation of *The Mabinogion* (London: J.M.Dent, 1906) page 362
8   Discussed by John Anthony West in *Serpent in the Sky,* (Illinois: Quest Books, The Theosophical Publishing House, 1993) page 184 ff
9   Murry Hope, *The Sirius Connection* (Shaftesbury, Dorset: Element Books Ltd, 1996)
10 The time is precisely specified by Robert Bauval and Graham Hancock in *Keeper of Genesis* (London: William Heinemann Ltd, 1996) as 10,500 BC when there was "a unique celestial conjunction involving the moment of sunrise, the constellation of Leo, and the meridian-transit of the three stars of Orion's belt..." page 218
11 ed. Norris J. Lacy, *The Lancelot-Grail Reader* (New York: Garland Publishing Inc., 2000)
12 Geoffrey of Monmouth, *The History of the Kings of Britain,* trans. Lewis Thorpe (Middlesex: Penguin, 1966) pages 228-229

CHAPTER EIGHT
Gwenevere's abductions

It was suggested in the previous chapter that the attitude of the Faeries towards Gwenevere's marriage with Arthur may not have been entirely favourable. Whatever we might make of the episode of her attempted abduction and the substitution of the false Gwenevere into Arthur's marriage bed, it would seem that the presence of the second Gwenevere was certainly made the most of by those Faeries who were apparently not at all keen that the union between Arthur and Gwenevere should take place. As an isolated incident this would not be sufficient to indicate whether this was typical of the Faery attitude in general or was simply an opportunist faction taking advantage of the situation. But whatever the broader view of the reunion between the two races may have been, members of the human race must realise that it is certainly not a foregone conclusion that the Faery race as a whole was either cognisant of the advantages of such a union or in agreement with it. As far as they were concerned there were many disadvantages, and this attitude may well still prevail.

We must again remember that just as there are many levels of evolution and consciousness demonstrated within the human race so also are there within the Faery race, and it is not for us to say who is 'right' from either point of view. But as far as this study is concerned, our particular interest lies with those of each race who constitute what may be called the Priesthood, and there is a Faery Priesthood just as there is a human Priesthood. That is to say, there are those among each race who are aware to a greater extent than many of their kin of the wider implications of the further evolution of their race within the Divine Plan, and who are actively working towards what they perceive to be its best future direction in accordance with the Will of God.

On a more immediate level, it is rarely asked whether or not Gwenevere herself actually *wanted* to marry Arthur. Given the social climate in which these stories were recorded this isn't anything unusual, and the legends are certainly silent on this point even though we are assured that Arthur desired union with Gwenevere. In fact we have no reason to assume that Gwenevere had not already formed a partnership with one of her own kind before she entered the human world. If she already had Faery lovers, and there is some evidence that she did, they would understandably be none too keen on the idea of her marrying a human. This idea is certainly well supported by the many stories in Celtic mythology in which a female Faery makes a brief union with a human man only to be taken back into Faery by her former Faery partner.

One of the most remarkable things about Gwenevere is that she was abducted from court and castle with astonishing regularity. The probable total of her disappearances as they have been recorded in the legends which have come down to us is a number which has some significance: fourteen. But whatever the greater significance this number may or may not hold in relation to her abductions, one's first thought has to be that to be captured this many times was really rather careless! It testifies to a consistent and determined effort on the part of the Faeries to put a stop to her life in the human world and reclaim her as their own. Also demonstrated, of course, is the equally determined effort on the part of one or two of Arthur's Knights, notably Gawain and Lancelot who regularly brought her back, that they should not be allowed to do so.

If Gwenevere was human, a more obvious explanation for these frequent abductions would be the kidnapping of the Queen by a rival petty King as a means of consolidating his claim to land or to the throne. History and myth both provide examples of a rival nation or group using a Queen as a figure-head for their own purpose, one of the most obvious being that of Mary Queen of Scots who for most of her life became the focus of various attempts to remove the Protestant Queen Elizabeth I from the throne and to restore the Roman Catholic faith, with Mary as its Queen and earthly representative. But there is little to be gained simply by removing a Queen to another land or country unless it is either to use her as the centre of focus for a rival faction, or to employ the tactic of distracting the King's attention and luring him away from his Kingdom – which will then be seized by the rival claimant or faction. This does not appear to be the case with the abductions of Gwenevere; they are not carried out by a rival King or leader who is attempting to over-run or otherwise claim Arthur's Kingdom as his own, and there is no evidence of a band of rival human claimants who see Gwenevere as someone who might espouse their cause. These abductions do not appear to have been inspired by any political motive and they are not carried out by human rivals to Arthur's throne. In fact, apart from Mordred, Arthur seems to have experienced no serious claims upon his kingship after he had initially proved his right to the throne through battle, and after his marriage to Gwenevere. And yet these regular abductions continued throughout the marriage: they are the most pronounced feature of Gwenevere's life and so we must look a little deeper to find the reason behind them.

It is possible that there is a correspondence between the disappearances of Gwenevere and that of Goddess figures from other mythologies, most notably that of Persephone who disappeared, literally, from the surface of the earth every year to spend six months as the Queen of Pluto, King of the Underworld. Such a correlation is certainly a reasonable attempt to make more sense of Gwenevere's disappearances and it furnishes her with the respectable background of the yearly vegetative cycle. It aligns her with the rhythm which is personified by all Earth-mother Goddesses and it would make a good deal of sense if she could be equated with the nature-inspired cycle of the Maiden, Mother and Crone and the three-fold aspect of the Goddess, or as the Summer Queen and the Winter Queen. It is true that there are stories of her going a-Maying, but the correspondence ends here, for she does not appear to have become a mother and she did not attain sufficient age to become a wise old woman. In fact she seems to have stayed a maiden all her life in the greater, if not the literal sense of the word: the Virgin Queen. And there is another difficulty with this theory in that Gwenevere's disappearances do not take place at yearly intervals (or indeed at any regular interval) such as that of Persephone's sojourn in the underworld. Each disappearance is brought about by a different abductor and there seems to be a different reason behind each attempt. It is only when we look at them in turn that we begin to find a pattern, and the meaning behind these puzzling episodes begins to emerge.

The Prose Lancelot describes the second abduction of Gwenevere.[1] (By this time the relationship between Gwenevere and Lancelot is well underway, a tale which is so familiar that it needs no repetition here.) The story tells how the false Gwenevere, who has for some time disappeared from the scene, reappears with a vengeance for she sends a messenger to the court at Camelot and claims again that *she* is the real Gwenevere and that it was she who was joined to Arthur in wedlock at the church of St Stephen. She insists that she was that very same day taken and cast out, while the 'false' (i.e. 'real') Gwenevere was put in her place. The reaction among those who hear this is understandably of great concern; all that is except for one knight, Galehaut, who is on close terms with Lancelot. On receiving the news he is said to feel sorrow for Lancelot, but at the same time he is joyful, because this means he will now be able to retain his close friendship with Lancelot (and Gwenevere) more openly than would be the case if Gwenevere was still with Arthur. It is details such as this which invest these stories with moments of striking realism.

Galehaut is given some prominence in this story. He is the son of the Fair Giantess, Lord of the Faraway Islands and prince of the land of Sorelois. Clearly he is not human, but Faery, and rules a Faery Kingdom similar in nature to Carmelide. He is one of the few male Faeries in these or other stories who is able to move freely in and out of the human world. He easily forges a close friendship with Lancelot who, having himself been brought up by the Faery Lady of the Lake is also able to travel freely in and out of Faery. It is this ability that enables him to regularly retrieve Gwenevere from her Faery abductors. In confirmation of their shared land of birth we are told that Galehaut and Lancelot are actually buried in the same grave, which is perhaps another way of saying that at their death they both return through the same gateway to their country of origin.

The nature of the triangular relationship between Lancelot, Galehaut and Gwenevere is of some interest, and when trouble looms in the guise of the false Gwenevere it is Galehaut who immediately steps in with some very practical help: he offers to give her refuge in his Kingdom of Sorelois. In offering a solution to Gwenevere's plight he also sheds some interesting light on the relationship between the human and Faery worlds at this point in the story, as these events take place some time into Arthur and Gwenevere's marriage.

It would appear that Galehaut and Lancelot's shared kinship in Faery prompts Galehaut's unusual attitude towards Gwenevere's love for Lancelot. Unlike the rest of the court, and indeed the rest of the world who raise their hands with shock and horror, he appears to understand their love and finds nothing wrong, sinful or even worthy of comment in it. In fact he offers them both his loyalty and is pleased that Gwenevere is no longer with Arthur, because this means that she can now openly be with Lancelot.

If Galehaut's attitude is indicative of the Faeries in general then it would appear that they considered Gwenevere's union with Lancelot to be more acceptable than her union with Arthur. An odd echo of this is found in the suggestion in some versions of the story that Arthur, rather than riding (presumably into Lyonesse) to collect Gwenevere himself and bring her to his Court, sent Lancelot to do the job for him. It would seem that Lancelot was able to make the journey into Faery and escort Gwenevere into the human world while Arthur was not. Perhaps Arthur was not aware of the risk he took in making Lancelot Gwenevere's escort in this vital journey between the worlds.

To return to the claims of the false Gwenevere, it appears that Arthur was completely taken in by her. Acting with almost indecent haste, as soon as he heard her claim to be the real Gwenevere he proclaimed her as the rightful Queen and rejected his wife, announcing that she would be brought to trial for treason at the Feast of Pentecost. It is at this point that Galehaut (accompanied by Gawain who is also of the Faery race and therefore a suitable accomplice in his intended course of action) stepped in to take the real Gwenevere to safety by escorting her out of the human world and into his Faery Kingdom of Sorelois.

In fact Galehaut took things further than this, and it would seem that he was prompted by more than a simple desire to provide a temporary haven for Gwenevere until things were sorted out with Arthur. The land of Sorelois did not have a Queen, and as soon as Galehaut had taken Gwenevere back with him to Sorelois he declared her its Queen, ensuring that she was acknowledged as such and given due homage by his people. Gawain, obviously in full agreement, waited until he had seen that she was properly recognised and that due oaths of fealty had been sworn, and then returned to Arthur's court satisfied that Gwenevere was now properly established in her rightful place, at least for the time being.

Galehaut and Gawain acted very promptly after the sudden reappearance of the false Gwenevere, but it has to be said that their actions were not what one might expect. Clearly they, at least, are able to distinguish one Gwenevere from the other, but rather than taking the obvious course of trying to persuade Arthur to respect his true wife and not be taken in by the false Gwenevere, they seize the moment to achieve with great speed what we can only suspect might have been their aim all along. The rapid installation of Gwenevere as Queen of Galehaut's Faery kingdom when she has just been disgraced and rejected by Arthur in the human world is certainly over and above the call of duty on Galehaut's part, particularly as there is no hint of a physical relationship between him and Gwenevere. Galehaut and Gwenevere are not lovers, so it can only be assumed that he and Gawain are restoring Gwenevere to her rightful position in the Faery world for the time being and that this is something they had hoped for all along.

Gwenevere remained Queen of Sorelois for three years, during which time Arthur kept the false Gwenevere as his concubine. We are offered little information as to whether he knew that he had made a mistake and was now living with an impostor, or that he did know but didn't care. There is some suggestion that he did know, for it was reported by one Bertelay that he was not willing to give her up for anybody, a comment which rather gives the game away. If it was perhaps the case that the false Gwenevere was human and not Faery then it would not be surprising that Arthur preferred this new domestic arrangement. After several years of marriage to Gwenevere the disadvantages of living with a Faery must have become only too apparent to him!

We might be tempted to ask whether it really mattered which Gwenevere was Arthur's Queen. Actually, it mattered very much, although Arthur did not appear to be mindful of this. And here he made a grave error, for his indifference to the consequences of his actions put into jeopardy all that Merlin and the previous PenDragon dynasty had worked for. The consequences of the three-year period in which the real Gwenevere was not with Arthur at the centre of his kingdom were far-reaching indeed: "*everything on earth rotted.*" And not only did everything rot, but a great 'interdict' or restraint was placed upon the land, such that no body could be buried in consecrated ground during that period, unless it was done in secret. In other words, during Gwenevere's absence from Arthur's Kingdom the land was cut off from spiritual sustenance and protection, the normal sanctity afforded by holy ground was no longer available and the creative and fertilising energy of the cycles of renewal were withdrawn. The land was plunged into calamity and Arthur's disregard for his marriage with Gwenevere sets his kingship and his kingdom apart from the normal patterns of life, health and growth.

One can only guess what Merlin had to say about Arthur's wilful disregard of his destiny! Driven by his lust for the false Gwenevere, the consequences of his behaviour could not be without detrimental effect. These are no 'fairy stories' in the sense of pure make-believe; the characters who live and move in them are representative of the highest working-through of the collective destiny and purpose of these islands. Arthur was surely not ignorant of what he was supposed to achieve, nor of his place in the plan, nor of the significance of his marriage with Gwenevere, but his choice to ignore all this brought calamitous results and his kingdom was reduced to the desolation normally associated with the Waste Land of the Grail legends.

The story of the Grail and its significance for Faeries and humans alike is discussed in greater length in Chapters 12–14. But in brief, the mysterious and sacred vessel known as the Grail was guarded by the Grail King who suffered from an unhealed wound. His condition was linked to the condition of his land, and it is implied that this was laid waste as a direct result of his wounded condition for it did not support any life, either of plant, animal, human or Faery. The healing of the King and his land can only be brought about when a questing knight discovers the Grail castle, sees the Grail, and asks what it all means.

In the period in which Arthur's kingdom lies in a state of waste and rotten-ness we have what seems to be a parallel situation with the Waste Land of the Grail legends. But there are some important differences. The Grail King, who has been wounded by a spear, is unmarried; there is not a Grail Queen. Arthur, on the other hand, is married but has not been wounded, and no questing knight is needed to put things right within his kingdom. In contrast to the situation which has befallen the Grail King who must passively wait until someone arrives to initiate the action needed to change things, it is Arthur himself who alone has the knowledge and ability to rescue his kingdom from its state of rotten-ness, and he chooses not to do so.

Arthur represents Everyman, and in many ways we all have the same responsibilities as were carried upon his shoulders. He has all the knowledge he needs to enable him to distinguish between true and false, and the truth in this instance is intimately connected with his acceptance and realisation of his destiny to build a bridge between the human and Faery races, and of the true nature of the Faery being he has married. The episode of the false Gwenevere presented him with his first major test in this respect: the opportunity to chose between the more difficult path of his true purpose or the easier life with the false Gwenevere. The deeper meaning behind this episode is relevant to humanity as a whole, which also knows of the existence of the Faery race but chooses to ignore it. The consequences of our forgetting are, in a sense, the same as the rotten-ness which afflicted Arthur's kingdom. We and our physical world are very much the worse for our state of divorce from the Faeries who also inhabit it.

The story continues by describing how although Arthur took the false Gwenevere with him wherever he went, he would not sleep with her anywhere except in his own room. One cannot help wondering why the author felt it necessary to include this odd detail and as to what significance it might hold. In fact, the act of intercourse between a human and a Faery brings us to the very heart of the matter. The first plot to substitute the false Gwenevere was intended to prevent this moment of union from taking place. Whether the act of love takes place between two humans or between a Faery and a human it brings all worlds and all levels together for a brief moment. Any mismatching of the levels, any lack of synchronisation between the planes, and the mesh which holds the forms together is placed under pressure. Perhaps the problem was not with Arthur but with the false Gwenevere: that it was *she* who could not permit the act of love to take place unless she was within the walls of the chamber which kept her in close proximity with her confidante Bertelay whose presence, along with his herbal potions, seems to have been so necessary to her.

This takes us into difficult waters, but we must wade through them as best we may. This section of the Prose Lancelot is dealing with the actual mechanics of moving between one level of manifestation and another. For humans to enter the Faery world it is necessary for them to raise their level of vibration. For most people this is generally done by directed imagination and by the elevation of consciousness upon the Inner Planes so that the senses begin to function at a higher level. The persistent practice of these disciplines will eventually take effect upon the physical body, and as is well known, the health of the physical body is dependent upon the health and integrity of the subtle bodies. For a happy few, the step between the human and Faery worlds is just that: a step. Hence the stories of those such as Thomas the Rhymer who entered Faery whether he would or no, and for those such as he, the veil between the worlds is virtually non-existent.

For Faeries, of course, the process is very different. We have already seen that those such as Galehaut, or Gawain, or Culhwch, are able to move between the worlds with apparent ease, but for Faeries to function within the human world it is necessary for them to step *down* their level of vibration. Some idea of what this entails may be realised if we try to imagine how we might interact with the world of an earthworm, or a piece of rock. The idea quickly loses its attraction! And indeed just as the habit of raising one's consciousness to the higher planes can only have a beneficial effect so the habit of lowering one's consciousness will have the opposite effect.

This process is described graphically in the Prose Lancelot. One night, after having quarrelled with some of the noblemen of Arthur's court, the false Gwenevere withdrew to her quarters. But a transformation of the most unpleasant kind began to overtake her body. The first symptom was that she lost all her physical strength, an indication that the vital energies which supported her physical body were under attack. The process of withdrawal of vital energy continued so that her muscles gradually became paralysed with the exception of her eyes, and her flesh began to rot from the feet up.

One begins to wonder at this point exactly who or what this 'Gwenevere' is, for the graphic account of this unpleasant decay does not accord with our usual perception of either a Faery or a human being. While the real Gwenevere appears to have adjusted reasonably well to the physical world, perhaps by retaining a certain amount of the phantom-like transparency which is reflected in her name, the false Gwenevere seems to have had more difficulty. Like the act of love, the act of death also brings a soul to the gates between the worlds. At any rate, she and Bertelay presumably both soon died, for nothing more is heard of either of them. Presumably, also, Arthur's kingdom returned soon to its former verdant state following the death of the false Gwenevere and the restoration of the real Gwenevere to his side. It would seem that another crisis was over and all was once more as it should be in Camelot.

The discussion of the details of this episode in the life of Gwenevere has revealed several apparent inconsistencies in the behaviour of the main characters. It may be argued that as these stories are not history as such, to attempt to interpret the characters' behaviour in the light of normal rationality is bound to run into problems. But at their root, these stories are memories of magical rituals; memories which have been many times elaborated, embellished and deliberately 'occulted' or veiled until their core is all but obscured. Their magical core remains, and many of the apparent inconsistencies can be taken as indications to aspects of that inner truth.

The episode in which Gwenevere spent three years in the Faery kingdom of Sorelois was the first of many attempts on the part of the Faery race to take Gwenevere back as their own. Following the disappearance of the false Gwenevere, these attempts rapidly grew in frequency.

The second successful abduction, also described in the Prose Lancelot, is the better-known attempt instigated by Meleagant.[2] Often confused with Mordred, Meleagant is popularly assumed to be 'evil' since, at least at first sight, he appears to pose a threat to the stability of Arthur's Kingdom. Certainly there is far more sense of a deliberate plan in his abduction than the attempt made by Galehaut whose actions seem mainly to have been a genuine attempt to keep Gwenevere safe.

Meleagant is the son of Bademagu the King of Gorre who was re-crowned King every year upon the Feast of Mary Magdalen. Gorre, like Sorelois and Carmelide, is one of the Faery kingdoms which these stories reveal to have been much closer to the physical land than is now the case. This particular episode also provides further information as to the nature of the Faery Kingdoms and their relationship with the human world because the inhabitants of Gorre play a noticeably more active role in the story.

This 'abduction' is heralded by a visit from the Lady of the Lake to her protégé, Lancelot of the Lake. The Lady of the Lake is the power behind many of the more significant interchanges between the two worlds of human and Faery, the most obvious example being the occasion on which she presents Arthur with the sword Excalibur. Her status is over and above all the Faery Kingdoms, and these do not necessarily work in harmony together any more than do their physical counterparts. The Lady of the Lake is the Faery counterpart to Merlin, but while Merlin spends long periods of time working within the human world, the Lady of the Lake only makes brief appearances and is seen in many different guises. She could be regarded as the High Priestess of the Faery Priesthood, and her appearance at this point in the story alerts us to the fact that something of especial significance is about to take place.

It is interesting to note that after Merlin's intervention in the first attempted abduction of Gwenevere on her wedding night he then withdraws from the scene. It is as if the responsibility for overseeing, and sometimes manipulating, the unfolding of the events between human and Faery now falls to the Lady of the Lake, although it has to be said that while Merlin would appear to be impartial in his dealings with the inhabitants of the two worlds, the Lady of the Lake is rather more biased towards the Faeries. Perhaps such positive discrimination was considered necessary in the greater scheme of things, but at any rate while Merlin was responsible for setting up the pattern in which these events were to unfold it is the Lady of the Lake who now takes the initiative from within the Faery world and sets things in motion.

She finds Lancelot living rough in the countryside near Tintagel, where he is in the throes of a madness which has been brought about by the disappearance of Galehaut. She also reveals something of her close relationship with Lancelot. Certainly he is favoured by her in a manner that she does not extend to others, not even to Arthur whom she treats with rather short shrift. Lancelot's great friend Galehaut has recently died, but she refrains from telling Lancelot of his death in case it makes him feel worse. Instead, she keeps him by her side throughout the winter in order to ensure that he comes to a full recovery. Her reasons for doing so are not entirely altruistic, for she has a plan that will necessitate the full co-operation of both Gwenevere and Lancelot, and she needs to get him fit for the task. As soon as he has recovered she tells him that he had better get to Camelot with all good speed because on Ascension Day Gwenevere is going to be abducted at the hour of nones, or three o'clock in the afternoon. She tells Lancelot that if he is present at that hour then he will be able to rescue her, even though she will be taken to a place from which nobody has ever been rescued before.

It should be noted that she does not suggest to Lancelot that if he arrives on time he will be able to *prevent* the predicted abduction from taking place, but rather that even if he does manage to get to Camelot on time, it will happen anyway! His actual task is to get Gwenevere back from where she will have been taken, even though such a rescue has never been successfully made before. This curious prophecy reveals that the forthcoming events, which she has obviously known about for some time, are far from a simple escapade in which Gwenevere is taken from one world to another and then retrieved. What the Lady of the Lake has planned, for she is the moving force behind these events, is a complex exchange in which the two worlds of human and Faery will be forced into a closer relationship with each other. The actual 'abduction' is nothing less than a ploy by which the Lady of the Lake, working through Meleagant and Lancelot, is hoping to bring about a sequence of events designed to effect a mutual exchange and understanding between the worlds. Thus the stakes are considerably higher than in the previous attempted abduction.

Meleagant arrives at Camelot just as the Lady of the Lake predicted, but rather than immediately seizing Gwenevere and carrying her off, he first establishes the connection between the main characters in these events. He states that he has come to the court in order to prove his honour against Lancelot, and he refers to their joust of the previous year in which Lancelot was wounded.

Lancelot has not yet arrived on the scene, and Meleagant is told that no-one has seen him for a long time. He strides away, frustrated, but then turns at the door and unexpectedly announces that many of Arthur's knights, ladies and maidens are imprisoned in Gorre, but that no attempt has ever been made to rescue them.

This fact does indeed seem to be news to Arthur, who shows no awareness that any of his people have disappeared and does not come up with any suggestion as to how he might retrieve them! It is Meleagant who proposes how this might be accomplished, suggesting that one of Arthur's knights should escort Gwenevere to the edge of the forest and try to defend her against him. If this knight does manage to defend her successfully, then Meleagant will not only free all the human captives in Gorre, but both he and his father will become Arthur's men. If on the other hand Meleagant wins the duel, then the outcome is rather less clear, because he tells Arthur that "…this won't stop you from doing all that is within your powers, nor me from doing what I can."[3]

Here we have the outward appearance of a challenge which accords with the knightly code of conduct, but in fact is an indication of a very important episode of interaction between the two worlds of Faery and human, and of the re-balancing which the Lady of the Lake intends should take place between them. As we have seen before, on an immediate level the story makes little sense. How can a large number of Arthur's knights and ladies disappear without anyone noticing that they have gone? If Meleagant had been able to capture a large number of human prisoners without anyone missing them, then why risk everything by coming to Arthur's court and telling him about it? And why would he need human prisoners anyway, since he was not at war with Arthur?

The real challenge in Meleagant's statement is to our own perception of the reality of his Faery kingdom of Gorre. Like Arthur, who as in the previous episode stands for humanity as a whole, we find it hard to accept that there are large numbers (or indeed any) humans who are alive but living somewhere other than our own physical world. Arthur's response to Meleagant's claim is quite significant, for his reply is to the effect that what can't be cured must be endured. This serves to reveal that he has not yet arrived at the point where he is able to initiate any action which might change the situation or in any way improve the relationship between Faery and human, and it has to be said that his position is that taken by humanity from his time onwards. These stories mark the point when the division and distance between the two worlds had reached a critical point, and the Prose Lancelot seems to express the same incomprehension between them that was to prevail for the next thousand years.

In fact Meleagant's claim that many humans were living within the Faery world is accurate, although the term 'prisoners' is misleading. When we start to think outside the limiting conceptions of time and space we can begin to appreciate what he means. His statement should be understood in terms of consciousness rather than actuality, for there are many whose physical body may be extant within the human world but whose consciousness is such that they are also present within the Faery world. When we think of artists, poets, musicians, film-makers, children and adults who say they see Faeries, not to mention all those who in recorded history and legend who have walked between the worlds, and those who have been dubbed 'fey', then we start to understand what Meleagant means. The real nature of his challenge is to draw Arthur's attention to the Faery world and to get him to acknowledge its reality, and he does so in a manner most likely to attract Arthur's attention by suggesting that Gwenevere might be taken there.

Meleagant, under the aegis of the Lady of the Lake, is opening up a way between the worlds through which Arthur and those he represents may travel, if they wish to do so. He may also be seen as a representative of the Faery Priesthood, about to enter into a ritual of passage between the worlds in which Lancelot and Gwenevere will also play an important part. The Lady of the Lake has chosen well, for what is to take place will depend in no small part on Lancelot's love for Gwenevere and it is this emotional power which will drive him on into Faery.

Meleagant, having fulfilled his part of the deal, returns to his own land. It is now the task of Lancelot, driven by his love for Gwenevere, to follow through what has been set up by Meleagant and the Lady of the Lake. In doing so he undertakes a challenging initiatory journey which involves considerable sacrifice on his part. Gwenevere's role appears to be passive, but the forces which she represents are pivotal to the entire process. Were it not for his love for her, Lancelot would not pursue her into Gorre and, in so doing, open up the way for others to follow. Were it not our desire for that 'something else', for some lost enchantment, for some memory of other, blessed lands and for our forgotten ancestors who have already reached the world of the Shining Ones, then we too would not seek them but remain in our own isolation. Over and above this, the unfolding story makes clear that the passage between the worlds can only be made in love and respect, not idle curiosity.

Just before he leaves Arthur's court, Meleagant sets out the possible outcomes of this adventure, and these are worth looking at before we follow Lancelot on his journey. The initial action will take place in the forest into which Gwenevere is taken, symbolic of that area of consciousness which borders the two worlds. The fight which is about to take place between the representatives of the two worlds represents more than a simple joust. Gwenevere stands at the point of balance between human and Faery, and the contest for her is symbolic of the relationship between them. If the representative from Arthur's court successfully defends Gwenevere, then this will demonstrate the desire of the human race to retain their connection with Faery, their wish not to lose their Faery Queen but to keep her and what she represents at the heart of their kingdom. If this desire is strong enough then she will stay with Arthur and the way between the worlds will continue to open up, providing a means of passage for human seekers to enter into the Faery kingdom of Gorre. Simultaneously, it will allow Meleagant and Bademagu to travel more easily into the human world and to find a place within that world. They will thus become "Arthur's men."

If, on the other hand, the representative of the human race does not demonstrate this desire sufficiently strongly and loses the symbolic fight, Gwenevere will be lost to the human world; she will be escorted back to Gorre by Meleagant and will withdraw for ever from the human race. Clearly much depends on the outcome, and in the next chapter we will explore just what this entails.

1   Norris J. Lacy, ed., *The Lancelot Grail Reader,* (New York: Garland Publishing Inc., 2000) pages 143-168
2   ibid, pages 180-212
3   ibid, page 182

CHAPTER NINE
The Ritual of the Knight of the Cart

The episode in which Lancelot follows Gwenevere into the Faery kingdom of Gorre is often called "The Knight of the Cart."[1] It is an account of a journey of initiation into Faery which culminates in a ritual of high magic undertaken between human and Faery, although of course all of this is disguised in story. Many of the Arthurian legends are memories of magical rituals which have later been put into story and this is why, if you attempt to reconstruct them as such, they so readily reveal their origin. This is not to say that they have not been altered during the course of many thousands of years; many details have been added and changed in their long development through many countries and in many hands, but the subject matter which informs and inspires them remains the same.

Meleagant's challenge to Arthur, in the traditional terms of ritual, is the statement of intent which precedes any formal piece of magic. The purpose of this definition of terms and boundaries is to ensure that all who are taking part in the ritual will begin to make the necessary mental preparation, withdraw their focus from the outer world and bring their attention onto the matter in hand. The potential raw material for a ritual is almost infinite, but much of its effect in performance will depend on the focused concentration of those taking part. If an Arthurian ritual is about to take place it will not help matters if its participants' minds are wandering on the slopes of Mount Ida or in the lotus pools of Egypt. The ritual intent in this instance is to open a way between the human and Faery worlds through the laying down of what have been called tracks in space. These may be thought of as shining pathways of energy in the subtle planes of existence, although they operate in exactly the same way in which a path is formed on the physical plane. When someone treads through a grassy meadow for the first time then the indentation caused by that action makes it more likely that the next person who crosses the meadow will follow the same line, and so on, until a permanent path is formed.

Having defined the terms of what is to follow, Meleagant then retreats from the human world represented by Arthur and goes to stand at the borders between that world and the Faery world, which in this and many other instances is represented by a forest. Many of Meleagant's own Faery kind have also assembled there and thus the main characters in the ritual are gathered together, named, and their purpose stated for all to hear.

However, the exact moment of the start of the ritual was set down by the Lady of the Lake: the hour of nones on Ascension Day. At the beginning of the story, Lancelot has not arrived at Camelot and therefore anything which happens before this time will not be a part of the ritual. This, too, is a ritual tradition that makes obvious sense: everyone taking part in a ritual must not only be in the same place but must start at the same time! The time is set by the beings of the Inner Planes working through the Lady of the Lake. The place is defined by the two worlds of human and Faery represented by Arthur and Meleagant respectively, and these can perhaps be imagined as the two great interlocking circles of the geometrical form of the Vesica Piscis. The nature of the events which will unfold during the ritual have been kick-started, as it were, by the catalyst of Meleagant's challenge to King Arthur, Faery to human.

Although Arthur's reaction to Meleagant's challenge is "what will be, will be", Kay, who is traditionally characterised as being somewhat abrupt in nature, unexpectedly and prematurely takes matters into his own hands by insisting that he should immediately accompany Gwenevere to the edge of the forest. Arthur is reluctant to allow this to happen and Gwenevere appears to be even more distressed by Kay's proposal, weeping so bitterly that she is unable to speak. At first glance her reaction might be brushed aside as typical female behaviour: Gwenevere is understandably upset at the thought of having to leave her comfortable home in order to hang around at the edge of a forest while a couple of men hurl blows at each other. But Kay's precipitous action is endangering the whole endeavour. He is about to start things going before the agreed time and it is not his place to do so! This is not simply a matter of convenience for the participants but is part of the contract with the beings of the Inner Planes who will empower the forms set down by the ritual. If signals are given to them that things are underway before the agreed time then there is a very real danger that the rehearsal will turn into the ritual itself. Consequently when the real ritual starts, much of the energy has already been dispersed and the ritual itself will be reduced in power. Kay's emotional reaction is very unfortunate, and he blunders into matters that he obviously does not properly understand. Gwenevere, who as the Priestess of the ritual will bear much of the consequences of his untimely action, is understandably speechless!

However, Arthur allows Kay to do as he wants, and Kay takes Gwenevere to the edge of the forest where he encounters Meleagant. Meleagant then makes a formal, ritually empowered contact with Gwenevere, first by asking who she is (as if he didn't know) and then by lifting her veil. Again, this could be interpreted as a conventional action of the time, but in the customs of ritual Meleagant's 'lifting of the veil' signifies that Gwenevere is now taking an active part in the ritual proceedings rather than being a mere bystander. By removing her outward veil of humanity Meleagant has revealed her inner Faery identity, simultaneously lifting the veil into the Faery world as a whole. Gwenevere has been revealed for her true self and as the representative of Faery within the human world. Her role in this ritual is to mediate the inner powers not only of the world of Faery but also, as we shall see, the stellar world which empowers Faery. It is Meleagant who, as leader of the ritual, is responsible for instigating Gwenevere's role.

Three of the main characters of the ritual have thus been identified. We know who Arthur is and what he stands for. We know who Meleagant is, where he comes from and what he stands for. We know who Gwenevere is, so far as the ritual is concerned. Kay's role is as yet uncertain, but his presence will later prove to be of great significance.

Meleagant suggests that they should all move into a clearing where they will have more room to fight, and it is at this point that Lancelot appears and takes charge of the proceedings. Using the same technique of question and answer, he asks Kay who he is and what his purpose is. Again, this is not for Lancelot's benefit; Lancelot knows perfectly well who Kay is, but the purpose is to make a formal statement of intent which will be heard by those upon the Inner Planes. All four of them have moved away from the human world of the court and to the place between the worlds symbolised by the clearing in the forest. Once there, Meleagant and Kay fight. Meleagant defeats the hapless Kay who is carried off in a litter and appears to have been removed from the proceedings as fast as possible. Lancelot is now free to take up the challenge, and he puts up a brave fight with Meleagant and some of Meleagant's knights, but in spite of his best efforts Meleagant and Gwenevere soon disappear into the trees and fade from his sight.

There is a curious air of inevitability about this scene that betrays its ritual origins. Somehow we know that Kay will lose his fight with Meleagant. Somehow we know that Lancelot will inevitably fulfil the precise terms of the prophecy of the Lady of the Lake by arriving in time to witness the disappearance of Meleagant and Gwenevere into Faery but will not manage to stop them. Meleagant's actions are equally governed by the laws of the ritual, for when his knights come to assist him and it begins to look as if they might overpower Lancelot, he tells them to go away and leave Lancelot alone! This is hardly the action of one keen to win a fight at all costs! And in spite of the assistance of Gawain who also now arrives on the scene with fresh horses to give speed to Lancelot's pursuit, we know that he is not destined to catch up with Meleagant and Gwenevere for some time yet.

After this initial skirmish, everything is now set for the story to unfold in the manner of a quest, and following the dismissal of the unfortunate Kay it is Lancelot who must prove his strength, perseverance, desire and purity of motive before his goal will be achieved. The subsequent scenes describe how he is tested in these qualities. If his motive for wanting to enter the world of Faery is merely curiosity, or lust for Gwenevere, or if he lacks endurance and gives up at the least challenge, or in any way shows lack of faith, then he will not have the qualities necessary to take on the task of holding open the way between the worlds of human and Faery. The same is true of any who take this journey, and the challenges which Lancelot is about to face are those which are encountered by any seeker of the Mysteries of Faery and human.

Lancelot pursues Meleagant and Gwenevere through the forest until he is at the point of exhaustion, but is not able to catch up with them. However, having thus proved his commitment to the task, he now faces his second test. Deep within the forest, he comes across a cart which stands on a broad, grassy path. A dwarf is sitting on the cart. Lancelot asks the dwarf if a knight and a lady have passed that way. The dwarf indicates that he has seen them, but he first wants to know if Lancelot *greatly desires* to know where they are going, thus challenging Lancelot as to the strength of his resolve and will to continue. Lancelot's response is prompt and unequivocal, for he tells the dwarf that he does want to know, more than anything else. The dwarf's reply, on the other hand, is less than straight forward because he tells Lancelot that if he gets into the cart then he will not be taken to where Meleagant and Gwenevere are, but to a place where he will *learn the truth about them.* The dwarf has revealed that the object of the quest is not simply to locate Gwenevere and bring her back, but to discover certain aspects of wisdom which will then, through him, be made available to humanity in general. Lancelot climbs into the cart.

But by doing so he sets himself apart from the accepted bounds of normal society and, so the writer tells us, his reputation will thus be destroyed and he will be disgraced in every country. We are told that it was everywhere the custom that anyone who rode in a cart would lose all status accorded to a knight and would thereafter never be received in court. Whether or not this is actually so (and the fact that it was considered necessary to explain it to the reader suggests that it may not have been commonly known) we are told that Lancelot is now stripped of his former status and privileges. This is standard practice within any Mystery School where much of the training is designed to bring the neophyte to an awareness of the illusion of the apparent realities of the mundane world. Such actions as the symbolic removal of jewellery or the wearing of robes is intended to strip initiate and neophyte alike of any outward signs of personality or outer-world status. Lancelot cannot enter the world of Faery encumbered with the outward trappings of a Knight of the Round Table, and the customs, preconceptions and behaviour of the human world will not help him in his quest. By indicating his readiness to enter the cart he has shown his willingness to relinquish these material comforts and human habits in pursuit of his goal.

Gawain, who has followed Lancelot through the forest and who now comes upon the dwarf and the cart, is also asked by the dwarf if he would like to ride in it. He answers that he would never do such a thing and chooses to ride behind it, following where Lancelot has led. Gawain is no mere accessory to these events: he has taken this journey into Faery many times before and his role is to act as guardian and mentor to Lancelot who is undertaking the ritual journey for the first time. He doesn't need to make the symbolic sacrifice of riding in the cart.

The three of them continue on their journey. Dusk falls, and with the waning of the light comes another challenge. They arrive at a castle where the inhabitants jeer at Lancelot's lowly position and pelt him with stones. Gawain, adopting the role of devil's advocate, tempts Lancelot with the option of relinquishing the cart and continuing his journey on the back of one of the horses that he has brought with him. Lancelot refuses to take the easy option, and so they pass on, through the castle grounds. He has been tested as to whether or not he would give up his quest under the pressure of misunderstanding or antagonism from those about him, a very real test for anyone entering the Mysteries.

They arrive at a second castle where every inhabitant, young and old, chases after Lancelot in order to hurl more insults at him, but this time the dwarf drives the cart into an enclosure surrounded by high walls. He tells Lancelot to get down from the cart and to go to sleep in this enclosure, for this is the only way that he will discover what he wants to learn. At first a little reluctant, Lancelot decides to stay, and this is evidently the right decision for straight away two maidens descend from a high tower to meet him. Their descent from the heights indicates that they are representatives of a higher order who have come to assist him and to offer him a challenge beyond that which has already faced. They recognise Gawain and welcome him with joy, confirming that he is no stranger to these things! He has already passed this stage in the ritual journey.

Lancelot now has to make certain choices, and these are symbolised by three beds which are offered to him by the maidens. The middle of the three is the most splendid, and covered with a cloth of gold stars, but Lancelot is warned that if he sleeps in it he will be in for a difficult time. He chooses to take it.

The tests of the "Perilous Bed", and there are several such beds in the Arthurian legends, are those in which the Shadow is faced, recognised for what it is, defeated, and its strengths incorporated into the psyche. It is when the initiate is 'asleep' and the daytime defences of the personality are no longer in place that the full force of the Shadow can be seen, often taking on strange or animal-like shapes. Perhaps the most notable of all these beds is that found in the Ship of Solomon, made ready for all those who would follow in the lineage of the Western Mystery Tradition. Yet the initiate of the Mysteries who spends a night on such a bed faces more than his own individual shadow, and the nature of that which confronts him is likely to contain elements of the collective unconscious of the folk-soul of his nation. This collective shadow is traditionally referred to as the Dweller on the Threshold. The difference between the two is that while the individual who seeks self-knowledge is likely to encounter only his own Shadow upon his journey of self-discovery, those who undertake to serve within the magical Priesthood of their race are likely to have to confront rather more than their own repressions.

Thus we find that the test which is given to Lancelot lies at the heart of these Mysteries between Faery and human. Lancelot is literally run through by a symbol which links the Faery race with the Christian Mysteries: the spear, pivot of the Mysteries of the Grail. While he sleeps, (or, in ritual terms, enters into meditation) a spear with a white shaft and red tip descends from the roof like a thunderbolt. It bursts into flames, pierces through the bed-clothes and strikes Lancelot upon his left side in a manner which suggests a direct correlation with the Spear which pierced the side of Christ. Lancelot's challenge is not only not to show fear, but to continue in the face of whatever terrors may be summoned up by his own subconscious, and by his reaction to this sudden bursting through of the symbolic heart of these Mysteries.

In fact he responds with calmness, bravery and common sense. He puts out the flames, hurls the spear away from him into the middle of the room and then goes back to sleep! His apparent indifference to the violence of the phenomenon that bursts upon him reveals the virtues of discretion and discrimination. It is as if the strength and power of the symbol of the flaming, blood-tipped spear has broken through into his consciousness but it cannot, even by Lancelot, be grasped at this time and it is not appropriate for him to try to do so. His only proper course of action at this time and place is to put it aside until the time comes when he is better able to comprehend and deal with the full force of its power and Mystery. We shall encounter the Spear later, in the Castle of the Grail.

But Lancelot has little respite, for he is woken by the dwarf who shouts to him to come to the window. He sees a procession of knights and ladies in the meadow far below. Among them is Kay, still carried on his litter, and Meleagant who is leading Gwenevere on a white horse. This stately procession has a solemnity that betrays its ritual origin. But Lancelot is nearly driven to despair by the tantalising glimpse of the Queen, so near yet so far, and the realisation that she has spent the night in the same castle. He is about to jump from the window when Gawain, ever watchful at his side, pulls him to safety. Perhaps unconscious of the service which Gawain has done him by preventing him from abandoning his proper quest in pursuit of his love, Lancelot races out of the castle, but Meleagant and Gwenevere have disappeared from sight. The dwarf also disappears. But having proved his dedication, Lancelot is now able to continue his journey on horseback, an indication that his former status has been returned to him. His destination is Gorre, the land of King Bademagu and Meleagant.

After riding for some time without further adventure, Lancelot encounters a damsel who gives him some detailed instructions on how to find and enter Bademagu's land. There are two entrances, she says, both of which involve crossing over a dangerous bridge. One way is called The Water Bridge. This strange bridge runs *under* the water and has the same depth of water above it as below it. The other is called the Sword Bridge, because it is as sharp as a sword. In esoteric terms, Lancelot is being offered two approaches to the Faery Kingdom that lies at the centre of the ritual. The 'watery' way appears to be easier but its appearance is deceptive. Once on the bridge the seeker may become lost in a confusing mirrored world of illusion where it is not easy to distinguish above from below. The sword, on the other hand, presents the more difficult road of the spirit which cuts through illusion, but offers a very narrow path that does not allow for mistakes or a faltering step. Lancelot chooses the way that leads to the Sword Bridge.

In terms of the ritual journey, Lancelot is about to approach the Inner Temple and the area of Gorre that he is about to enter is laid out in a pattern typical of a Temple of the Mysteries. Once he has successfully passed over the bridge he will reach a place called "The Land Beyond" whose four-square boundaries are guarded at each corner by a castle. Customary ritual practice divides the Temple circle into four quarters, each representative of one of the four directions of the compass and of one of the four elements of earth, fire, air and water.

But before he reaches the aptly named Land Beyond, the intensity of the ritual is heightened as Lancelot encounters a symbol which serves to open up further Inner levels. He comes across a comb that Gwenevere has dropped in his path, and which contains some of her hair. There is great significance in this apparently conventional love-token. Esoteric Hebrew theology makes much of the symbolism of the hairs upon the beard of God, but there are other instances which lie closer to the spirit of this story. Percivale's sister Dindrane wove a belt for Solomon's sword with her hair and thus made an enduring connection between her own body and the sword of the spirit of the Grail Kings. But the real significance of the comb and strands of hair is that it opens up the stellar levels that lie behind, and empower, the Faery world.

The connection is revealed by the legend of Berenice's hair. Berenice, a Ptolemaic Queen of Egypt, pledged to sacrifice her hair if her husband was safely brought home after his battles with the invading Assyrian hordes. When he did indeed return safely she kept her word and, cutting off her hair, placed the tresses in the nearby Temple of Venus. The Goddess Venus herself took up the tresses and carried them up into the starlit sky where she spun them into a new constellation. The constellation thus formed, the Coma Berenice, lies between the constellation of Leo and the bright star Arcturus, and this wonderful stellar imagery adds a deep symbolism to Lancelot's discovery. Venus represents the 'higher self' of earth, and her powers are very much connected with the working through of those higher impulses into earth in a way which has equal relevance for human and Faery. The constellation of Berenice's Hair forms a stellar gateway, for it is said that behind it lie a thousand hidden galaxies, each hosting a myriad other worlds. And here also is a perfect link to Gwenevere, for the constellation of Coma Berenice was once considered to be part of the constellation of Leo. Just as the separation of the Little Bear from Draco is the stellar equivalent of the descent of Arthur from Uther PenDragon so the separation of Coma Berenice from Leo symbolises Gwenevere's emergence from her father Leodegrance.

The symbol is offered to Lancelot for him to make what he will of it, and he takes it to his heart. However, there is more preparation in store before he finally enters the Faery world. In addition to the opening up of his awareness of the stellar levels he must also now make a formal pledge of his allegiance to the work of the Mysteries and of his service to the Great Work which they represent.

Lancelot arrives at a church within a monastery where he discovers a number of tombstones. They mark the graves of Galahad (not the usual Galahad, but a son of Joseph of Arimathea) and twenty-four of his companions; also the tombs of Gawain, and of Lancelot himself. Whoever lifts the lid of the most richly decorated tomb is destined to release the prisoners within Gorre. The apparent confusion of names and as to which generation of Galahads is referred to is an indication of the continuity over many years of the underlying ritual. Although the names Galahad and Lancelot may once have belonged to individuals, during the course of time they have become attached to a role or office within the ritual. The episode gathers together some of the many threads of this tradition prior to Lancelot's crossing of the Sword Bridge. It links the present events with what has happened in the past, while also looking forwards in time to the Grail stories. This is a customary ritual technique, for within the bounds of the magical Temple past, present and future are as one. A ritual is concerned with archetypes, patterns, and Inner realities and not with individual personalities bound by space and time. The Priesthood who represent those archetypes within the ritual must extend the boundaries of their consciousness to take in the greater picture.

Several minor adventures follow in which it becomes apparent that Lancelot's impending presence in Gorre is now not only predicted but that the awaiting 'prisoners' are strengthened by his approach. The passage between the human and Faery worlds works both ways. When Faeries enter the human world, changes occur. When humans enter Faery, changes also occur and these will be especially felt by those Faeries who already have human connections.

Lancelot finally arrives at the Dolorous River which forms the boundary of Gorre. Here he encounters a Ferryman whose role is more than that of the silent oarsman who takes his money and rows his boat. The toll in this instance is not a fixed token but varies according to what the Ferryman chooses to ask! A comparison may be made with the encounter between Arthur and the Lady of the Lake in which she asked for whatever she desired in return for the sword Excalibur.

This particular test is a subtle one. Lancelot's immediate aim is to enter the Faery Kingdom of Gorre which lies at the heart of this Mystery and represents the highest point of the ritual. Yet he must not be glamorised by the Faery world and its enchantments nor confuse its inhabitants with Gods and Goddesses. If Lancelot allows the Ferryman to make an unreasonable demand of him in return for getting him there then Lancelot is not making a realistic assessment of the Faery race or of his own task. He would successfully reach the Faery world but would have failed to see beyond it to the greater picture and, ultimately, would fail in his quest.

Unlike Arthur, Lancelot wisely refuses such an open-ended contract. His greater understanding of the world of Faery makes him wary of such a demand. Another fight ensues in which Lancelot gains the advantage over the Ferryman and leaves his opponent begging for mercy. At this moment a young woman rides up and begs Lancelot, as a favour that will bring him great honour, to cut off the head of the ferryman because he has been 'treacherous' to her.

Lancelot's tests are coming thick and fast, for he is now placed in a moral dilemma. He would not normally refuse to grant mercy when it was requested, but neither would he normally refuse the request of a lady when it was within his power to grant it. Her un-nerving request is not without its parallels in the Arthurian and Grail mythos: the Lady of the Lake demands of Arthur that he gives her the severed head of Balin in return for her gift to him of Excalibur. A parallel may also be made with Salome's request of the head of John the Baptist. Lancelot tries to find a way out of the situation by offering the ferryman another chance at a fight, generously lessening the odds by giving him a new shield, but he quickly overcomes him again. He cuts off the ferryman's head and gives it to the young woman who, it would appear, has a task to perform which lies beyond that of mere revenge. She grabs the head, jumps onto her horse and races off with it until she reaches a well, ancient and very deep, and throws the head down it!

A well is not normally a good place to put a decomposing head. But this is a ritual, and such actions must be interpreted accordingly. The deposition of the ferryman's head within the depths of the well adds another dimension to the episode. The stellar levels of awareness have been opened up through the episode of Gwenevere's hair and its connection with the constellation of Coma Berenice, and now the corresponding connection with the deep earth is established. The Celtic belief in the powers held within the head is well documented. We can see it behind the story of the severed head of Bran which, after entertaining his followers with song and prophecy for seven years was eventually buried under the White Mount of the Tower of London. Ancient well-shafts have been found to be oriented on certain stars in the same way in which the so-called air-shafts in the pyramids are focused on certain significant stars. The ferryman's head, now deep within the earth, reflects and focuses the incoming stellar influences at this crossing-point into the other world. Lancelot is therefore literally at the axis of heaven and earth: he is now not only crossing from the human world into the Faery world but also standing, within the terms of the ritual, over the 'vertical' flow of energy between deep space and deep earth. It is revealed at this point that the young woman is Meleagant's sister.

Lancelot pauses before the river, which is not wide, but very deep. And here the reader is granted the first description of the fabulous country which lies upon the other side. He looks across the water to where the city of Gorrun stands upon the other bank, beautiful, magnificent and unearthly. Gwenevere is now safely within a castle in this city, and at the same moment as Lancelot reaches the edge of the river she comes to a window in one of the castle's towers and looks out across the river towards him. In a ritual performance this would be a very powerful moment. Lancelot makes his preparations for crossing the Sword Bridge as best he may, and begins to move over it inch by inch, receiving many sharp cuts in the process, until he reaches the other side where he wipes his blood upon the grass.

On arriving at the other side he straight away encounters King Bademagu, who up until now has been an invisible presence in the ritual. It is of no little significance that this character is only revealed when Lancelot has reached the other side of the bridge. He is of a very different world and cannot be perceived until the reader, with Lancelot, has reached the world of Faery. Bademagu asks Gwenevere to identify the knight who stands upon the edge of his kingdom. Lancelot still wears his helmet which in symbolic terms serves to indicate that he is still functioning at a lower rate of vibration than Bademagu. Gwenevere tells him that she believes him to be Lancelot of the Lake, whereupon Bademagu offers an interesting appraisal of the situation. He says that of all the knights of Arthur's kingdom it is Lancelot whom he loves the most. He also tells Gwenevere that it is because of her relationship with Lancelot that he holds her in the regard he does, since her husband's ancestors had caused great harm to his ancestors.

And in this statement, made at the moment of Lancelot's entry into Faery, we are given in a nutshell the situation which Lancelot has come to remedy. Bademagu does not specify precisely which of Arthur's ancestors have done harm to his own and the statement perhaps does not refer to the immediate past. Arthur's more immediate and historical ancestors were, as we have seen in earlier chapters, closely and sympathetically linked to the Faery world. But Bademagu is of very ancient stock indeed, far older in time than his son Meleagant, and the root word 'magus' within his name suggests his real status. When he speaks of Arthur's ancestors he is referring to ancient feuds and battles between human and Faery of time before memory, not the more recent actions of Uther, Ambrosius or Ygrainne who came into the world in order to try to solve the very problems to which Bademagu refers.

Bademagu shines through the story in a manner which is very reminiscent of Tolkien's Elven race. He possesses the wisdom of the Elves and displays their understanding and serenity, and while his son is representative of the more headstrong, ego-driven Atlantean race, Bademagu is of the older, Lemurian age. He assesses the situation that has come about by Lancelot's entry into Gorre with a dignified and rational overview where his son Meleagant is more inclined to rush headstrong into it with fists and sword. Bademagu comes to greet Lancelot as he stands wiping the blood from his wounds upon the grass, and tells him that he will place him under his protection, so that the only person he need fear is Meleagant. This is perfectly true: Bademagu has no axe to grind even though he is aware of the age-long conflict between Elves and Men, and he stays free from any of the more immediate battling between Lancelot and Meleagant.

Soon it becomes evident that Lancelot's purpose in travelling to Gorre has very little to do with the release of the so-called prisoners who have received increasingly scant attention in the story and are now almost completely forgotten. Nor, even, is the aim of his journey to rescue Gwenevere. She is clearly not held captive by Meleagant and could return to the human world and Arthur's Court any time she chose – although that is beside the point.

Now that Lancelot has reached the city of Gorrun, all the main characters are gathered together. Bademagu, Meleagant, Gwenevere, and Lancelot are present. Gawain, who has acted as Lancelot's mentor now disappears into the background, but another important character comes forward: Kay. As mentioned earlier, this is not Kay's journey of initiation and he has certainly suffered for having jumped the gun, as it were, when he tried to attack Meleagant in the forest. But for a reason not explained at the time, Meleagant put Kay on a litter and had him carried into his castle in Gorrun. Kay's role in this unfolding ritual drama is to take over the role of Everyman from King Arthur. Often, Arthur stands for Everyman, but Arthur is also King. He cannot himself travel to Faery because he must remain at the head of his human kingdom of Logres, and in this ritual journey which takes place between the worlds he has to stay at the centre of the human world. If we think in terms of the two interlocking circles, Arthur must remain in charge of the human circle. But Kay can take his place and represent Arthur's qualities within the Faery world, and indeed he does just that.

Initially nothing seems to have changed after Lancelot's crossing of the Sword Bridge. He and Meleagant fight (again) but Bademagu and Gwenevere decide that this approach will solve nothing. Bademagu separates them, and demands that a solution should be reached upon a higher level. But it seems that the chief movers in this story are not yet capable of attaining that level, for Meleagant's only response is to protest that Bademagu is interfering in his private battle. They eventually reach an uneasy truce in which Meleagant and Lancelot agree that Meleagant can go to Arthur's court and summon Lancelot to fight with him whenever he wants, and Gwenevere agrees that if Meleagant wins the fight she will again go with him into Gorre.

But this half-baked solution only leads round in circles, although it has to be said that as a prophecy of what will happen in the future between the human and Faery worlds it is uncannily accurate. The unresolved tension between Faery and human does still exist, Gwenevere is still pivotal in the 'contest' between the two worlds and finds no real home in either, and it is the lot of Lancelot and those who follow in his path to continue to travel between them until a permanent resolution is reached.

The catalyst for the resolution is provided by Gwenevere, and it is entirely appropriate that at this moment, when it really matters, she steps out of her previously passive role and initiates the final sequence in the ritual. When Lancelot has recovered from his latest fight with Meleagant he goes to her in the full hope that she will give him proper recognition and reward for all his hard work. Her only response is to tell him that he has wasted his time. Lancelot is understandably shocked and disappointed! But Gwenevere is acting neither through coyness nor in the conventions of courtly love. Just as the initiate in the Eleusian Mysteries was confronted at the end of his journey with the revelation that "There is no God", or the initiate in the Egyptian Mysteries reached the empty chamber, or the Qabalist reaches the sphere of Daath on the Tree of Life, Gwenevere is instrumental in informing the seeker that when the apparent goal of the arduous and testing journey is reached, it is no longer the goal. The seeker has only reached the stage where he or she realises that everything they thought was real, is an illusion.

And in confirmation of this, there follows an episode in which Lancelot and Gwenevere each believe the other to have died. The significance of the final twist of these apparent deaths is to indicate that they have each, at this point, 'died' upon one level of reality and have now both now attained a higher level of consciousness. The consummation of the ritual is not that Lancelot and Gwenevere make love in any physical sense, but that, each representing their respective worlds of human and Faery, they bring about a union between them at the highest possible level. The reader and the other ritual participants are not included in this final act of magical mating, but the events which lead up to it indicate something of what is involved.

Although Gwenevere can come and go from her room in the castle at will, rather than suggesting that Lancelot should enter her room in the normal way through the door, she shows him, to the left of her bed, a window covered by iron bars. On the other side of the window is a garden surrounded by a crumbling wall. She tells Lancelot to wait until dark and then to come to her in her bedchamber which, for some strange reason, she shares with Kay.

Once night has fallen, Lancelot climbs out of the window in his own room, crosses the garden, scales the crumbling wall and then manages to remove the iron bars from out of the window frame without making a noise and without waking Kay. After spending the night with Gwenevere he returns the same way at dawn, replacing the iron bars as silently as he has removed them. However, he had injured his hands in the process, and they bled in Gwenevere's bed. Lancelot himself appears not to have noticed that this was happening and Gwenevere, we are told, mistook the blood for perspiration because it was dark.

In the morning, Meleagant visits Gwenevere in her bed-chamber as is his custom, and notices the blood on her sheets. But he also notices that Kay's unhealed wounds (which were, as we recall, received some considerable time previously in his fight with Meleagant) had been bleeding more heavily during the night, an apparently customary occurrence. He assumes that Kay, who is unable to move or even speak because of the severity of his injuries, has spent the night in Gwenevere's bed.

What are we to make of this? Why is a man sharing the Queen's bedchamber when the castle must surely have had rooms to spare? Why doesn't Lancelot just walk through the door? Why are Kay's wounds still bleeding after all this time? Why is there no sign of a nurse, or of any suggestion that Gwenevere is tending to his wounds? Why did Meleagant go to so much trouble and effort to get Kay there at all when it would have made a lot more sense to have left him in the forest? When we subject the story to such rational questions it is in danger of becoming almost farcical, but we must remember that its real meaning is disguised behind such apparent nonsense.

We have said that Kay represents the presence of Arthur and the voice of humanity, but the truth lies deeper than this, for the real purpose of Kay's presence is his human blood which is being spilt in the Faery castle of Gorrun. It is through the constant bleeding of his wounds that the presence of the blood of humankind is, literally, brought into the very heart of this ritual in this castle of Faery. While Lancelot makes the journey into Faery by taking on the trials which confront all those who seek to follow in his path, he is by nature of his birth already halfway there. Kay, on the other hand, represents humanity at its least receptive to the Faeries. While his only way of reaching the Faery kingdom is by literally being carried there, once he has arrived, his presence serves to bring about a constant flow of human blood, and the life-energy which is found within that blood, into Bademagu's Faery world. His abrupt actions have resulted in an act of personal sacrifice which holds talismanic significance, and which in some respects is comparable to the Wounded King of Grail legend.

We must remember that the castle of Gorrun is a magical Temple. Gwenevere's bedchamber is not a room for sleeping in, but lies at the centre of the Temple where the heart of the magical and ritual activity is found. Kay must therefore also remain there, at the centre.

Lancelot's entry into the Inner Temple can now be seen as the final part of his initiatory journey. His crossing of the Sword Bridge had only taken him into the Outer Court of Faery. The further test initiated by Gwenevere still lay before him, and it was only when he had passed this that he was permitted to enter the Inner Court which, in the terms of the story, is Gwenevere's chamber. Even then it is not a matter of walking straight in through the door. He must find his own way to Gwenevere.

The nature of that which still bars Lancelot's way enforces his return to the very concepts with which this study is concerned. In Chapter One we looked at the significance of the Garden of Eden in which the final separation between human and Faery was recorded in the Bible. In order to achieve a union with Gwenevere as Queen of Faery, and this act of magic is the ultimate aim of his journey, he must first find his own way back into the Garden in which human and Faery first became separated, then find his way through it *and out the other side*. By virtue of his long journey he is more than half-way there, and this is symbolised by the fact that the wall surrounding the garden is crumbling: he is not confronted by an impenetrable barrier but has already begun to break down the walls. When he has returned in spirit to the time and place of the Garden of Eden he has arrived at the point at which human and Faery went their separate ways. Yet even this is not enough, for another barrier, that of the iron bars, still lies between him and Gwenevere. Gwenevere is now not only the Queen of Faery but she represents the stellar beings that inspire her world, and the final barrier between her and Lancelot presents the ultimate metaphysical challenge.

The description of the iron bars across the window makes no sense on a literal level. Iron bars cannot be pulled out from a stone encasement without effort or noise unless they are only lodged in place, in which case there would have been no point in them being there. But since this is a Faery castle which does not exist on the physical plane there is of course no stone or iron there at all, although it has often been said that iron is one of the greatest symbolic barriers between human and Faery. Once Lancelot has entered the Garden he must go further back in time and space and reach behind the veils of creation itself. The iron bars which appear to be an obstacle are not, and the encasement of the stone window which appears to hold them in place, does not. And yet these apparent barriers serve their purpose. The journey back through consciousness into the far distant source of our being is barred to all but those who are as dedicated and determined as Lancelot.

1   The two versions referred to throughout this Chapter are:
ed. Norris J. Lacy, *The Lancelot-Grail Reader* (New York: Garland Publishing Inc. 2000)
Chrétien de Troyes, trans. W.W. Comfort, *Arthurian Romances* (London: Everyman, 1986)

CHAPTER TEN
Why Faeries marry Humans

The preceding chapters have tended to show Gwenevere playing a passive role in the dramatic events which unfold around her. The ritual of the Knight of the Cart gives little away as to her character, preferring to depict her almost entirely in her role as Priestess of the Faery Mysteries. In this and the many other such rituals hidden within the stories of Arthur, the Knights of the Round Table and the Grail, the personalities of the individual characters are of far less importance than the universal and archetypal forces they mediate within the ritual. But is this a true indication of Gwenevere's state of existence in the human world, or is there any evidence to show that she might have played a more positive hand in her destiny?

As we have seen, one of the most remarkable features of her life was that she was abducted from Arthur's court many times over, and although we have looked in detail at one or two of these episodes there are number of others.[1] Several of the lesser-known stories are particularly interesting, and help us to gain a better picture of Gwenevere herself rather than Gwenevere as a Priestess and mediator of archetypal forces, and some of them even offer us glimpses of her Faery family. Unfortunately most of the versions of the Arthurian mythos which were originally written in English or have been translated into English tend to be the very ones which have pared away much of the recollection of her former life. It is the lesser known, still untranslated chronicles such as *Diu Crône*[2] which contain the more interesting information as regards Gwenevere's Faery background. The accounts which have achieved popularity tend to be those which emphasise the human side of the stories at the expense of the Faery perspective.

One of the better known of the abductions so far not discussed is that attempted by Melwas, ruler of the Summer Country, who captures Gwenevere and takes her to his City of Glass, a location which can readily be equated with Glastonbury. Melwas's stronghold is surrounded by marshland, a feature of the natural landscape which surrounded Glastonbury before it was drained and which also appears in several other versions of the abduction stories.

This time it is Arthur himself who searches for Gwenevere. He searches for a year before he finds her, but manages to rescue her safely, with the help of Saint Gildas who is responsible for telling this particular story. While this tale is interesting for its specifically Avalonian setting and for the unusual appearance of Arthur as the one who rescues his wife, it would appear be a Welsh version of the Meleagant abduction and does not really provide us with any significant new information. However, it should be noted that the story makes no suggestion that Gwenevere was ill treated by Melwas, nor that she was unhappy with the situation, and this fact becomes increasingly more evident as we look at some of the remaining abductions.

In the *Perlesvaus*[3] we are given one of the best indications of Gwenevere's family. Following her death, a certain Madeglans of Oriande, who lives in the "far North", claims that he is her next of kin. He therefore requests that her dowry of the Round Table should be returned to him, or alternatively that Arthur should now marry his sister, the oddly named Jandree. We are given no information of the nature of their relationship, but something may be inferred. Presumably Madeglans is not Gwenevere's son, nor is Jandree her daughter, or they would be named as such, so they are probably her brother and sister. But the nature of the relationship is less important than the fact that Gwenevere had a next of kin at all, and the hierarchy of human blood relationships is not applicable to Faery families which consist of a large, interconnected group of like beings all of whom could be described as brother or sister.

The episode is also significant in raising the question of what happened to the Round Table after Arthur's death. As Madeglans is of the Faery race his claim that the Table should be returned to them after the ending of the PenDragon era would seem to be perfectly justified, and an indication that its work within the human world was now over. The Table represents far more than a mere piece of furniture and when it no longer has an appropriate human guardian then it must be returned to the Inner Planes and the Faery world from which it originated. Madeglan's suggestion that Arthur should now marry another of the Faery race is also interesting for it does reveal some continuing understanding from the Faery point of view of the purpose behind Arthur's marriage.

A little-known poem, the *Lanzelet* of Ulrich von Zatsikhoven,[4] offers some rare insights into Gwenevere's ancestry. This telling of the story introduces King Valerin of the Tangled Wood, who lives in a shining castle at the top of a high mountain. The castle is surrounded by mists and can only be approached by a single road through a forest that is inhabited by serpents. Clearly this is no human king and no ordinary forest. Valerin appears at Arthur's court and announces that Gwenevere belongs to him because she was pledged to him as a young girl. Lancelot, as usual in the right place at the right time, fights a duel with Valerin, and defeats him. Valerin rides away, but on a later occasion when Arthur is hunting the white stag in a forest, he attacks again, and this time successfully carries Gwenevere away with him.

However, the poet informs us that Gwenevere did *not* enjoy her stay with Valerin. Again it is Arthur who attempts to rescue her, although he has to enlist the help of the enchanter Malduc who is able to cast a spell upon the forest and overcome the serpents that surround the castle. Valerin has put Gwenevere into a deep sleep, although one wonders why he should. But if Gwenevere was unhappy in Valerin's care then perhaps this action was necessary to prevent her from escaping. As it is, Arthur wakes her, and kills Valerin. Malduc knowingly remarks that if Gwenevere had gone to Valerin of her own free will, his life might have been spared. It would seem that Gwenevere is happy with some of her abductors but not with others. She was apparently only content to be carried off by her own kind if she liked them, which seems fair enough!

Diu Crône (The Crown) was written in c.1220 by Heinrich von dem Türlin, but tantalisingly is for the most part as yet untranslated into English. It provides us with many more of the names of Gwenevere's family, and the author of this version of the story has some especial insights which make his version unique. Here, Gwenevere has a sister called Lenomie, a brother named Gotegrin, and her father is called Garlin of Galore. We cannot help but note the similarity between Garlin and Garlon, the latter being an important character in the Grail legends and who will be discussed in more detail in Chapter 13. But more to the point, a character named Gasozein le Dragoz accuses Arthur of taking Gwenevere from him and of keeping her captive, in Britain, for seven years!

Gasozein is clearly of the Faery race, and we are at last given an unequivocal description of the situation from the Faery point of view: *that it is Arthur who has abducted Gwenevere from the Faeries.* This makes so much more sense of the otherwise inexplicable series of abductions of Gwenevere by the Faeries, which are now shown to be a persistent attempt on the part of her kindred to remove her from the human world and restore her to her own kind. Gasozein is described in some detail by Gwenevere who tells how he wears only a white silk shirt with red hose, that he rides a white horse, and carries a white shield and red spear. He spends each night at a ford which is marked by a black thorn tree, all the while singing songs to his love, Gwenevere. This is the ford between the worlds, reminiscent of the ford at which Morgan waited until discovered by King Urien.[5]

Arthur and his companions ride to the ford, and meet Gasozein. He claims that he is Gwenevere's real partner, having had her love from the time that she was born. He and Arthur agree to fight a duel for Gwenevere, but just before this takes place Gasozein asks for the proceedings to be drawn to a halt and says that Gwenevere should be allowed to decide whether she prefers to stay with Arthur or Gasozein. But Gwenevere seems unable to make the choice.

There are deep issues at stake here and ones which Heinrich seems to be fully aware of. Gwenevere is indeed *not* able to decide; she is *not* able to exercise free choice, nor can she move freely and at will between one world and another. She has to exist predominately *either* as Faery *or* human, and too much has happened already for her to return to the Faery world of her own volition. In obvious desperation she resolves the issue by unexpectedly denying all knowledge of Gasozein, which in effect amounts to a denial of the existence of the Faery world.

At this, Gasozein immediately leaves, but Gwenevere's brother Gotegrin now appears on the scene, seizes Gwenevere by the hair and rides off with her into a wood. One may wonder whose side he is on, for he is about to kill her when Gasozein reappears in the nick of time, sweeps Gotegrin up into a tree and himself rides off with Gwenevere.

It may well be that Gotegrin was incensed that Gwenevere denied her own people at such a crucial moment, but of course if she had decided to return to Faery with her lover Gasozein then the entire story would have ended there and then. If, in company with other Faeries who find themselves in a similar position Gwenevere had said "Sorry, Arthur, I'm just not enjoying life here with you any more and I've decided to go back home" then we begin to realise just how much depended on Gwenevere staying within the human world. As it is, Gwenevere and Gasozein are about to consummate their love when Gawain rides up and puts a similar question to her: "Is this situation brought about by your own free will?" Gwenevere's answer has to be "No," and so in an attempt to resolve the matter in the time-honoured fashion Gawain and Gasozein fight until they are both exhausted.

The stalemate between Gawain and Gasozein is a true symptom of the underlying problem, for no amount of fighting can bring a resolution to the issue at stake: that of Gwenevere's inability to choose freely between the worlds of Faery and human. We are tempted to ask whether Gwenevere *chose* to live in the human world and marry Arthur, but the concept of free will is even more difficult when applied to those who are not of the human race. Faeries do have free will, but not as individuals.

Their freedom of choice is not differentiated between each separate soul because they themselves do not as a general rule have that individuation. One may well ask how many of the human race really exercise or are even aware of the extent of their free will, but never the less it is there to be exercised. This lack of individual free choice lies at the root of much otherwise inexplicable Faery behaviour, not least that of Gwenevere.

At a personal and individual level Gwenevere probably did not make the choice to become human and marry Arthur. If she had done so then that conscious decision to incarnate as a human would have shone through her actions and resulted in a stronger personality and more directed sense of purpose than she appears to demonstrate. This raises the deeper issue of whether Gwenevere's exile in the human world could bring about the desired effect if she herself was not a willing party to it. So far as we are told she shows no resentment, but neither does she give the impression that she whole-heartedly espouses the task for which she has been chosen. Inevitably she comes over as a pawn rather than a leading player in this game of chess between the worlds, and talismanically this cannot have a beneficial effect on the final outcome.

As it is, Gawain and Gasozein agree to go to the Castle of Caerdoel until they have both been healed, and then start all over again! The situation is finally brought to an end when Gasozein declares that he had lied when he said that Gwenevere loved him. Under the circumstances this is probably the only available solution, and his statement should be recognised as a generous reaction. It certainly releases Gwenevere from an impossible position, although in the final analysis and the greater scheme of things it solves nothing when the Faeries retreat in this way.

Although this is one of the most significant abduction episodes, there are many others. In addition to those already discussed, the Prose Lancelot mentions two other attempts. The first is by King Lot of Lothian, and takes place a week before Arthur's marriage to Gwenevere. Lot is here named as one of the twelve kings who are hostile to Arthur. Following a battle which takes place between them, Arthur captures Lot's wife and son, who in this version is Mordred. (Sometimes Mordred is said to be Arthur's son.) The explanation for this attempt at abduction is unusual because it is so normal! Lot's reason for wanting to capture Gwenevere is a simple and understandable act of revenge, and an attempt to get his own wife and son back again in exchange for Gwenevere.

Another unlikely abductor in the Prose Lancelot is Bors, and it is very out of character for this honest-hearted Grail winner to attempt such an undertaking. But Bors has promised a certain Lady that he will attempt to capture Gwenevere, and he reluctantly keeps to his promise although he is defeated in the attempt by Lancelot. Another surprising abductor is King Urien of Gorre, a story told in the *Livre D'Artus*.[6] He captures Gwenevere while Caerdoel is on fire, but again it is Gawain who rescues her. The *Livre D'Artus* also describes another of Gwenevere's lovers, Gotengos (his name is very similar to that of Gotegrin) who also appears in the Vulgate Cycle.

Among this bewildering plethora of captures and rescues, several distinct patterns emerge. First, with the exception of Valerin, none of the abductors shows any attempt to overpower or ill-treat Gwenevere or even, with the exception of King Lot, use her as bargaining power. In fact she seems to be treated with great respect, is acknowledged as a Queen in Sorelois, and rarely restrained. There is no attempt to take advantage of her, or to threaten Arthur and his kingdom by using her as hostage. In the great majority of cases it is those of Faery blood who are responsible for abducting Gwenevere and it would therefore seem that their only motive is simply to take her back to her own land. Next, it is always the same few characters who act as intermediaries between the worlds in the attempt to bring her back to King Arthur: occasionally Arthur, often Lancelot, but usually Gawain. Gawain seems to be one of the very few who is able to recognise the greater plan behind Gwenevere's marriage with Arthur and he consistently rises above the tug-of-war between the worlds. He has no personal interest in thwarting the intentions of the Faery world because he has no personal relationship with Gwenevere. When he rescues her from her abductors and returns her to Arthur it is simply in order to support and maintain her presence within the human world for as long as possible. This very fact alone casts some interesting light on aspects of Gawain's character and his role in the stories that has not previously been recognised.

In Lancelot's case, the obvious explanation for his behaviour is that he is Gwenevere's lover, but since Lancelot was himself either of Faery blood or at least had a very close relationship with Faery as a result of his up-bringing by the Lady of the Lake, it would actually have been of personal advantage to him to follow her into Faery and stay there with her rather than bringing her back to Arthur and his world.

In fact Lancelot didn't appear on the literary scene until the late twelfth century, and is first seen in the works of Chrétien de Troyes. This is not to say that Chrétien invented the character he called Lancelot. His Lancelot emerges fully fledged from a background of several traditions, one of which he especially personifies: that of the archetypal good knight, brave and courteous but of uncertain parentage, who appears upon the courtly scene having until then been fostered by an other-worldly mother. But unlike the writers of the Vulgate Cycle who clearly were aware of the background of the magical and ritual tradition to their stories, Chrétien chose to emphasise the purely human aspect of things, and it is his interpetation which has gradually taken supremacy in the general perception of Lancelot's story.

It is not hard to see why Chrétien should have included a very human Lancelot in his re-telling of the Arthurian mythos and chosen to place him so centrally. His Lancelot provides the tension, drama and inevitable tragedy of a human love interest which the legends had previously lacked, with the possible exception of the more peripheral adventures of the Cornish Tristan and Ysolde. But he did his job so well that Lancelot-and-Gwenevere quickly became a unit, and a very appealing one at that, taking centre-stage so effectively that for ever after no other writer has been able to rend asunder the couple which he so successfully brought together. The Arthurian story is now unthinkable without the triangle of Arthur, Gwenevere and Lancelot at its centre, but the unfortunate effect of Chrétien's human slant is that it takes us yet another step away from their original meaning. Inevitably legends change and adapt in their telling in order to reflect the demands of their time, but in this instance the change is to be regretted. There is never very much depth to be found in the tangles of a human love-triangle, and in this case it serves only to emphasise the human-ness of Gwenevere while making any real understanding of her Faery origins even less likely. Chrétien's Lancelot is the final nail in the Faery coffin.

It cannot be denied, however, that he offers his readers a way to make sense of Gwenevere, and without Gwenevere there would be little point to Lancelot. Instead of a lack-lustre wife who never really fulfils her role as Queen she becomes a perfectly understandable human figure who is caught in a tangle of human desires. Once she has fallen in love with Lancelot she furnishes the story with its central emotional tension. We are given sufficient information about her to satisfy any curiosity we may have had about her actual function in the stories: she is Arthur's wife but she loves Lancelot, and because we know what she does, we assume that we know who she is.

And this is by no means the only advantage of making Gwenevere human. As a result of her adultery, it is said, the ideals of the court and the Round Table are brought into disarray; everything that goes wrong is her fault, just as it was Eve's fault back in the Garden of Eden at the beginning of time. As a literary device and pseudo-religious comment this is a master-stroke, but what is gained by the humanisation of Gwenevere and her love-affair with Lancelot is achieved at the expense of her real purpose, and in the final analysis this contrived human triangle is of little consequence beyond that of human mores and amores. It grabs our attention, but blinds us to the deeper message of the story.

The inspiration for the Arthur-Gwenevere-Lancelot triangle may well have been the earlier but little known triangle of Arthur-Gwenevere-Mordred. Mordred is linked with Gwenevere by several of the major chroniclers including Wace, Lawman, Geoffrey of Monmouth and Malory, and this three-cornered relationship is actually of much greater interest. But Mordred's parentage is not certain, and some chroniclers say that he was the son of Arthur and Morgan. Perhaps because this presents something of a problem, he is generally considered as malevolent and no proper study has been made of him. His relationship with Gwenevere has similarly tended to be ignored. There are few obvious bad guys in the Arthurian stories, and the tendency has been to force Mordred into this vacancy to a greater extent than may be warranted by the facts. He has become demonised like his half-sister Morgan, although it is true to say that they each perform a similar, and often disruptive, function. The question is whether this was 'motiveless malignancy' or whether there was a genuine Inner initiative behind their actions. There are certainly traces of a split within the Priesthood which may have stemmed from a justified disapproval of or disagreement with Merlin's plans. But Mordred's role cannot be ignored: he is at the centre of it all; a catalyst to some of the most important events in the Arthurian court just as Balin later functions as a catalyst in the Castle of the Grail.

Perhaps another reason for our discomfort with Mordred's character is that he doesn't seem to come from the same place as Kay, or Gawain, or Lancelot. In fact there is a group of characters at the centre of the Arthurian legends whose ancestry is uncertain, yet who share similar names and have a similar 'feel' to them: Morgan, Mordred and Morgawse. Morgan and Morgawse are both Ygrainne's daughters, yet they are not the daughters of Uther PenDragon, nor are they are the daughters of her first husband Gorlois, and a third husband is never mentioned. Their strength and influence suggests that they represented a line of the Atlantean Priesthood descending with Ygrainne but which was at odds with much that was taking place.

In an environment in which Arthur's own conception was arranged by Merlin and the long arm of Atlantean magic, it is not unlikely that there were other contemporaneous attempts to influence the course of events through magical mating. When it became apparent that Arthur and Gwenevere could not produce a child, an alternative to either Arthur or Gwenevere had to be found if the entire initiative was not to fall at the first hurdle. Marrying Arthur and Gwenevere was only the first step; the most important part of the whole venture was the line of children, half human and half Faery, which it was hoped they would engender. It is most unlikely that the whole initiative would have been abandoned simply because of one failed attempt. Too much was at stake, and too much effort of preparation had been made. Arthur had offspring by other, human women, but these children could not provide the desired result of a marriage between the worlds. Another Faery partner had to be found for him, although Madeglan's suggestion that Arthur should marry Jandree was obviously not greeted with much enthusiasm!

Morgan, Ygrainne's daughter, was the obvious choice. Morgan was of Faery blood, yet there are vital differences between her and Gwenevere. Morgan has far more definition than Gwenevere. Like the other Priestesses of the Lake, she acts more positively and speaks more loudly; she has adjusted much better to the conditions of the physical world. Yet the contrast between Morgan and Gwenevere reveals the range and variety of the Faery world. It seems that perhaps Gwenevere is of purer, earlier Faery blood and cannot adapt well to human physicality. Morgan is of the Faery/Atlantean Priesthood and is therefore more skilled, as are others of that Priesthood such as Merlin, in moving between the worlds. Obviously one of purer blood would have been the first choice, but when this attempt ran into difficulties then an alternative had to be found.

But the problem with the mating between Arthur and Morgan or between any human and Faery, is that that the natural laws of the human world have to be respected and observed by those who wish to function in this world, and this arrangement violated one of the fundamental laws of the human condition. In the human world there are very good reasons for avoiding incestuous relationships. This does not in itself make Mordred 'evil' as such, but certainly provides an open door for unbalanced force to enter, and there is no doubt that much of Morgan and Mordred's behaviour is disruptive of the status quo of Arthur, Gwenevere and the Court. Since the attempted union between Arthur and Gwenevere clearly wasn't succeeding there must have been an understandable frustration within the inner Priesthood to clear the stage for the next attempt while Arthur was still alive. One can only speculate as to what might have been planned, but there was clearly an impatience that since a successful mating had now been achieved between a human and a Faery (Arthur and

Morgan), their child Mordred should be allowed to get on with things. Much of Morgan's apparently disruptive behaviour can be interpreted in the same light, such as her attempt to seize the initiative by stealing Excalibur.

In common with other Faeries, Mordred seems to have matured very rapidly, and there is some evidence to suggest that his intended partner was Gwenevere. An early Welsh tradition states that Gwenevere actually left Arthur for Mordred,[7] offering a rare instance of Gwenevere taking matters into her own hands by leaving Arthur of her own volition. Her unusual action lends some weight of significance to the man of her choice. Why did she choose Mordred? The obvious answer can only be that he was much nearer to her own race than Arthur. *The Alliterative Morte Arthure* states that he and Gwenevere had a child.[8]

Later versions tend to confirm this early tradition. Geoffrey of Monmouth describes how when Arthur was away doing battle with the Romans he left Gwenevere and Mordred in charge of his kingdom, only to discover later that they were living together adulterously. Again one wonders why Arthur chose Mordred to take his place at Gwenevere's side. It is not as if he didn't have other sons even though none were Gwenevere's.[9] He returns to Britain and defeats Mordred.[10] Wace describes a similar scenario[11] but suggests something of the emotional charge behind these events by telling us that Mordred was greatly in love with Gwenevere but had understandably kept his feelings to himself. Wace says nothing of Gwenevere's feelings towards Mordred but, when describing how they later lived together as lovers, significantly does not offer any suggestion that Gwenevere was coerced into the situation, and it does rather sound as if the two of them were equally happy with the arrangement. Mordred retreats to Cornwall in guilt and fear when Arthur returns, and we get a brief glimpse of the difficult situation he is in by virtue of the circumstances of his birth, and by the mounting pressure upon all who were involved in these events.

In the *Lyr Myreur des Histoires*[12] Mordred is said to have survived the battle with Arthur only to be pursued and attacked by Lancelot, presumably out of jealousy over Gwenevere's behaviour with Mordred. But this version of the story concludes with a startling new twist. Lancelot kills Gwenevere, and then incarcerates Mordred with her dead body, which, we are told, Mordred eats before he finally dies of starvation!

Unless this is a grotesque attempt to add cannibalism to Mordred's already plentiful sins of incestuous birth and adulterous life, the episode is so bizarre that it must surely house a truth which has later been misinterpreted. The story appears to refer to a memory of a bricked-up cell which contains Mordred's body and Gwenevere's clothes, or of some other faint but identifiable trace of her presence. If it was commonly assumed that the two occupants of the cell were human, cannibalism would be the only possible interpretation, and since Mordred was dead he was in no position to defend himself against such a charge. But we have the benefit of the knowledge that at least one of the occupants was Faery, and this throws a very different light on things, for dead Faeries leave no corporeal remains.

However, apart from these faint memories of her relationship with Mordred, Gwenevere appears to have taken little positive action in relation to the Faery world. There are many other Faery women who do have a clear role to play, notably the Lady of the Lake and those who work with her in Avalon. But the essential difference between the Ladies of the Lake and Gwenevere is that none of the Ladies of the Lake retain a constant existence within the human world. There are many strong Faery maidens who ride out from Avalon into the human world and up the very steps of Arthur's court to throw down their challenge of a sword, a demand, or a taunt, but having done so they quickly return to their own land. Nor does Gwenevere make any reaction to such appearances from her own world. It is as if it is enough for her simply to *be* a Faery within the masculine-oriented human world of the Court of Arthur, to survive, and to endure.

Again we must turn to other sources for illumination, for there are a number of stories which are far more explicit about the tensions which are caused when a Faery female within the human world makes contact with a previous Faery lover. One of the best of these is the Irish legend of Étaín and Mider which was used by William Sharp in his verse-drama *The Immortal Hour*,[13] later so powerfully set to music by Rutland Boughton. William Sharp's choice of this story is profoundly moving and evocative in itself, but his unparalleled understanding of the character of Faery serves to illumine many similar stories, not least that of Gwenevere.

The Immortal Hour opens with the darkly disturbing character Dalua, the Faery Fool, the Son of the Wandering Star. The wandering star is Venus, and this connection places Dalua within the tradition of Manus such as Melchizedek who act as mediators between Venus and the Earth. Dalua appears to hold considerable power over the Faery race in a manner which can be compared to Merlin, but he affects their lives and destiny in a manner that offers no easily discernible meaning or purpose.

There is an apparent randomness about his influence; he is a cosmic loose canon whose purpose is thus fundamentally different to his apparent counterpart of the Divine Fool in Christ.

> "I have come hither, led by dreams and visions,
>   And know not why I come, and to what end," [14]

His state of forgetfulness, of not-knowing, is expressed by all those of his race in this drama.

Later, Étaín, a Faery, is found wandering in the same dark wood in a similar state of forgetfulness. She has only just arrived upon the mortal earth and for a brief moment she is able to remember something of the fair place she has come from. She sings of her memories in the now famous song: "How beautiful they are, the Lordly Ones" and vows that she will return to her own land. But now she is in the human world her memory quickly fades, and soon all she can remember of her former life is her name. Dalua likens the Faery race to sheep led by an unknown shepherd, a comment that evokes a comparison with Christ as Divine Shepherd, although the Faery Dalua lacks a heart.

Étaín is discovered in the dark wood by Eochaidh, King of Eire, who sees in her the object of his heart's desire and the answer to his dreams. He has yet to learn that he will only achieve what he wants, through death. Étaín follows him to his court and they live together for a year. At the end of the year, Eochaidh holds a great celebration to mark the anniversary of his happiness. But Étaín is full of foreboding and asks to be excused from the gathering. A stranger appears in the hall: Mider. He describes himself as the first son of a King whose land lies beyond Eochaidh's realm. Although he is not permitted to tell them his name and lineage, in order to introduce himself he sings ecstatically of the love-making of Dana and Aed, the Faery first mother and father, "…when the world swayed and the stars swung … and Oengus, Lord of Love, Son of Wisdom and Death was born." [15]

Mider asks for a boon: that his lips should touch Étaín's white hand and that he should sing a song to her. We are reminded of Gasozein's song to Gwenevere at the ford. Eochaidh can hardly refuse such an innocent request, and Étaín is brought to the celebrations. She looks troubled, and is wearing the same clothes that she wore when she first appeared out of the Faery world in the dark wood. As soon as she is touched by Mider and hears his ravishing song of Faery her memory floods back, and she remembers everything. But this very fact makes her continued existence in the human world impossible, and she walks away from Eochaidh, with Mider, back into their own land.

The story is a re-telling of a well-known Irish legend, but William Sharp makes a poignant explanation of the 'forgetting' which overtakes Étaín. He suggests that Étaín can only survive her allotted time in the human world *because* she has forgotten: that her earthly existence is dependent on this forgetting. Through Mider's briefest touch and his evocative song of the Lordly Ones the restoration of her memory of what she once was, and from whence she has come, is so strong that it makes her continued existence within the human dimension untenable.

This all rings very true. It is this same condition of forgetfulness which has overtaken Gwenevere, and which makes a great deal more sense of her apparent passiveness. Gwenevere does not know who she is, or where she has come from, and her continued existence within the human world depends to a large part on the maintenance of this state. This rather begs the question as to whether this is true for all Faeries who exist for a prolonged period of time in the human world. But we should not assume that there is one rule for all. Just as it is easier for some humans to enter the Faery world so it is equally the case that some Faeries possess greater abilities than others to survive in this world. As we have noted before, there are problems in sustaining the right level of vibration at a consistent rate over a prolonged period. The 'false' Gwenevere was not able do this after her confidante Bertelay had died. The Faery messengers from the Lady of the Lake only make fleeting visits, literally riding into this world and out again just as most humans only fleetingly visit the Faery world through their imagination. Only the most skilled magicians such as Merlin and Morgan are able to maintain a more persistent presence in both worlds, and neither of them is seen constantly within the human world.

There is also a problem of consciousness, although the two factors are related. There is little point in acquiring the ability to alter your vibratory rate such that you are able to walk in and out of another world if you are not able to comprehend what you are doing when you get there. If humans manage to do this and walk into the Faery world without knowing what they are doing, and there are many tales of those who have unwittingly done so, then not a great deal is achieved. Similarly, it is questionable whether Étaín achieved very much of lasting effect during her time with Eochaidh. But on the other hand the very fact of her existence, even though of short duration, achieved something simply because of its profound effect on Eochaidh himself who, as King, may have transmitted some of this to his people.

Experience of the Faery world has the potential to bring about a huge change in consciousness which will profoundly affect the life of those who undergo the experience, and who in turn affect the lives of others as a result of their increased wisdom. The tales of Faeries who enter the human world and form a relationship with a human tend to dwell more on the subsequent passion and tragedy of the event rather than the small increases in wisdom and understanding which may be the more lasting result. History loves a love story, but the small advances in human understanding which may result from it are not so often recorded.

We may equally ask 'how it was' for Étaín, or for Gwenevere, or any of the Faery females who appear to find themselves doing time on planet Earth without much awareness of why they have come. It may well be that such realisation is not given arbitrarily by those who guard and govern these passages of interchange between the worlds. Consciousness, whether human or Faery, has many layers of veils and limitations. There are Faeries who, in their own world, have opted to incarnate within the physical world but who are then not able to cope with the realisation of that decision. This was certainly the case with Étaín and probably with Gwenevere. To some extent she knew what she was doing, but was not able sufficiently to integrate that knowledge within her waking consciousness to fully engage with her previous world, or to actively work in co-operation and further the combined destinies of those two races. Nevertheless there was within her a steadfastness which ensured that she remained within the physical world and served her purpose as best she may for many long years even though it must have appeared to offer her very little.

As a final example of a marriage between human and Faery, we shall turn to the story of Yder, for tradition names him as a Faery lover of Gwenevere. Unlike many Faeries, Yder's ancestry is well-documented and, like Gwenevere, he was part of the attempt to bridge the worlds. Loomis[16] speculates that his name, which is sometimes recorded as Edern, may derive from the Latin 'Aeternus', meaning Eternal, or Immortal, and which would be an entirely appropriate name for a Faery. He comes from a remarkable family which shares many characteristics with that of Ygrainne's immediate ancestors, reaching back into the pre-human, stellar world.

His father's name is Nudd which means "Night", putting him firmly in the realm of the earliest and most ancient of beings. Other variants of his name are Nuc or Nut, which latter is of course, and perhaps not co-incidentally, the same name as that of the ancient Egyptian Goddess of the star-filled sky. But while the conservatism of the ancient Egyptian religion means that the Goddess Nut is still the Goddess of the star-filled sky, the gradual process of humanisation to which our native Shining Ones have been subjected means that the Celtic Nut or Nudd is now little remembered, and in the story of Yder [17] he is virtually indistinguishable from any human man.

Nudd is much better preserved in Irish mythology, where he is known as Nuada, one of the earliest Kings of the Faery race of the Tuatha dé Danaan. An evocative part of this legend describes how, after his hand was cut off in battle, it was replaced by one made of silver. This image of the silver hand emerging from the dark arm of night as the bright, fertilising star-fire beautifully evokes the creative stellar force. Nuada later succeeded to Lugh, a Sun God, in the familiar manner in which earlier stellar races give way to solar-based civilisations.

In the Welsh version of this story, Nudd's most famous son is Gwyn. Gwyn ap Nudd, who has already appeared several times in these pages, means "White son of Night," another name redolent of the white Faery star-fire. According to some sources his mother is Nwyvre, whose name means "Firmament". However, other sources [18] identify her as Tywanwedd, one of the family of Amlawdd Wledig and Gwen PenDragon! There is no real contradiction here, for the same principles are exemplified, but the suggestion that Yder's mother is Ygrainne's sister certainly brings him right into the heart of this family.

In the Romance which bears his name, Yder is born in Caerdoel, a well-defined Inner castle that is often also associated with Uther PenDragon. [19] The author of this Romance is markedly anti-Arthur and pro-Faery. Here, Nudd's wife is not "Firmament" but an un-named woman who is presumably human and who may yet be Tywanwedd as clearly they are both part of the human/Faery Priesthood. Their marriage is symbolised by a ring divided into two separate halves.

Nudd leaves one half of this broken ring with his wife before he disappears, taking the other half away with him. It is Yder's task to re-join the two halves, and this task of re-forging the links in the severed destinies of Faery and human is played out through his quest to rediscover his father. As it happens this quest soon takes him to the court of Arthur, and it is at this point that the story reveals that whatever the nature of Yder's personal quest there would appear also to be a connection between him and Gwenevere, because Arthur takes an instant and apparently irrational dislike to him. In the absence of any other reason we can only assume that Arthur feels threatened by the intrusion of a brother of the King of Faery into his court, and this is confirmed by the ensuing events.

The more immediate cause of Yder's quest is Queen Guenloie, a maiden whom he has met at the outset of his adventures. Despite the similarity in names, Guenloie is not the same person as Gwenevere, although her name does reveal her to be of the Faery race. Guenloie and Yder fall in love at first sight, but at Guenloie's request he temporarily leaves her in order to achieve his destiny in the human world. His first encounter there is with King Arthur who not only takes a dislike to Yder but, as we have seen before, tends to display a particularly poor attitude towards the Faery world in general.

Yder first comes across Arthur in a wood, where Arthur is out hunting but has managed to lose his way. Yder kindly helps him to discover his bearings, and for good measure also kills two knights who suddenly appear on the scene and start to attack Arthur. Thus at the outset Yder demonstrates his willingness to serve in the world of men and to prove his allegiance to the king of that world. But once they have come out of the wood and returned to the safety of the court Arthur unexpectedly refuses to reward Yder in the accustomed manner for having saved his life, and chooses instead to ignore him completely. Yder is surprised at this unexpected snub, as is the reader, for every convention dictates that Arthur should make a formal recognition of Yder's act of service by offering him his protection in the form of a knighthood. The writer is making a deliberate point, and in order that it is not missed, it is quickly backed up by another example of Arthur's intolerant behaviour towards those of the Faery world.

A young girl arrives at the court from the nearby Castle of Maidens, and brings a challenge to Arthur. The message comes from the Lady of the Castle of Maidens who informs Arthur that she is under attack from the Black Knight, who wants to take her captive. But the situation is not as obvious as it might at first seem, for the girl is at pains to point out that her Lady is in fact perfectly well equipped to resist all such attacks without any help from Arthur. She is not asking for practical help, but wants to make the point that since the Castle of Maidens is in the gift of Arthur he should not have let his neglect of such matters allow the threat to have arisen in the first place. But now he has done so, the girl tells him, the Lady is thoughtfully offering him a chance to save his honour by staging the outward show and appearance of a rescue which she doesn't actually require! It seems that Arthur isn't interested even in saving his own face, let alone the Castle of Maidens, and he tells the girl that he hasn't got time to do anything at the moment as he is off to lay seige to Rougemont Castle in order to punish its owner, Talac, for not recognising him as king.

This episode makes clear just where King Arthur stands in his relationship with the Faery world. He has put his desire for recognition of his earthly status before his first duty of responsibility towards the Faery world, before a promise made to a Faery Priestess, and also to his duty to the Inner Mysteries which are represented by the Castle of Maidens. The imminent fight with Talac of Rougemont does not appear to be in response to any actual threat to the security of Arthur's person or kingdom but is simply a result of Arthur's indignation that Talac has not given him the respect he would have hoped for. The maiden tells him exactly what she thinks of him, angrily pointing out that Arthur had already made a commitment to the Lady of the Castle of Maidens before he got involved in petty feuding with Talac and that he has got his priorities wrong. And indeed, the disgrace which would fall to Arthur if it should become known that he had neglected his proper duty as a King would be very serious.

Yder was also greatly upset when he heard what had happened and realised that Arthur had broken his promise. Disgusted at the treatment he had received from Arthur and by what he has just witnessed, he rides away. Yet his appearance seems to have acted as a catalyst, for the situation now rapidly comes to a head. As soon as he has left the court he decides to place his allegiance with Talac, and fight with him against Arthur. His presence on Talac's side adds considerable weight to Talac's effort and he and Talac are so successful that Talac's sister gives Yder a new set of clothes in recognition of his service to them.

In the inner language of these stories this is an indication that Yder has now been fully integrated into the human world, so much so that Guenloie who is 'camping' nearby (that is to say she is watching the events from her own world) is no longer able to recognise him. But things do not end here and fuel is added to the fire when Kei, who earlier in the story had been described in negative terms even by his normal standards, stabs Yder in the back. This final act of treachery brings everyone to their senses for as a result of Kei's actions Talac and Arthur are reconciled. Yder survives the attack, but is taken to a convent to recuperate.

Gawain suggests that they visit him, and Gwenevere proposes that she and Arthur should go also. Arthur begins to question Gwenevere relentlessly as to what she would do if she were to lose him. The scene could be straight out of a modern soap opera. Gwenevere does her best to stem the rising tide of jealousy by telling him that under such circumstances she wouldn't live another day, requesting very sensibly that he should stop this distressing line of questioning. Arthur replies that he will stop just as soon as she gives him the answer he is looking for, putting forward the supposition that if someone forced her to take another husband in fear of her life, who would it be?

Gwenevere eventually admits that if she found herself in such a terrible position, and if Yder would accept her, he would be the man who would least displease her. She might have been wiser to remain silent, for this only serves to confirm Arthur's worst suspicions.

The episode is remarkably realistic in its passion and immediacy, and feelings are running higher even than the apparent circumstances would explain. The quarrel between Arthur and Gwenevere exposes a considerable depth of emotion, and it is perhaps unique in its comment on 'how it felt' for Arthur and Gwenevere. Here, they are rounded, believable characters who have to cope with living at the sharp end of an experimental marriage between the races engineered by Merlin. And in this version of events the author is clearly on the side of Gwenevere.

A subsequent episode sheds further light on the situation. Gwenevere is later found in the company of young women of noble birth, and sends one of them to find Gawain and bring him to her. The girl delivers a cryptic message to Gawain to the effect that the Queen has summoned him because there is no bishop in the Castle who is responsible for separations. Gawain is with Yder, who has recovered from his injuries, and Yvain the son of King Urien who is at least half Faery. The two of them accompany Gawain to Gwenevere's presence, but as soon as they sit down with her a large, angry, blind bear blunders into the room. The bear is not, of course, a real bear but a metaphor for Arthur, who in his jealous rage is blind to the presence of the Faery world and displays only the raw aggression of his baser animal counterpart rather than the enlightened wisdom of his ancestors.

Yder confronts the bear, preventing it from reaching any of the others by clasping it tight and squeezing the air out of its body. He then grabs it in an arm lock and hurls it out of the tower window so that it lands head first in the ditch at the bottom. Arthur, we are told, is again in a forest while this remarkable scene unfolds, but the message could hardly be plainer. In modern terminology we might call it a psychic attack caused by extreme and unbalanced emotion: one which Gwenevere anticipated and for which she appealed for help from those of her own kind.

After this episode the story is largely devoted to Yder who survives another attack from Kei, finds his father, marries Guenloie and probably lives happily ever after. Of all those whose name has been linked with Gwenevere, Yder would have been one of the most suitable of partners.

Yet had this been so, neither might achieve their destined tasks within the world.

1   They are listed by Kenneth G. T. Webster, *Guinevere: A Study of her Abductions* (Milton, Massachusetts: The Turtle Press, 1951)
2   Heinrich von dem Türlin, *Diu Crône*, ed. G. H. F. Scholl (Suttgart: Bibliothek de Littevarischen Vereins, Vol XXVIII, 1852)
3   Trans. Nigel Bryant, *The High Book of the Holy Grail* (Cambridge: D.S. Brewer, 1996)
4   Ulrich von Zazikhoven, ed. K. A. Hahn, *Der Lanzelet* (Frankfurt, 1845)
5   The meeting at the ford between Urien and Morgan is discussed by Wendy Berg and Mike Harris, *Polarity Magic* (St Paul, Minnesota, Llewellyn Publications, 2003) pages 163-165
6   Freymond, *Livre D'Artus* (Zeitschrift für Französiche Sprache und Litteratur, XVII, 1895) cited by Webster, pages 13-14
7   G. T. Webster, *Guinevere: A Study of her Abductions,* page 2
8   Cited by Ronan Coghlan, *The Illustrated Encycolopaedia of Arthurian Legends* (London: Vega, 2002) page 185
9   Arthur's sons have been named as Loholt, Llacheu, Borre, Arthur the Little, Mordred, Rowland, Gwydre, Amr, Adeluf, Morgan the Black, Ilinot and Patrick the Red, and his daughters as Melora, Ellen and Gyneth. See: Ronan Coghlan, *The Illustrated Encyclopedia of Arthurian Legends* (London: Vega, 2002)
10 Geoffrey of Monmouth, *The History of the Kings of Britain* trans. Lewis Thorpe (Middlesex, Penguin, 1966) page 259
11 Wace and Lawman, *The Life of King Arthur,* trans. Judith Weiss and Rosamund Allen (London: J.M. Dent, Everyman Paperbacks, 1997) page 72
12 Quoted in R. H. Fletcher, *Arthurian Material in the Chronicles* (Boston: Ginn, 1906)
13 Fiona Macleod, *The Works of "Fiona Macleod"* arranged by Mrs William Sharp Vol VII: *Poems and Dramas* (London: William Heinemann, 1910)
14 ibid
15 ibid
16 Roger Sherman Loomis, *Celtic Myth and Arthurian Romance,* (London: Constable, 1993) page 349
17 Ed. Alison Adams, *The Romance of Yder* (Cambridge: D.S.Brewer, 1983)
18 Referred to by Lady Charlotte Guest in her translation of *The Mabinogion* (London: J.M Dent and Sons Ltd, 1906) page 307
19 See John Darrah, *Paganism in Arthurian Romance* (Cambridge: D.S. Brewer, 1997) page 221

CHAPTER ELEVEN
The Dolorous Blow: The Sword and the Stone

The unresolved fight between Gawain and Gasozein offers a vivid microcosmic image of the macrocosmic 'fight' between the two worlds of human and Faery represented at this stage in the Arthurian story. At this point, nothing can be resolved, nothing can move on, only acted out in a repetitive cycle punctuated by periods of withdrawal or positive animosity. As things currently stand, this still tends to be how the human and Faery worlds relate to each other.

A possible way out of the impasse is attempted by Gwenevere's brother Gotegrin when he attempts to kill her. This impetuous act would certainly have sorted things out on one level: Gwenevere would have been released from a difficult existence in the human world, Gasozein would not have to fight for Gwenevere, the endless attempts to retrieve her would no longer be necessary, and the by now crumbling edifice of the union between Arthur and Gwenevere would have been brought to an abrupt close. But to short-circuit things in this way would not do, and fortunately Gotegrin is prevented from carrying out his threat.

It has to be said that Gasozein, in common with all the other Faery abductors, doesn't really help matters in his effort to re-claim Gwenevere because he is not looking beyond the immediate event. For him and his kind, matters are simple. He was not part of Merlin's plan, he did not want his betrothed to exist apart from him in a completely different world, and he intended to get her back. The eventual magnanimous retraction of his claim to Gwenevere, although easing the situation for a while, fails to address the underlying problem. The Faery attitude to Merlin's plan is made clear by Gasozein and all of Gwenevere's Faery abductors: they don't agree with Merlin's experiment, they don't want Gwenevere to remain in the human world and they don't recognise the validity of Arthur as King. And in any case, Merlin has long since disappeared from the action, Arthur generally gives the impression that he doesn't understand much of what's going on, and Gwenevere has lost her memory!

If all this were not of such importance it would have something of a farce about it. But the situation is far graver than is perceived by either Arthur or Gasozein. There are those within the Faery and human Priesthood who perceive that the severance between the two races of beings, both inhabitants of Earth, cannot continue if evolution is to run its course. Gawain is the chief representative of this belief, for he works constantly to maintain the situation brought about by Merlin and to keep Arthur and Gwenevere together even though he has no personal reason to bring Gwenevere back each time she is taken away.

It is Gawain who puts the vital question to Gwenevere: "Are you doing this (i.e. attempting this union with a human) of your own free-will?" The answer, from Faery and human alike, must eventually be a convincing "Yes". As it is, Gasozein returns to his own kind where he presumably waits until Gwenevere will one day return to him. Gwenevere returns to Arthur but produces no children. Arthur produces Mordred, who kills Arthur and is then himself killed. It is rarely acknowledged that the Arthurian legends are a catalogue of failure, yet until this reality is admitted, we cannot move on. We have arrived at the same stalemate as Gawain and Gasozein, and our period of retreat into Caerdoel has lasted too long.

The lancing of the situation attempted by Gotegrin holds considerable symbolic significance, yet his action operates at too low a level to bring about any real change. As with any stalemate, a real solution can only be achieved by an intervention from a higher level, and one which will be recognised by both sides. Although Merlin initiated these events, only someone greater than he can bring them to a resolution. So let us now broaden our perspective, and look for that One. To do so, we must become like the Knights of the Round Table who, when their mundane tasks within the kingdom were completed, turned their attention to the higher realities of the Grail.

Much has been written about the Grail. But although the commentaries and interpretations of the original stories flow as richly as ever, the actual stories of this mysterious and sacred object were committed to paper within a very short period indeed. They appeared out of the blue at the end of the 1100s AD, and by the mid 1200s their profuse but brief flowering was more or less complete. However, many of the Grail chroniclers insisted that they were recording an older tradition, and there can be little doubt that this was true.

The phenomenon of a sudden outpouring of a hitherto secret tradition occurs from time to time, and last occurred in the final quarter of the 20th century when a tide of revelation of information hitherto kept locked behind the doors of esoteric fraternities was unleashed upon the general public. Volumes of newly revealed information (not infrequently peppered with wild speculation) of the Western Mystery Tradition: its beliefs, its practices, its Temples, its liturgy, and in particular the real identity and message of Jesus, were for the first time laid before the public. Those who take an interest in these things and did not resist the temptation to accumulate some of this printed material now look at their bookshelves which groan under the weight of twenty years' of revelatory information, and ask: "Yes, but now what? What are we to do with all this?"

There is a close connection between these two creative outpourings of previously hidden knowledge. The first was concerned with a vessel, the San Grail, which was said to have contained the blood of Jesus. The second was concerned with the actual nature of that blood: the Sang Real or True Blood. The first period of revelation set forth the stories, legends, rituals and symbolism connected with the Grail, but the second period of revelation has taken us closer to the reality which lies behind them. Briefly, the Grail legends may be summarised thus ...

The Grail is guarded by a King who lives in a mysterious castle that is hard to find. Those that do find it witness a variety of strange events including a procession that appears to be part of a ritual connected with the Grail, and a group of artefacts which usually includes a sword, a spear, a dish and a stone. Indeed, sometimes the Grail is described as a cup or chalice, and sometimes a dish or stone. The Grail King is sometimes called the Fisher King or the Wounded King. He suffers from an incapacitating wound that is related to the wasted nature of his kingdom, which has been deserted by its people and in which nothing grows. In spite of the barrenness of the King's land, the Grail itself is a source of unfailing physical and spiritual abundance, and it nourishes those who find the castle and sit at its table. All, that is, except the Grail King – although no-one asks why this should be so. The healing of the Grail King depends on the actions of those who discover the castle and, on witnessing the Grail procession, ask the right question. Only then will the King will be healed of his wound, the land become green and fertile once more, and its people return. The King will be released from his position as guardian and the 'questor' will become the new Grail King. Simple!

Yet not so simple. Because the seeker, usually Percivale, eventually *does* manage to find the castle and ask the right question although on his first visit he is too excited to remember what it is. But the question is no secret: it is "Whom does the Grail serve?" And we all know the answer: "The Grail serves the servants of creation." It must have been asked, and answered, a thousand times over by those who read and ponder on this legend. Yet nothing has changed! The story remains the same, the King is still wounded, the question still asked and answered, the land still laid waste and unpopulated.

This in no manner denies the obvious and lasting benefit of a legend which provokes deep thought and questioning and is a source of spiritual nourishment and enlightenment. There is no doubt that many who meditate on the meaning and symbolism of the Grail have greatly benefited from doing so, and its Inner reality is unquestionable. But it is so easy to become enticed, like Percivale, by the plethora of characters, symbols and imagery with which it is associated and by the intellectual satisfaction of cross-referencing one version of the story with another that we, too, fail to ask the right question.

The Grail question is no longer the right question, and we need to move on. The legend, once designed to be a catalyst for change, is now stuck, and we are perpetuating its stuckness. We know the question and we know the answer, yet we continue to ask it. The Grail Question no longer serves us, neither are we served by the answer "It serves the servants of creation", which sends us round in circles upon a treadmill that sounds full of esoteric promise but gets us nowhere. The answer only tells us "I'll help you if you help me," or "I'll believe in you if you believe in me," which of course is true, but it is also true of God, or of Isis, or of any Inner Plane guide, or of one's own self, or one's own consciousness. In short, it is no answer at all. If the Grail stories are to be more than a fascinating riddle there must be something more to be discovered. Gotegrin's attempt to bring the situation to a resolution points us in the right direction but, as we have said, he was acting at too low a level to cause any real change.

One very real turning point was brought about by the so-called Dolorous Blow in which a knight killed, or injured, the Grail King. The episode of the Dolorous Blow represents the nadir of the Arthurian legends, the point at which the entire initiative finally hit the floor in apparent complete failure. Yet, as the cosmic cycle reaches the lowest point of the involutionary cycle, so does the evolutionary path become available, opening up the possibility to move onwards and upwards if we properly understand its meaning.

Nothing is the same after the Dolorous Blow has been struck. In Malory's version of this story, Balin, who has discovered the Grail Castle, gets into a fight with the Grail King but finds himself without a weapon, so he grabs a spear which is lying on the altar in the chapel. He kills the King with it. As a result of his action the castle and all its inhabitants immediately disappear, and an enchantment falls upon the land.

The enchantment of this Dolorous Blow is still working its effect, for it is as if a thick veil has been drawn across the scene and its significance is still far from understood. But we are moving ahead too quickly, and must look at the events which lead up to this, for they were set into motion long before the hapless Balin wandered into the Grail Castle. In Malory's account it is Arthur who is the instigator of the train of events which lead directly to the Dolorous Blow, these events all stemming from his lack of understanding of the symbolic significance of his sword which was gifted to him by Faery. As the sword was one of the four Faery weapons gifted to humanity this was unfortunate indeed, and it is from this point onwards that the four Faery weapons of sword, spear, cup and stone come to the forefront of events.

Arthur had not one, but two swords, and those familiar with the symbolism of the Tarot will know that Two Swords are not propitious. The first sword was broken in inauspicious circumstances. Malory describes how King Arthur gained possession of his first sword, the one which he pulled out from a stone before he was crowned King. "...against the high altar, a great stone four square, like unto a marble stone and in the midst thereof was like an anvil of steel a foot on high and therein stuck a fair sword naked by the point ..."[1] This is clearly no ordinary sword forged by the local blacksmith but a gift from the inner worlds of Faery and intended solely for Arthur. His Kingship is ratified by the very fact that he alone could withdraw the sword from its hold of iron and stone. But having acquired it, he uses it in a frenzy of killing in order to subdue the numerous petty kings of the land who refused to recognise him.

The sword was a gift from Faery as an indication of their acceptance of Arthur, and as a means whereby he could make bridges between the worlds. But Arthur has no understanding of this, and unfortunately sets the tone for his future relationship with the sword such that even Merlin has to rebuke him. This first sword quickly gets broken, and the manner in which it is broken is important because it indicates that Arthur's sense of his own destiny is 'broken' or fundamentally flawed. It is not broken in the battlefield because as a Faery weapon it could not be broken by any mortal, but in a location which forms an entrance to the Faery world: by a fountain in a forest. An unknown knight has set himself up by the fountain and kills or maims anyone who comes that way. He is the guardian of the fountain and prevents any who are unworthy or unaware from riding roughshod into the Faery world. In fact this knight is King Pellinore, and it may perhaps be said that he is a little over-zealous in his duty for he seems to leave little room for negotiation!

But Pellinore is a much older figure than Arthur, and seems to be one of the Lemurian, Elven race who has remained within the human world and yet who no longer seems to fit very easily within it, as if his time was 'out of joint'. He is of the same kind as Leodegrance, or Bademagu. His first appearance in this story gives little clue to the central role he and his family are eventually to play in these events, for it is his children Dindrane and Percivale who will eventually become foremost among the Grail Seekers. For the moment, Arthur and the reader are not aware of this even though Merlin, who is accompanying Arthur, is fully cognisant of the fact.

When Arthur encounters him at the fountain, Pellinore states that they should fight not with swords but with spears.[2] He does not say why, but his request holds particular relevance to his position at the fountain as guardian of the Faery world, because the spear, not the sword, is the Faeries' defensive weapon. Pellinore is stating his position as a King of Faery and asking Arthur to recognise him as such and fight on equal terms. But Arthur reaches for his sword, indicating that he either does not recognise that Pellinore is of the Faery world or, if he does, he prefers to ignore it and to impose the sword, the weapon of the human world, upon him. Pellinore again insists that they use spears, and eventually Arthur reluctantly agrees. It is only when they have fought for some time and all their spears have been broken that they continue with swords.

Pellinore then easily breaks Arthur's sword into two pieces. He tells Arthur that he, Arthur, has not understood the significance of their fight and does not realise that he is now in danger *whether Pellinore kills him or not*. Pellinore offers no further explanation of what he means by this enigmatic statement, but it is clear that he is availed of a greater knowledge than Arthur of the significance of this encounter and that Arthur is in grave danger of failing in his task.

The power to break a sword such as Excalibur (Malory refers to both this sword and Arthur's later one by the same name) is of no little significance. Excalibur, being a Faery sword, can only be broken by another Faery sword. It is only through the fortuitous intervention of Merlin that Pellinore, who is on the point of killing Arthur and thus bringing everything to a premature end, is cast into an enchantment and falls to the earth in a great sleep. It is a narrow escape for Arthur, but his first close encounter with a Faery has not found him acting with the wisdom he ought to have displayed, and the sword which he was destined to own throughout his life has, as a result, been broken in two by a Faery King. This is not a good start.

Pellinore is the King of Listenois, a Faery Kingdom akin to Carmelide or Sorelois. But he is no 'ordinary' Faery King because his Kingdom of Listenois is the kingdom in which the Grail Castle is located. Indeed in many versions of the story he *is* the Grail king. The distinct properties and locations of the Faery Kingdoms are not often realised. A useful analogy can be made with the more physically obvious Brughs or mounds of Ireland into which the Faery race of the Tuatha dé Danaan retreated following the invasion of Ireland by the human race of Milesians. Each Brugh became identified with a particular member of the Tuatha dé Danaan, most notably the Brugh na Boyne, or Newgrange, which at first was inhabited by the Dagda and then by his son Oengus. We can find the same association between Glastonbury Tor and Gwyn ap Nudd.

The Faery kingdoms of Britain possess the same distinctive properties, and in the many versions of the Grail story it is Listenois which is solely and persistently identified as the Faery kingdom in which the Grail Castle is situated. Our habit of ignoring this fact is unhelpful, for it encourages us to ignore this very precise and specific link with Faery. We instead relegate the Grail Castle to a generalised, non-specific Inner, imaginary or archetypal location, each of which categories also carries the inevitable implication 'not quite real'.

Further light is cast upon this episode of the broken sword by the more fully worked out thread of "The Sword That Was Broken" in Tolkien. In *The Lord of the Rings* and *The Silmarillion* the broken sword was named Narsil, which means "red and white flame",[3] suggesting the symbolism of the united blood of the human and Faery races. It originally belonged to the mighty Elendil, one of the greatest Kings of Númenor/Atlantis, and the foremost of those who survived the cataclysmic flood which caused the great Change in the world. When the flood engulfed Númenor, Elendil and a few other survivors took to their ships, eventually landing upon the shores of Middle Earth where Elendil was later recognised as the first High King of Gondor and Arnor, the two great kingdoms of Middle Earth. In the Last Alliance between Elves and Men, he fought the evil Sauron but was killed, and it was at the end of this Last Alliance that Narsil was broken into pieces. However, unlike Arthur's broken sword, Narsil was not lost and the shards eventually came into the safe-keeping of Elrond, who held them at Rivendell until the time was right for the sword to be re-forged and given to Aragorn. Aragorn, as those familiar with *The Lord of the Rings* will know, stepped out of obscurity to assist in the Wars of the Ring and, when the One Ring was destroyed, was recognised as the rightful King of the re-united Kingdoms of Gondor and Arnor. The re-forged sword was given back to him in recognition of the significance of his Kingship

The importance of the underlying symbolism of Narsil, "red and white flame", is that it represents the line of descent from the Atani ("Elf-friends") into modern times. The Atani, of whom Elendil was one of the greatest, were those of the race of Men who were closest of all to the Elvish race and were the most influenced by them, taking on many Elvish virtues such as wisdom, clear-sightedness and longevity. They represent the most harmonious and mutually beneficial relationship which can be achieved between the Elves and Men, each race preserving their own identity, yet united at a higher level. The link between them became increasingly thin after the sinking of Númenor/Atlantis, but was restored by Aragorn who displayed the highest of their virtues and ruled over his united kingdom in this light. A further correlation might perhaps be made with Narmer, the Pharaoh who united the two kingdoms of Egypt, the white Upper Kingdom and the red Lower Kingdom.

But the correlation between Aragorn and Arthur is equally clear (not least in their habit of talking to wizards) and although Arthur is a much later figure in history than Aragorn the task he was intended to achieve was no less.

To return to Arthur, we lack the early history of his first sword, although there is no doubt it had a history. Such swords as are withdrawn from a block of stone by one person alone are not intended to be temporary stop-gaps until something better comes along: they are swords of destiny. It is unfortunate to say the least, that Arthur was unaware of this and managed to get it broken in a misguided fight with King Pellinore who was arguably the last person on earth he should have been in conflict with. And if this were not trouble enough, while Arthur's first sword was given freely to him, its replacement came with conditions attached.

Merlin steps into the breach and arranges for Arthur to receive his second sword, for it is most certainly in Merlin's interest that Arthur should be armed with a sword which, if not the one originally intended, is at least empowered by Faery magic. There follows the famous episode in which Merlin takes Arthur to a lake from which appears an arm, clothed in white samite, brandishing a sword.[4] The owner of the arm is not the Lady of the Lake herself, for she is seen walking towards them across the water. Merlin explains that she has come from a rock deep within the lake. The Lady of the Lake tells Arthur that the sword belongs to her, but she will let him take it. Arthur steps into a barge, rows himself across the lake, takes the sword and its scabbard, and rows back to the shore with his prize.

But the Lady of the Lake tells him that she will require something in return for the sword. The elements of this episode make a wonderful story: the arm, "mystic, wonderful," clothed in white samite appearing from the depths, and the Lady of the Lake herself walking across the lake to meet him. But like Faust, to whom Mephistopheles was altogether far more obvious in his devilishly unreasonable demand for Faust's soul in return for what he could offer him, Arthur also did not stop to question at this time just where this bargain might lead him. He was being offered a bright sword from a beautiful Faery just when he needed one, and the temptation to take it without question was too much. And, as the Lady of the Lake reminded him, he was also being given an even greater gift than the sword: the scabbard which would provide immortality. Whoever bore it would never bleed to death from his battle-wounds. But Arthur's acceptance of this sword, although coming very early in his reign, marks the beginning of the end. His bargain with the Lady of the Lake is the start of the chain the events which lead to the Dolorous Blow.

Not long after, when the Arthur and his court were gathered at Camelot a damosel of the "Lady Lile of Avelion" entered in to the gathered company. The Lady Lile of Avelion of course is the Lady of the Isle of Avalon, the High Priestess of Avalon. Avalon is another of the Faery Kingdoms, but distinguished from the others in several respects. It too is a distinctly defined inner location, and has acquired a particular association with the physical area of the landscape which centres on Glastonbury, with its Tor, Abbey and Chalice Well. Each of these physical features provides an entrance to Avalon: broadly speaking the Tor gives access to the elemental beings, the Abbey gives access to the Christian connections and the Chalice Well gives access to the inhabitants of the Faery world. But Avalon is particularly distinguished from other Faery Kingdoms in that it is one of the main locations of the Faery/human Priesthood.

The damosel in the service of the Lady of the Isle of Avalon proves to be, as we have seen so often, the catalyst for a period of interchange between the worlds. It is as if, periodically, there is an explosion of accumulated energy from the Faery world and the herald of this is a maiden who brings challenge and confrontation with certain realities which have been ignored for too long. The damosel of the Lady of the Isle of Avalon brings challenges which confront our deepest preconceptions about the Faery world. We should not assume that every impulse from the Faery world, or indeed any Inner world, is all sweetness and light, and this particular episode is heavily laden with intolerance, violence and hatred. After announcing who has sent her, the damosel lets fall her cloak to reveal that she is wearing a great sword. Arthur comments rather unpleasantly that it doesn't suit her.

It is not right to assume, however, that this or any Faery-given sword actually originates from the Faery world. They take etheric form in the Faery world, and the various Faery beings who present these swords into the physical world are the envoys of a higher truth. Such swords are not always used wisely by human *or* Faery, and just as the humans who hold these magical swords may use them for unfit purpose, so do their various Faery owners also misuse them, ignorant of their higher purpose. That is not to deny the gift of the many swords from Faery to human, but the gift is not so much the actual weapon itself but the qualities with which the sword (and scabbard) have been invested by Faery. Some of these qualities are good and some are not so good, although these terms in themselves are relative to the world from which they are viewed. Faery morality is not the same as human morality, and neither is perfect.

The damosel announces that she is bound to wear the sword until a knight who is without villainy, treachery or treason is able to remove it from the scabbard. Surprisingly, none of the knights in the court fit into this category, not even Arthur, although they all make the attempt. Indeed we may well ask if there is any likelihood that the damosel will ever find such a perfect human being. But again, we must not forget the previous history of this sword. It was not forged within the Faery world but is the symbol of a spiritual impulse which began upon the highest planes of existence. The meaning behind her quest for a perfect human is that *if* such a one existed then the weight of unbalanced force which was carried by the sword might stand a chance of being corrected. And as is soon explained, this sword has accumulated a great deal of karma by reason of its previous use. It would therefore be better if, now the sword has come into the physical world, it was taken up by someone who would not add their own unresolved burdens to its weight.

Just as only Arthur was destined to pull his sword from stone, so only the one destined to carry this sword will be able to remove it from the scabbard. As it happens, the only knight who manages to withdraw the sword from the scabbard is one called Balin, yet he has just been fetched out of prison where he had been incarcerated for the slaying of a knight, so he is clearly far from perfect. But in effect, Balin's name was written on the sword, just as Galahad will later become the only knight able to pull 'his' sword from another stone, which in this instance is floating down a river. It was Balin's sword because it was his particular destiny to carry it out into the world and achieve some very thankless tasks.

What had given shape and form to the unbalanced force carried by the sword was something which lies at the heart of these matters: a lover's contract forged *between the worlds*. The Faery damosel had fallen in love with a human knight. Her brother, for reasons which are not given but we may guess at since the implications of any Faery/human alliance are profound, had taken strong objection to this union and had dealt with it in summary fashion by killing the knight. His sister the damosel (described later as 'false' with the chauvinism of the time which condoned her brother's action as being perfectly acceptable!) was understandably not prepared to accept this interference and asked her mentor, the Lady of the Isle of Avalon, to deal with what had happened.

The solution offered by the Lady was perfectly in accordance with the morality of Faery, in that she empowered the sword such that it should only be drawn from its scabbard by one who would later kill the damosel's brother. It is easy to overlook the fact that in this instance the wrong has been done by a Faery to a human and not, as is more often the case, the other way round. The Lady's action may seem harsh, but there is no doubt that on a talismanic level it would restore the breach between the worlds which had been caused by the killing of the knight. If we imagine the situation to be reversed, and a human punished for killing a Faery, then we may begin to see the decisive strength of the Lady's action.

The curse which lies upon the sword and scabbard is not a matter to be taken lightly, nor with any self-righteous censorship of human morality, but as an example, if an extreme one, of the dynamics between the worlds. This eye for an eye justice is not simply blind revenge but indicates that there is a balance between the two worlds which must be preserved. There is jealousy here, and there is revenge, but what lies beneath these human concepts and human words of interpretation is the fact that any alliance between the worlds, especially one of love, carries a significance and weight beyond its immediate sphere. When such a relationship is destroyed, particularly through the murder of one of those involved, such an action causes ripples of effect which are profound and far-reaching through both the worlds, and must be righted.

Ultimately the way forward, the way in which the worlds of human and Faery may be reunited, can only happen through loving kindness. It is essential that we should understand and love those of the Faery world just as they must come to understand and love those of human world, not in a sentimental or desirous way, but through the love which imposes no conditions. Faeries also love, but our human love is coloured with the constructs of death and time whereas theirs is not. Our perception and experience of love is often closer to desire than love, the love which must *have*, the possessive love which is limited by time, because time's limit imposes the need to have it all now because it will not be there tomorrow. These are the limitations of the containment of place, or containment of person. Faeries, barely touched by time or the limitations of physical form, do not experience the death that causes desire.

As soon as Balin draws the sword from the scabbard, the damosel asks him to return it to her.[5] It was sufficient that he should have withdrawn the sword: the action was enough in itself. The talismanic power of grasping such a Faery sword and removing it from its scabbard cannot be overstated. But Balin, like Arthur before him, is only too keen to keep such an apparently wonderful prize and insists on holding on to it. The damosel warns him that this is a most unwise choice, because if he keeps the sword he will use it to kill the best friend that he has, the man he loves most in the world, and the sword will then be the means of his own destruction. Having been given all the information he needs to make a free choice Balin now has every opportunity to step aside from the sword's unhappy burden. But his pride in the possession of a Faery sword is his undoing, and he immediately announces his intention to leave the court and set out upon adventure.

Even while he is making preparation, the Lady of the Lake herself appears and, making clear the intimate connection between these events and her gift of Excalibur, she chooses this very moment to claim the gift promised by Arthur when he took his sword from the lake.

It is as if the possibility or the latent potential of these events has been firmed into a certainty by Balin's choice to take the sword rather than return it to the damosel. If he had done so perhaps all would have been well, but he did not. Arthur, at this point, again shows a similar disregard for the true significance of Excalibur because he casually tells the Lady of the Lake that he has forgotten its name! And yet the name of a sword encapsulates its power and purpose and he should have committed it to heart. The meaning could hardly be plainer. The Lady of the Lake has to remind him that it is called Excalibur ("cut steel") but it is evident that Arthur has not yet made it his own; he has not yet aligned his personal will with the spiritual will symbolised by his sword. Nor did he anticipate the gift which the Lady of the Lake now demands in return for her gift of Excalibur. She asks to be given either Balin's head, or the damosel's head, one or the other.

Astonishing as this request might have been to Arthur, the reader is equally taken aback by her explanation for this demand. It is as if the veil between the worlds has been torn open by Balin's possession of the sword, and an age of suspicion and enmity is pouring through unchecked. The Lady of the Lake explains that Balin had killed her brother, and the damosel had caused the death of her father. Somehow we find it difficult to grasp the concept that they could have been killed, or even that the Lady of the Lake has a brother or a father in the first place. We find ourselves reluctant to accept this challenging idea of Faery murder. It confronts too many of our pre-conceived notions about the nature and reality of the Faery world, although readers of Tolkien will have less difficulty in realising that violence and treachery form as much a part of it as they do of the human world. Much of *The Silmarillion* is taken up with descriptions of the enmity and division which marked the early history of the Elves. As it is, we begin to realise that both Balin and the damosel are part of a much larger perturbation between the worlds than may have been immediately evident, and the events which are now unfolding in Arthur's court are far more extensive than a petty quarrel.

Balin's response to the Lady of the Lake is equally startling, for he retorts that the Lady of the Lake has killed his mother by causing her to have been burnt. And before we have time to wonder what further enmity can be revealed between human and Faery, Balin cuts off her head. Thus this shocking sequence of events is brought to a temporary conclusion, albeit a most unhappy one. Balin takes the head, referring to the Lady of the Lake as his "most foe" and sets off to kill King Rience, Arthur's enemy, hoping that this might somehow bring him back to Arthur's favour.

But Balin has now become the Knight with Two Swords, a most unfortunate destiny indeed. Not only is he of divided spiritual will, but he carries the burden of two swords from two different worlds and races: one of his swords is from the human world, the other from the Faery world. Unable as he is to unite the worlds through love he instead is destined to carry the weight of their separation, and as the dire consequences of his actions unfold we begin to see that this is no Fairytale.

1   Thomas Malory, *Le Morte D'Arthur,* ed. Janet Cowen (London: Penguin Books, 1969) page 15
2   ibid, pages 52-54
3   All translations from Elvish taken from: Robert Foster, *The Complete Guide to Middle-Earth* (London: Unwin Paperbacks, 1978)
4   Thomas Malory, *Le Morte D'Arthur,* ed. Janet Cowen (London: Penguin Books, 1969) pages 55-57
5   ibid, pages 60-66

CHAPTER TWELVE
The Dolorous Blow: The Blood and the Spear

Although we do not meet Balin until the moment he is brought out of prison, it soon becomes obvious that he has a 'history' with the Faery world.[1] We have not been told of this before, but what we now learn does not sound good: he killed the Lady of the Lake's brother. Moreover, his first action on being released from prison is to kill the Lady of the Lake herself. We find this hard to accept, perhaps because we imagine that such beings as the Lady of the Lake cannot be killed or perhaps, because the Lady of the Lake doesn't disappear from the story even after having been killed, that somehow it didn't really happen. But 'The Lady of the Lake' is the title of an office: she is the Priestess of an inner Order, not one single being but one of a succession of High Priestesses. There is no reason to doubt the veracity of what Malory says, and to assume that this is a metaphoric murder is to miss the point. But it is equally hard to accept Balin's statement that the Lady of the Lake had not only caused the death of his mother through burning but had been the cause of the death of many other good knights. This challenges our belief that somehow such Faery beings as the Lady of the Lake ought to be above such behaviour.

This remains a perplexing episode, and one which is unique to Malory. Malory himself offers his readers no further information as to the background to these events and, typically, allows the reader to come to his or her own understanding of them. However, they are part and parcel of Malory's other major innovation at this stage of the story, one which relates to the Dolorous Blow. In almost all other versions, the Grail King (or Kings, for there are many in the line of those who hold this title) was wounded at a much earlier period in time. The actual nature of the wound, and the manner in which it was received, and by whose hand, varies considerably from one account to another, but there is a consensus of belief that it occurred a long time before the reign of Arthur. Malory is therefore making a radical change when he places the event within Arthur's reign where he deliberately sets it against a background of misunderstanding, enmity and murder between Faery and human. Malory's unspoken message is clear: this is happening here and now.

Balin represents some of the worst of our human thoughts and actions towards the Faery world: a mixture of disbelief, misguided idealism and even violence. He therefore takes on a significant weight of collective responsibility and the expurgation of collective guilt as, whether he will or no, he gradually finds his way towards the Grail Castle. Yet he is not an evil man: he is initially introduced as a good man, though poor, and poorly clothed. His reply to the damosel's objection that he looks too shabby to fit her requirements of perfection is made with honesty and dignity: that a knight's courage and fitness for a task are not always conveyed by his outer appearance. Easy as it is either to condemn him or to shrug off his misfortune, we may all consider ourselves guilty of the 'violence' that we cause to the Faery world by our disregard, disbelief and lack of realism.

Having left the comparative seclusion of Arthur's castle Balin sets out to find what adventure he can, but he carries the sword of the Lady of Avalon and his every move, although made with the best of intentions, inevitably draws him deeper into the mire. The outcome of previous unbalanced forces manifests as misfortune and disaster which are inexorably drawn to him.

His first encounter is with a knight named Lanceor who is envious of Balin's new sword and has sought him out in order to kill him and take it as his own. Lanceor has pretended to Arthur that his real motive for seeking Balin is to revenge the wrong that Balin did by killing the Lady of the Lake, and therefore has Arthur's blessing for what he is about to do. Again, Malory's unspoken message is clear: the King is involved in this, and condones this unwise action. Lanceor picks a fight with Balin, but Balin kills him. No sooner has Lanceor fallen to the ground than his amour, Colombe, rides up and sees what has happened. She takes up Lanceor's sword and falls to the ground in a faint. Concerned for her safety, Balin tries to take the sword from her grasp before she hurts herself, but she has it in too tight a grip. When she realises what he is trying to do, she jams the pommel in the ground, throws herself upon the blade and dies!

In a short space of time Balin has been the cause of two deaths yet can hardly be blamed for either of them. Full of despair, he rides into a forest where he meets his brother, Balan. They decide to seek out the evil King Rience who is posing a threat to Arthur, and drive him from the land, an undertaking which Balin hopes will restore him to the favour of the King.

But the death of Lanceor and Colombe has yet to reveal a greater significance, for now King Mark of Cornwall rides up, sees the bodies and declares that because of their great love he will not rest until he has buried them under a rich tomb. He searches the country to find one that is suitable, and on discovering the perfect stone has it inscribed with a memorial and proceeds to bury the bodies under it. No sooner has he accomplished this than Merlin also rides up and announces that the place of the tomb will not only mark the grave of the two lovers but will be the location of the greatest battle between two knights that ever was or ever will be! And Merlin proceeds to write *their* names in gold upon the tomb, these being those of Lancelot and Tristan. Finally, almost as if to add insult to injury, Merlin turns upon Balin, who must by now be wondering what on earth is going on, and tells him that it is his fault this has happened because he should have been quicker in stopping Colombe running onto the sword.

On one level this is almost comical in its hyperbole. Each succeeding character appears to be set on outdoing the others in proving the molehill to be a mountain. Balin has simply done the best he can in the circumstances, yet his very presence is acting as a vortex that attracts misfortune and enmity from an ever-widening circle of influence. These are the symptoms of the working out in the physical world of the accumulation of many ages of mistrust and enmity between the human and Faery worlds. The curse-bearing sword that Balin now holds will continue to bring such disasters to his hand, and the story is by no means over yet.

Merlin predicts what will happen in the near future, although he is obviously not giving away all he knows. He tells Balin that because he failed to stop Colombe from running onto the sword he, Balin, will cause a wound to the truest knight and man of most worship that is alive, a wound which will not heal for many years. Because of this Dolorous Stroke, three kingdoms will fall into poverty and misery for twelve years. Balin replies that if he thought that this really was the case then he would kill himself at once, but Merlin disappears without answering. Indeed, there is little answer that he can give, for they are all in the grip of something which will not be resolved simply by Balin's taking of his own life.

So far as Balin is aware, his only reason for seeking battle with King Rience is to rid Arthur of a troublesome neighbour and to regain his favour, but Rience is the tip of the iceberg of threats to the stability of Arthur's kingdom at this time, and we must remember that just as Arthur stands for Everyman, so his Kingdom is Everyland. Balin and Balan overcome Rience and send him to Arthur, who is pleased with what they have done. But Arthur is then threatened by Rience's brother, the malevolent Nero, whose Castle Terrabil is a veritable fortress of unbalanced force. And as if this was not bad enough, Arthur is also under threat from King Lot of

Lothian who, understandably aggrieved that Arthur has slept with his wife Morgawse (Arthur's half-sister) is threatening to add his army to that of Nero.

It is no coincidence that these multiple threats to the stability of Arthur's kingdom are all happening at once. Many, many years of misunderstanding between human and Faery have been lanced by the Lady of the Lake's demand that Arthur's side of the bargain with the Faery worlds should now be honoured, and things will get still worse before they improve.

The threat from Nero is not given an extensive explanation in Malory's account. It is another example of the compression of many years of history and pre-history which form the background to Arthur's life but of which the Arthurian chroniclers, concerned only with comparatively recent history, make little or no account. Malory describes in one short phrase the real extent of the battle with Nero, describing it as not one battle but ten, in which Nero commanded a host of men which was far greater than Arthur's. Such a struggle is not a minor border skirmish. It is the memory of an epic and long drawn-out battle of cosmic proportions in which Nero is the manifestation of cosmic forces of malignancy. He is comparable to Tolkien's Sauron, and his Castle Terrabil is the equivalent of Sauron's stronghold of Mordor. If one bears in mind the extent of the battle in which Sauron is finally defeated, and the forces which are brought to this battle on both sides, then this will give some indication of the magnitude of Arthur's ten battles in front of the gates of Castle Terrabil.

Finally, only the unbalanced forces channelled by King Lot remain to be dealt with. Lot is killed by Pellinore, who is later killed by Gawain, thus ending that particular cycle of mishap. Twelve kings who fight on Lot's side are also killed, and Merlin makes a gilded image of them, each holding a taper of wax which burns continually. He warns that when he dies these flames will be extinguished, and that this will be a sign that the initial phase of his work will be concluded and the greater adventures of the Holy Grail will be ushered into being. It is Merlin's continued close involvement in Arthur's reign which keeps the flames alive. A statue of Arthur stands over the twelve defeated kings as a statement of his triumph, like Hercules standing over the twelve signs and forces of the zodiac, providing a perfect symbol of the unity and cosmic reflections of the Round Table. For the time being Arthur's kingdom is securely established as a reflection of cosmic order, but the greater task of the relationship between the human and Faery kingdoms still remains to be addressed.

All will be resolved within the Grail Castle, whose influence now draws Balin towards it like a magnet. Malory offers a number of hints as to the nature of the Inner significance of the Grail Castle, particularly in his increasing references to the significance of the Mystery of Blood.

Merlin again warns Arthur to take great care of the scabbard because, no matter how deeply he may be wounded, he will not lose any blood if he has the scabbard with him. On one level this would seem to be a clear statement of fact: if Arthur holds the scabbard he will not lose his life through loss of blood even if he is injured in battle. But it is not quite as simple as that, because Merlin then refers to a future battle in which Arthur's son Mordred will fight against him. This, as we know, is when Arthur will die of the wounds caused to him by Mordred, so it would seem to give the lie to Merlin's prognosis. But 'loss of blood' refers to something more subtle than a simple prevention of haemorrhage, and this reference to blood, and the properties of blood, heralds a change of level at this point in the story.

The bridging between the worlds of Faery and human involves not only dealing with the physiological properties of blood but with its more subtle levels of energy, which are very important to the understanding of the relationship between the two worlds. Although its etheric and spiritual significance are by no means fully understood, it is worth reminding ourselves exactly what human blood comprises. There are four main constituents: red cells, white cells, platelets and the more mysterious plasma. On a physiological level, the red cells are responsible for carrying oxygen to the body's tissues. The life-span of a red cell (and they die at the rate of a couple of million a second) is only three to four months, but they are constantly generated in the body's bone marrow. The red colour of human blood is due to the presence of haemoglobin in the red blood cells, haeme being an iron-bearing pigment which is able to receive oxygen from the lungs. The vital importance of the presence of the element of iron to the proper functioning of the red blood cells is particularly interesting from the point of view of this study because there is a traditional and persistent belief in the Faery aversion to iron which cannot otherwise be satisfactorily explained. The answer perhaps lies in the primary distinction between human blood and Faery 'blood', for human blood contains red, iron-bearing haemoglobin. Faery veins cannot carry red human blood; it is harmful to them.

The function of the white blood cells is to defend the body against infection. On the other hand, over-production of abnormal white blood cells results in the crowding out of other healthy cells in the bone marrow and results in blood disorders such as leukaemia. The third constituent of human blood is the platelets, and it is these which Merlin seems to suggest will be affected by the scabbard, for they are essential to the clotting process which stops the flow of blood after an injury. They trigger chemical reactions that lead to the formation of a mesh of strands of protein that trap and holds the flow of red blood cells and forms a clot. The scabbard therefore would therefore seem to hold magical properties that can directly affect and stimulate the properties of one of the four constituents of human blood. While this in itself is a most desirable asset to possess, it also begs the question as to what other magical means were once available to directly affect or change the qualities of blood. This is particularly important in Faery/human marriage when it comes to the matter of reproduction, which is perhaps the real purpose of Excalibur's scabbard.

The fourth main constituent of blood is plasma, which takes up more than half the total volume of human blood. Plasma is by far the most mysterious of the four ingredients, and is certainly the least understood. In a sense it is not blood as such but the substance which remains when all the blood cells have been removed. It is a straw coloured liquid which contains salt, proteins and other nutrients which regulate the volume of the blood. It would be more accurate to think of it as an essential supporting substance that flows with the blood, perhaps the physical manifestation of remote stellar influence and inspiration within the human body.

While human blood is red and Faery 'blood' is white, this does not mean that the substance of Faery blood is the same as the substance of human blood, or that Faery blood consists only of white blood cells. However, the life-carrying vehicle of the Faery form, the substance which performs the same life-sustaining function within the Faery body as human blood does within the human body, is white. The white stellar inspiration that supports Faery blood perhaps has some similarity to the plasma which supports human blood, and who knows but perhaps Faery blood is actually something very similar to plasma.

With this in mind, we return to the story ...

Arthur is sick, and lies down in his pavilion in a meadow. A curious sequence of events then unfolds in which the reader is spectator to a magical ritual whose purpose is obviously known by the participants but which is left to the reader to work out for him or herself. A sorrowing knight passes by and is questioned by Arthur as to the cause of his sorrow. He refuses to say, and rides on. Balin rides up, and Arthur instructs him to bring the knight back to him, whether willingly or by force, for he greatly wishes to understand the reason for his sorrow. Balin rides off and discovers the knight with a damosel in a forest, the area of interface between the human and Faery worlds. Balin is anxious to carry out his duty to Arthur, and requests that the knight should return to Arthur and explain what is grieving him. The knight replies that not only would Arthur be hurt by such an action but it would do Balin no good either, although he does eventually agree to accompany Balin back to Arthur provided that Balin will agree to offer him safe-conduct. Balin agrees to do as the knight asks, and they leave the damosel in the forest and return to Arthur. But no sooner have they arrived at his pavilion than an invisible man on horseback runs the knight through with a spear and kills him.

And with this stroke we are plunged into the heart of the Grail Mysteries. The knight reveals, with his last breath, that he knows that the name of the invisible man is Garlon, and asks that Balin should take his horse, return to the damosel, and continue with her in the quest that he was following, revenging his death if the opportunity occurs. Balin goes back to the forest, gives the hilt of the spear to the damosel and rides on with her.

They soon encounter another knight who, when he learns of their purpose, declares that he will ride with them. While they are riding by a churchyard, the invisible knight now reappears and strikes this second knight dead with a spear. Merlin rides up, and confirms that the invisible adversary is indeed the same Garlon.

Balin buries the dead knight under a rich stone, but on waking the next morning he finds that an inscription in letters of gold has appeared on it. It reads: "Sir Gawain shall revenge his father's death, King Lot, on the King Pellinore." This new inscription, which would appear to have no connection whatever with the knight who lies beneath the tombstone, suggests that Garlon's killing of the knights and Pellinore's killing of Lot are somehow connected, as if events which occur in the human world are mirrored by those in the Faery world.

What are we to make of all this? Is this a Mystery or just a muddle? Pellinore we have already met: he is King of the Faery kingdom of Listenois. But there is a close correlation between Pellinore and another King of Listenois who is known variously as Pellam, Pelles, Pellehan or Parlan, and who is also a Grail King.[2] And the last of these names, Parlan, is very similar to Garlon, who is the Grail King's brother. Amid this plethora of similar names there is a clear pattern: Pellinore, Pellehan and Garlon are brothers, and both are kings of the Faery Kingdom of Listenois, at the centre of which is the Grail Castle.

The same story is also taken up in the First Continuation to Chrétien,[3] although here it is Gawain who plays the role ascribed by Malory to Balin. And this time it is Gwenevere, rather than Arthur, who waits at the crossroads. A knight passes by her and refuses to stop. Gwenevere sends first Kay, then Gawain, after the knight, who eventually explains that he is on such an important mission that he cannot possibly delay his journey. Gawain persuades the knight to return, but as soon as they reach Gwenevere he is run through with a spear by the invisible opponent. Gawain takes up the dead knight's quest as did Balin.

What is the purpose of this strange charade? Certain knights have obtained knowledge of the existence of a Mystery of great significance, but it cannot be found in Arthur's Kingdom, and indeed does not appear to be accessible to Arthur who is either asleep or ill while others search for it. It is something which causes great grief and sorrow to those who know of it, but promotes an intense and urgent desire to seek it out. Not only does Arthur not know of this Mystery, but those who do have knowledge of it are most reluctant to tell him. If they are forced to speak of their secret knowledge against their will they are run through with an invisible spear.

Gawain reaches the forest. Night falls, and a terrible storm rages through the trees. He reaches a crossroads in the middle of the forest where he discovers a chapel. The door stands open and, hoping to escape from the weather, he enters. Inside the chapel is an altar on which stands a single golden candlestick which holds a brightly burning candle. But at Gawain's entrance, a black hand reaches through the window behind the altar and snuffs out the candle. This is accompanied by a voice that groans so terribly that the entire chapel shakes. Gawain rushes outside, where he finds that the storm has suddenly abated and the night is now clear and pure.

The chapel represents a Temple of the Mysteries which stands halfway between the worlds of human and Faery, and Gawain is presented with a sequence of events which challenges his conception of reality. What takes place in this Temple is designed to make both Gawain and the reader look at things from an entirely different perspective, as if from the other side of a mirror. The ability to do this is one of the pre-requisites of entering the Faery Kingdom of Listenois and of finding the Grail Castle at its centre.

The candle flame is extinguished by a force which reaches through from another world that lies behind the altar, and is strong enough to manifest within the world in which Gawain stands. The manifestation is described as a "black hand" but this is a metaphor for 'invisible' or 'difficult to perceive' rather than a synonym for evil. It is of the same nature as the invisible foe who kills Balin's knights with a spear. The gesture of putting out the light is accompanied by a voice which expresses a sorrow so forcefully that the sound of it also breaks through the veil between the worlds and is heard even in the Temple which Gawain has entered. A light has been extinguished, for which there is much sorrow in that other world. Someone has died, or been killed; his death has caused the flame to go out and is the reason for such sorrow, but it is not made at all clear *whose* life and death is symbolised by the flame on the altar.

Lest Gawain and the reader should jump to the conclusion that this act is the work of malignancy, on leaving the Temple Gawain discovers that the violent storm that was raging outside has now completely abated and the night is calm and clear: the opposite of what we might expect. The extinguishing of the light inside the Temple has not produced cosmic unbalance but brought about healing and harmony in the forest that surrounds the Temple. The death has caused much sorrow, but its effect is healing.

The Temple stands between the worlds. Gawain stands upon the threshold, neither in one world nor the other. On which side of the mirror does he stand? Is he in the human world, perceiving a death that has taken place in the Faery world? Or is he standing in the Faery world and perceiving a death that occurred in the human world? The answer is: 'both'.

Gawain leaves the chapel and rides on through the forest. When dawn breaks, he finds that he has ridden across the whole of Britain in a single night and has reached the shore of a great sea. This is not the ocean of the physical world, for stretching out into the water is a causeway planted on either side with evergreen trees, whose branches meet overhead and completely roof it in. Gawain can just glimpse a light burning at the far end of the causeway tunnel, but it is rocked by pounding waves, and the trees are crashing together in the wind. His courage falters, but his horse takes the bit between its teeth and gallops off down the causeway towards the light.

Even so, it takes many hours to reach the end but eventually Gawain reaches a great hall which holds a vast throng of people. They receive him with honour and, telling him that they have long yearned for his coming, place a cloak lined with white fur about him. Gawain's journey has been arduous, and evidently he is the first to have managed it successfully. But when the inhabitants of the hall have had the chance to take a proper look at him they start to whisper to each other that he isn't the "right one", and vanish.

Gawain has reached the Faery Kingdom of Listenois. The tunnel across the astral waters is the 'tunnel' of human consciousness which connects the physical world with the more subtle levels of being, and the human world with the dimension of Faery.[4] This can be entered through meditation or other altered states of consciousness, and the journey is not always easy, as Gawain has discovered. But the inhabitants of the world which Gawain finds at the end of the tunnel are not figments of his imagination. If they were, then their existence would depend on Gawain's consciousness of them, and the truth is quite the reverse: when they realise that he is not the man they had hoped to see then they disappear from his sight of their own volition.

Who had they hoped for? We are not told, although as the story unfolds it becomes clear that Gawain has not yet reached the stage where he is able to ask the right question: "*What does all this mean?*" But by their gift of a white cloak the inhabitants of the hall at the end of the causeway indicate that he may be one of their own race, or at least, one who has achieved some understanding of this white, Faery world. He has taken on the mantle of Faery.

Even though not "the right one", Gawain now becomes the observer of a magical ritual in which certain signs, symbols and actions are revealed to him. There are four parts to this Ritual. Each reader who sees these signs and symbols through Gawain's eyes becomes, through their participation, a Grail Seeker, but it is vital that each ask their own questions throughout the story.

The first ritual Gawain witnesses is a ceremony for the dead which appears to be closely linked with the symbolic death he witnessed in the chapel in the forest. Within the empty hall, a bier supporting a dead king now appears. The body is covered by a cloth of red samite which has a cross of gold thread embroidered in the centre. A great golden candlestick stands at each corner, each candlestick supporting a golden censer. Placed on the red samite is one half of a broken sword which is positioned over the dead man's heart. A procession of priests enters, and they perform a ritual which is described as the office of the dead. When the ceremony is completed, the hall fills with people who make bitter mourning.

The obvious implication is that this ceremony is the Christian Mass for the Dead, and indeed the author seems happy for us to make this assumption. But the text does not make any explicit Christian connection, and Gawain is now far from the human, Christian world. In fact there is every indication that the body is not about to buried but has been there for some time and is likely to remain there for some considerable time in the future! Clearly we are not witnessing a funeral, nor can the 'body' be a human corpse. The conclusion of the ritual is marked by a highly significant comment in the text: "*Li dious s'en vait, li cors remaint.* "The god disappeared, the body remained."[5] We are offered the suggestion that the purpose of this ritual may be equated with the transubstantiation of Christ's body in the Host of the Christian Eucharist, though again, this is not specifically stated. Nevertheless, the purpose of the ritual appears to be to invoke the living spirit of a god upon the body that lies upon the bier. It might be more helpful to think of the body as an image of God: perhaps a statue or carving which represents a deity. Yet who was invoked in the Grail Castle? We are faced with a conundrum: the most likely candidate would appear to be Christ, yet this can hardly be so.

The invocation of the god thus complete, this part of the Ritual is concluded and the next stage commences. More people enter, carrying white cloths which they place on tables which appear all around as if for a banquet. A tall and strong-limbed man, wise and noble, enters from a chamber to the side of the hall. He is a King, crowned with gold, and carries a sceptre. He reveals later that he is the Grail King. They all sit to eat, and are served by the mysterious Grail. No-one carries it, but it moves among them and provides them with seven courses of wonderful food, all in silver bowls. It is made clear to Gawain that the Grail provides not only physical but spiritual nourishment and that this is linked with the previous ceremony.

When they have all eaten their fill, the King asks everyone to leave and, left alone with him, Gawain now witnesses the next part of the Ritual in which he is presented with a series of symbols but not offered any explanation as to their meaning. He sees a spear at the head of the high table. The head of the spear is as white as snow and it is standing in a silver vase which holds it upright. Blood springs from the tip of the spear, which is covered by the pattern of previous flows of blood, but no matter how much blood issues from the spear's tip, the container in which it stands is never filled. The blood is channelled through a pipe made of emerald into another, golden pipe, through which it flows out of the hall. It is now up to Gawain to show, through a symbolic ritual action which he must now make, whether or not he has reached a sufficiently advanced stage in these Mysteries not only to understand what has been shown to him but that he can *use* that knowledge in appropriate action.

After the body, the cup and the spear, a fourth symbol is introduced: the sword. Gawain's sword had been taken from him on his arrival, and the King now returns it to him. This sword, we remember, was the one originally owned by the knight who was mysteriously killed in front of Gwenevere. The King begins to weep bitterly over the body which still lies upon the bier and draws Gawain's sword from its scabbard, but in doing so reveals that it consists only of the hilt. It is the other half of the sword that lies upon the body of the king on the bier. He requests, with great gentleness, that Gawain attempt to re-unite the two halves. Gawain tries to do so, but does not succeed. The King takes back the hilt, kindly telling Gawain not to reproach himself too much that he has failed. The sword, it is later revealed, is the one which was used to kill the dead king.

By now we have here a proliferation of swords, but they are united by a single thread of meaning. Arthur's first sword was broken by the Faery King Pellinore.[6] The sword carried by Balin of the Two Swords carried a weight of unresolved karma which had been brought about by a long enmity between the Faery and human races. The sword which had killed the king whose body now rests in the Grail Castle was broken in two at his death. One part remained with his body while the other part was carried by a succession of knights of the human world. The two halves can only be reunited when the Seeker comes to a full understanding of the Mysteries which were revealed to him in the Grail Castle. And behind all these events lies the talismanic action of Solomon who took the sword of his father David from the Temple and broke it in two.

The sword in the Grail Castle has become divided through an act of treachery. The dead king, and the Faery folk who are the people of the dead king, have become separated from the human beings who now possess the other half of the sword. One half is carried by the Faery world, the other half is carried by those who journey into the Faery world in order to join the two broken halves together. The questions and actions of those who make this journey will reveal whether or not they fully understand the significance of all that is shown to them there. They are offered the opportunity to heal the division between their races, but this can only come about if they reveal that they fully comprehend the Mystery which is shown to them.

Gawain shows that he is on the right track when he asks the meaning of all that he has seen. The king tells him that the spear is the one which pierced the side of Christ as he hung on the cross and that it will continue to bleed, in that hall, until the Day of Judgement. But he also says it has been the ransom of all those in that land, and speaks of the joy which the blow of the spear won for them!

Here is an explicit statement of the connection between Christ and the spear in the Grail Castle. But lest there is any doubt, this is not a pagan Mystery which has been 'Christianised' in order to make it acceptable to the contemporary public. The Grail King's statement that the blow which killed Christ was the source of great joy to them is not an expression of the orthodox Christian belief that Christ's death freed humanity from sin.

We would appear to be wading into ever deepening waters here, because there is an obvious correlation between the blow from the spear which killed Christ yet brings joy to the Faery race, and the Dolorous Blow of the Grail legend which wounds the Grail King and brings his land to waste. It is as if one mirrors the other, yet they are not the same, and unless we retain an awareness of the distinction between the two events and two worlds, the Mystery soon becomes a muddle.

The Grail King is about to reveal the name of the dead king when he sees that Gawain has fallen asleep. Gawain has done all he can for the moment. The King falls silent, and when Gawain awakens the next morning he is standing alone on a cliff above the sea; the castle and all those in it have vanished. But he stays in that land for a long while, during which time he learns that although it had become Waste at the death of their King, its fertility was restored when he asked to be told the meaning of the spear. But because he fell asleep, the land was still devoid of population.

Gawain neglected to ask the central question which would make sense of so much more of the Mystery: what was the identity of the dead King? In fact we do not learn of his identity until much later when Percivale reaches the Grail Castle and asks for an explanation of all he has seen. He is told that the dead king is King Gon of Sert, who is elsewhere called Goon du Sert, or Goon Desert, or Garlon. Garlon was killed through treachery and the sword used by his attacker broke in two at the moment he was killed. The Grail King, brother of Garlon, took up the sword and cut through his own thighs with it, severing the nerves.

Here then, at the heart of the Grail Mysteries lies a figure whose identity is vital to their meaning yet whose identity seems curiously indistinct. There is a confusion between the Grail King and the Wounded King. They often appear to be brothers, and indeed the concept of the Grail King's brother is a thread common to most versions of the story. Sometimes the two brothers seem to merge into one person while at other times they separate into two distinct characters. Yet the wound which is borne by one of them is intricately linked with the other, even, as noted above, self-inflicted as a deliberate attempt to mirror or reproduce the blow which killed the other.

We return to Malory to fill in the missing details, and find Balin still making his way to the Grail Castle. Balin and the damosel who now accompanies him reach the Castle Meliot, but as soon as Balin enters the portcullis falls down and traps him inside. The damosel, left stranded outside, is attacked by men of the castle who appear intent on killing her. Balin climbs up the tower and jumps down into the moat hoping to rescue her, but the men explain that they are only carrying out their custom of years, and have no wish to fight with him. They tell him that within the castle lies their lady who has been sick for a long while. The only thing that will heal her is for them to fill a silver dish full of the blood of a maiden who is pure, and also a king's daughter.

This is not simply a matter of loss of blood and subsequent transfusion, but something rather more Mysterious. Not any blood will do; it has to be of the right kind. The donor must be a king's daughter because only a king's daughter will possess the right type of blood. This is not superstition or illusion of grandeur, but simple fact. The phrase "daughter of a King" signifies a distinction between the blood of a mortal woman and the blood of a Faery. A King's daughter will be of the Lemurian, Faery race and only her blood will match that of the ailing lady within the castle.

The damosel with Balin obviously does not fit the necessary requirement, but in order that we do not miss the point of these events Malory now casts forward in time to explain that the lady within the castle will only eventually be healed by the blood of Percivale's sister, Dindrane, daughter of King Pellinore. The un-named lady therefore has a long time to wait because the event to which Malory refers does not occur until the concluding pages in the story of the Grail when Percivale, Dindrane, Galahad and Bors have achieved possession of the Grail and are taking it, in the Ship of Solomon, to the Holy City. They stop at the castle where the lady still lies sick, and Dindrane offers to let some of her blood into the silver dish. The lady is healed, but Dindrane dies.

If this episode is interpreted at a mundane level, several puzzles present themselves. Why, for instance, is it *only* Dindrane's blood which will heal the lady? It hardly seems likely that over the years no other virginal king's daughter passed by, or that one could not have been sought out and brought to the castle! Second, losing a small amount of blood, enough to fill a dish, does not kill you, and there is no obvious reason as to why Dindrane should have lost her life in this way.

As we have seen, Pellinore is of ancient Faery lineage, older even than the Atlantean Faery race. His blood is of the pure Lemurian strain of whom only a very few of survived into Arthur's time. However, his blood is carried by his offspring Percivale and Dindrane. The healing of the lady in the castle is therefore not a blood-transfusion in the terms of human physiology where a pint of blood can be lost without harm to the donor. Faery blood cannot be measured in pints or half-litres, and if the life-force of one Faery is transmitted to another then it is all or nothing. It is for this reason that Dindrane dies.

The lady's condition is as significant as her eventual healing, for she is a symbol of the predicament of all Faeries who are stuck in the human world and cut off from the source of their existence. Her situation may be likened to that of Arwen Evenstar in *The Lord of the Rings*. Arwen's father, Elrond, forecasts that if she persists in her desire to marry the mortal Aragorn and remain within Middle Earth rather than take the journey back into Far West with the remainder of her Elven kin, she will consign herself to a prolonged half-existence. After his death, her immortality will keep her in Middle Earth, not fully alive but unable to die, isolated from her own kind. Such is the condition of the Lady of Castle Meliot.

Balin's next adventure is also closely linked with the Mystery of Blood. A rich man offers him hospitality for the night. He tells Balin that his son was recently wounded at a tournament by a knight who then made himself invisible. Balin is of course now able to identify this knight as Garlon, but his host unexpectedly continues by stating that the only thing which will heal his son is some of Garlon's blood!

This is a curious statement in itself, and especially so given Garlon's apparently 'evil' behaviour up to now. So far as we know, the only person who possesses healing blood is Christ. And there appears to be a connection between the statement that Garlon's blood possesses miraculous healing properties and the Lady of Castle Meliot, who could also only be saved by a particular type of blood. It is at this point that Malory, restricting himself as ever to giving us the necessary facts but without offering any interpretation, reveals that Garlon is the brother of Pellam of Listenois, whom we know to be the Grail King. Balin vows that he will obtain some of Garlon's blood in order to heal his host's son.

Malory's Garlon seems to come from another dimension, another world beyond even the Grail Castle, and for which his 'invisibility' is a literary technique intended to convey something of the nature of his real identity. In Chrétien's account we only encounter Garlon long after his death, yet he retains a greater power over events than the living Grail King. Similarly, Malory identifies Garlon as one who commands considerable influence over what happens in the environs of the Grail Castle, yet who appears and disappears at will in the highly charged atmosphere of these lands which lie between human and Faery.

Finally, Balin and the damosel arrive at the Grail Castle. They are well received and are invited to a feast which is being prepared at that moment, but Balin is asked not to take his sword in with him. This is a Faery custom, and one which Balin would have done well to respect, but he insists that he will continue to carry his sword since it is the custom of his own (human) country that a man should keep his sword at a feast. In fact, he tells the servants that if he can't keep his sword then he will leave at once, and they reluctantly acquiesce.

This is a critical moment, and Balin's attitude proves fatal. Wisdom and common courtesy should have told him that he must observe the customs of his hosts, whether human or Faery. His refusal to do so parallels Arthur's refusal to use the spear rather than the sword in his fight with Pellinore. It is not just a matter of courtesy but is indicative of his denial of the existence of the Faery race or at least his blindness to them. And his refusal means that he carries his doom-laden sword into the heart of the Grail Castle.

Seated at the table, Balin asks that Garlon should be pointed out to him, and is told that Garlon, who in this environment is no longer invisible, is serving food to the assembled company. From what we have been told of him so far we might expect that Garlon was disliked and feared by those about him, but this is not the case, for he is described as the most marvellous knight alive. And we must not neglect to notice how strange it is that the brother of the Grail King should be taking the role of a vassal and serving food to those present. Perhaps this 'feast' is a disguised representation of the Grail feast and procession, in which case Garlon would be presiding over that ritual meal, perhaps even as the bearer of the Grail.

Garlon notices that Balin is staring at him and smites him on the face with the back of his hand, suggesting that Balin would do better to stop looking at him and to get on with eating and "with what he came to do". Unheeding of this piece of very reasonable advice, Balin cuts off Garlon's head! He then takes the hilt of the spear (the one used by Garlon to kill the damosel's knight) from the damosel and sticks it through Garlon's body, calling to his host of the previous evening that he could now obtain some of Garlon's blood with which to heal his son.

The Grail King Pellam tells Balin that out of love for his brother he will now kill Balin. In the fight which ensues, Pellam breaks Balin's sword, the sword which carried the curse of the Lady of Avalon. It is fitting that it can only be destroyed by Pellam/Pellinore who, we remember, also broke Arthur's sword. Balin, searching for a replacement weapon, runs through the castle until he reaches a chamber in which he discovers the Grail Hallows which lie at the very heart of these Mysteries. The chamber is richly furnished, and in it is a bed covered with cloth of gold on which a figure lies, seemingly dead. Next to the bed stands a table made of gold, which rests upon four pillars of silver. Upon the table stands a "marvellous spear strangely wrought". Balin, not stopping to question the significance of what lies before him, snatches up the spear and strikes King Pellam through both thighs. Pellam is not killed but falls down in a swoon. At this same moment the castle also falls to the ground, and Balin with it, unable to move for three days.

1   Balin's story is told by Thomas Malory in Book II of *Le Morte D'Arthur*
2   Listed by John Darrah in *Paganism in Arthurian Romance* (Cambridge: D.S Brewer 1997) page 103
3   Chrétien de Troyes, trans. Nigel Bryant, *Perceval: The Story of the Grail* (Cambridge: D.S. Brewer, 1982) pages 124-133
4   Physical counterparts of this can be found in the landscape, for instance in the causeway across marshland leading to an island excavated at Flag Fen in Cambridgeshire, where many broken bronze swords have been found.
5   Quoted by Emma Jung and Marie-Louise von Franz, trans. Andrea Dykes, *The Grail Legend* (Boston, Massachusetts: Sigo Press, 1986) page 246
6   See Chapter 11

CHAPTER THIRTEEN
Qui l'on en Sert?

The Dolorous Blow has been struck, the land surrounding the Grail Castle is laid waste, and the Grail King remains in his wounded state for many long years. Balin himself will soon be killed, mistakenly, by his own brother Balan. Everything waits for the one who will find the castle and set things right by asking an apparently simple question: "Who is served by this?"

Yet we must pause to ask why Balin's action should have caused such devastation, and then ask why such an obvious question should have the power to undo the harm he apparently caused. There is no doubt that Balin's hasty seizure of the Spear in order to defend himself against the Grail King was an act of sacrilege; it was a most inappropriate misuse of a sacred object. But there have been many acts of sacrilege in history, as often as not committed in the name of Good Intention, and they do not normally lay an entire country to waste for hundreds of years. The state of the Waste Land is that of a land struck by an atomic bomb, but while the contemporary reader is only too mindful of the prophetic warning thus offered, the fact is that the Grail chronicles almost unanimously describe the Waste Land as something which had already happened long ago.

Contrary to popular belief, the Grail Seekers do not set out on their journey with the deliberate intention of healing a perceived disorder within themselves or their world. Their journey is a journey of initiation, a ritual in which they may, or may not, discover the cause of the disease which affects the Grail King and his land, but this is by no means apparent to them at the outset. It is purely and simply the power of the Grail which draws them ever onwards: they do not know what it is they seek, or why. In fact Gawain, one of the Grail seekers, does not even intend to look for the Grail; he believes himself to be on an entirely different quest and it is only because his horse takes the bit between its teeth that he arrives at the Grail Castle whether he will or no. As many of those who have found themselves in pursuit of the Mysteries will vouch, this is often the way of things. The impulses of the Higher Self will somehow manage to reach through to the Personality even though it is deaf and blind.

Of all the versions of the Dolorous Blow it is perhaps Malory's which most firmly grabs the imagination. His masterstroke was to bring the event out of the distant past and put it right into the present time of the reign of King Arthur. In this way each of his readers gets to know Balin as the perpetrator of the Dolorous Blow, joining with him in the events which lead up to it, and becoming a witness and accomplice to every stage of the journey from Arthur's Court to the Grail Castle.

Thus we all become as Balin and are all part of the crime. Through Balin, we all strike the Dolorous Blow upon the Grail King. But, as we have seen, Balin is re-enacting an ancient ritual of redemption and, for us, takes on the burden of a supreme act of self-sacrifice. He is the instrument through which the situation of stalemate between Faery and human can be 'lanced' and healed, and simply by reading his story we too are drawn into the Grail Ritual and are offered the opportunity to discover how things may be put right. As participants in the ritual we must first pass the tests and find answers to the series of enigmas which open up before us, and unless we do so we will find, like Balin, that Good Intention is not enough.

To many seekers, the simple achievement of the Grail is in itself sufficient reason for the Quest. Drawn as surely upon the quest as were the knights of old, we find the combination of the challenges of the journey and the spiritual nourishment which it offers can seem reason in themselves. A. E. Waite comments: "Having passed through many initiations, I can say with the sincerity which comes of full knowledge that the Graal legend, ritually and ceremonially presented, is the greatest of all which lies beyond the known borders of the instituted mysteries."[1]

But there is more at stake here than a quest for personal spiritual fulfilment; a great deal more than this hangs in the balance. Finding the Grail is the just the beginning of the ritual, and in magical terms it could be said that it represents the Outer Court of the Grail Priesthood. Many Grail questions remain to be asked, questions which are urgently relevant to our own time and the future of the Faery and human races.

The Ritual of the Grail Quest stands in complete contrast to the normal initiatory process. In almost every other initiatory experience it is the initiate who is asked questions by the initiators who stand before him at the end of his journey and represent those who have seen the light face to face. Having proved his dedication and worthiness, the seeker is offered a revelatory or transforming experience which will open the doors to an accelerated process of growth and evolution to the benefit of all. But in the Grail Quest it is the initiate who has to ask the questions, and having done so, it is not he but the Grail King who is transformed! The resolution of the Mystery depends on the initiate. The Grail sustains us on our journey, but it is not the journey's end. We must ask more questions.

The first question is: *why is the Grail King wounded*?

The Grail Guardians consistently suffer from a wound which will not heal, and which is inseparably linked with their guardianship of the Grail Hallows. But there is no reason to believe that the Grail Hallows were in any way intrinsically malefic: far from it. This is not what we would expect from a close association with such holy objects. At the time in which these stories were written there were numerous appearances of the very same relics, such as Christ's blood, pieces of wood from the true cross, actual thorns from the crown and so on. Every new ecclesiastical venture was more than keen to make a claim to one or other of these artefacts in order to give especial credence to the clergy who owned them and the new church or cathedral which housed them. These relics, we may assume, did not bring calamity to those who guarded them, but were considered a potential source of healing and miracles.

Recent theories have tended to answer this question by attempting to identify the wounded Grail King with the archetype of the Wounded Healer, but this is not helpful. The Grail King is not possessed of healing powers. He does not bring healing to those around him, nor does he himself appear to reach any further stage of personal growth or enlightenment through his suffering. He simply waits until someone comes along to ask the right question, at which point he is either cured, or free to die. Indeed, far from bringing healing he seems to attract misfortune and woe, though why he should do so is not at all obvious. Nowhere is a convincing reason offered for this persistent wound, for which only an ill-defined understanding of the nature of 'sacrifice' is usually offered. Something here does not make sense.

The second question is: *Where* is the Grail King's wound?

The location of the wound is more often than not said to be in the thigh, or thighs. It is often suggested that 'thigh' is a euphemism for genitals, and that his castrated state is an explanation for the consequent infertility of his land. This would certainly accord with the Faery belief that the King, married to the land, must be without blemish. Ancient Irish history tells how when the Faery King Nuada lost his hand in the battle with the Fir Bolgs he was no longer acceptable to them as their leader and a replacement had to be sought. Yet while the Grail stories rest easily upon this background of Faery/Celtic belief it can hardly be said to apply to Joseph of Arimathea and his successors the Grail Kings, none of whom were 'kings' in the sense that they ruled over a known or named country, until Pelles/Pellehan, the last of the line, who ruled over the Faery land of Listenois. In addition, the frequent emphasis on the blow which wounded both thighs suggests a somewhat unusual physiology, and in any case the Grail Kings had no difficulty in fathering numerous progeny – even though there is not a Grail Queen!

So we are left with a strange assortment of facts. The King is wounded in the genitals but can still reproduce. His woundedness, according to *Faery* belief affects the land, yet it is not suggested in any overt manner that he is a Faery. His woundedness appears either to be hereditary or is mysteriously received as part and parcel of the role of guardianship of the Grail.

We have noted previously that there is also widespread confusion as to whether it is the Grail King or his brother who is wounded. On a purely literary basis this is a clumsy device. If these stories were only fantasy then such an odd confusion would never have arisen, so we must assume that its persistence throughout the stories is because it is a vital key to the mystery, even though encrypted in ritual form. It leads us to the third question: *who is the Grail King's brother?*

His role is crucial. He appears in almost all the Grail chronicles and is usually named Garlon Desert or Garlon Du Sert. But there is considerable variance as to whether he is dead and the object of a veneration which appears to equate him with Christ[2] or alive and, again like Christ, possessed of a miraculous blood which brings healing and restores life.[3] Clearly he is someone of very great significance yet he remains in the background, a mysterious and unexplained figure.

In fact there is a persistent confusion between the identity of the two brothers. The Grail Guardian is mirrored in a dark glass by his brother who is the same, yet not the same. One brother is wounded and one is implicated in that wounding, but there is disagreement as to which is which. In some versions Percivale is the son of the Grail King, but elsewhere he is said to be the nephew, rather than the son. If this is so, then this makes him the son of Garlon du Sert, and since Percivale is an eventual Grail Winner, the true identity of his father is rather important!

There is a consistent acceptance and acknowledgement of the brother's existence yet a reluctance to reveal his real identity to the uninitiated reader except through tantalising clues. But the real clue lies in his very name, for in speaking it out loud, "Garlon du Sert" we are almost speaking the Grail Question: "Qui l'on en Sert?" And when we have discovered who the mysterious brother is then we will be approaching the very heart of the mystery.

But before we do, there is a fourth question: *Why were the Grail Hallows removed from Jerusalem?*

The Grail literature falls broadly into two parts. The part with which most readers are familiar describes how the several knights set out from Arthur's court on a quest to find the Grail which is hidden somewhere in Britain. But there is an equal body of literature which describes how the sacred Christian artefacts of the Grail, along with the spear, the sword and the dish, were removed from the Holy Land and taken on their long journey west. They eventually arrived at their destination in Logres, where they were hidden from the common gaze. But given that Christ was a Jew living in the Holy Land, this was not an obvious course of action by any means. Why were the Hallows not left in the Holy Land? This early half of the story is understandably neglected in favour of the episodes which deal with the adventures of the questing knights, for it would appear to serve only as a prelude to the real story which starts with the challenges of the Grail Castle, but it contains much which is of great significance to us.[4]

Our particular interest starts with the first Grail Guardian, Joseph of Arimathea, although arguably there were even two guardians before him, whose contributions to the history of the Grail are brief but pivotal. The first was an un-named Jew who took the Cup which Christ had used to celebrate the New Covenant from the house of Simon, where Christ had held the Last Supper. After Christ had been arrested, the same man passed the Cup to Pontius Pilate, an action which throws an interesting light on Pilate's involvement in this early history of the Grail. It remained in Pilate's keeping until after Christ's death, when Joseph of Arimathea asked Pilate for his body and Pilate, giving him permission to take the body also handed him the Cup. Joseph used the vessel to collect the blood which was still flowing from Christ's wounds while his body was being prepared for burial.

This would appear to connect the Cup with the body *and* blood of Christ, yet is something very different from the concept offered by the celebration of the Eucharist. And it is at this moment that two major streams of thought diverge: exoteric Christianity on the one hand, and the esoteric belief which lies at the heart of the Grail stories on the other. The basis of the Eucharist celebration of the new Covenant instigated by Christ at the Last Supper is that of transubstantiation: that the bread becomes His body and the wine becomes His blood. In contrast, the Grail story depends upon the preservation of the original Cup, yet does not depend upon the doctrine of transubstantiation.

In fact the connection between the Cup and the blood of Christ is soon severed, for it is the spear which, according to the Grail stories, becomes the instrument through which Christ's actual blood continues to flow. And while the Grail stories affirm, in concordance with exoteric Christianity, that the Grail offers super-substantial nourishment, they do not identify these qualities with the forgiveness of sins which has become so central to Christian belief, but with the far more positive qualities of blessing, healing and spiritual enlightenment. The concept of the Covenant of blood-sacrifice as atonement for sin is not part of the Grail ideology, although the concept of the healing powers of Christ's blood is of paramount importance.

According to the story told by Robert de Boron, who so far as we know was the first to make a connection between the Grail and the Cup of the Last Supper, Joseph of Arimathea was thrown into prison soon after Christ's death. But he was visited by the risen Christ, who gave him the Cup which he had taken from Joseph's house. He is also said to have communicated certain sacred words to Joseph. These words, according to Boron, were written down in the "high book" of the mystery of the Grail which, though now lost, informed many other versions of the same story. Joseph remained in prison for many years, during which time he was sustained only by the Grail.

What transformation must he have undergone during these years in which he did not receive any physical sustenance? Joseph of Arimathea is familiar to all Christians as the man who took Christ's body from the cross and laid it in his own especially prepared tomb in the Garden of Gethsemane. As far as the Bible is concerned, his role ended there. But in the esoteric belief found within the Grail literature we find a very different man indeed, one whose task only just began at the moment of Christ's death. Joseph of Arimathea is the lynch-pin who connects exoteric and esoteric Christianity, one of the very few people to appear in both the Bible and Arthurian literature. He is the first of the line of Grail Guardians, and it is he who initiates the Grail's journey to its eventual destination in the Castle in Listenois. The changes he himself undergoes during this pivotal time are of great importance.

During his time in prison, Joseph becomes transformed from the physicality of the human condition into the body of light which is equivalent to that of Faery, sustained not by any actual food but by the spiritual light and sustenance contained within the Grail. The change undergone by Joseph of Arimathea during his forty years in prison also marks the time of change in form of the Grail itself. Initially identified with a cup, during this time it sheds physical form and thereafter is transformed into a light too dazzling to be perceived by mortal eyes. Consequently, from now on it is not described with any clear or precise definition but appears in all shapes to all people, yet consistently feeds them with a food more rare and nourishing than they have ever experienced elsewhere.

Boron tells how at first, when the Emperor Vespasian visited Joseph in prison after forty years, all he could see within the cell was a brilliant light. Eventually he released him, but he destroyed the Temple of Jerusalem, an actual event of AD 70.[5]

These two events are closely linked, for the destruction of the Temple of Solomon simultaneously marked the outward destruction of an ancient line of priesthood as far as Jerusalem was concerned, and the beginning of another, inner line of tradition which was removed from Jerusalem to be reborn in the islands of the West. The outer wheel had reached the end of its turning; the inner wheel began to move. Joseph of Arimathea and his companions left Judea, first travelling north by land to the "City of the Sun" and then by sea to Britain. Their destination, however, was not the outer, physical land of Great Britain but one of the Faery lands which can be accessed through certain gateways to be found in Britain, and through carefully constructed magical ritual: Listenois.

It cannot be emphasised enough that the Grail Castle and its inhabitants are not to be found within the physical, human world, yet neither are they symbolic or archetypal in the sense of only existing within the imagination. They are found in another, equally real world: that of Faery. The spear is not a symbolic or archetypal spear, but a real spear that has been taken from the human world into the Faery world, as are the cup and the sword. The answers which the Grail-seekers elicit concerning the spear and the cup do not reveal an archetypal or conceptual spear or cup, but ones which possess a particular, definite and real history.

It is the discovery of their origin, and of the reason why they have been moved to the Faery kingdom of Listenois, that is the object of the Grail quest.

It is has been suggested that the revelation of the Christian origin of the Grail Hallows is a device employed by the authors of these tales to provide such fantasies with a gravitas they would otherwise lack. Another frequently expressed opinion is that their 'Christianisation' devalues and rides roughshod over their Faery origins and, if only it were removed, their original significance would shine through. Yet the real message of the Grail stories is that the two are intimately and inextricably connected.

And this leads us to our final question: *Why was the Faery race entrusted with the guardianship of these sacred Hallows?*

According to the Grail chroniclers, the deepest secrets contained within the Grail Castle, revealed only to a very few and even then only after years of searching and questioning, were that the Grail and Spear were connected with Christ. But where can be the secret in this? Why should this knowledge have been so thoroughly removed from the sight of the questing knights when, as we have noted, sacred relics abounded in the world in which these stories were written?

The revelation which awaited those who asked the catalysing questions was not that these Christian sacred artefacts existed at all, but that they were held within the custodianship of the Faery race, and that it was to the Faery race that their quest had led them. In addition to the reversal of the normal initiatory sequence noted previously, here lies another mirror-like reversal of the normal sequence of events, for the removal of the Grail, Spear and Sword from the human world back into the Faery world is a reversal of the normal manner in which the Faery race offer their magically charged weapons to those of the human world.[6]

When the sword, spear, cup and dish which had all been intimately associated with the life and death of Christ were taken back into the Faery Kingdom, they were being returned from whence they came, just as the dying Arthur arranged for Excalibur to be returned to the Lake of the Faery Priesthood of Avalon. The Grail Hallows, as with all other Faery weapons, once their cycle of use had been completed within the human world, were returned to their land of origin. The cycle of movement is from Faery to human, then back to Faery. The quest is to realise this pattern, and the goal of the Grail Quest is to realise that these particular Hallows were used within the world by Christ.

The Bible makes reference to two streams of blood issuing from Christ's side: "But one of the soldiers with a spear pierced his side, and forthwith came thereout blood and water. And he that saw it bare record, and his record is true: and he knoweth that he saith true, that ye might believe."[7]

We find it easy to accept that one of the streams of fluid that came from Christ's side was blood, but the exact nature of the other fluid is less obvious. In fact John presents his readers with quite a problem when he states that two, differently coloured streams of fluid emerged from Christ's side when he was stabbed with the spear. From his insistence that this occurrence was observed by an eye-witness who spoke the truth and therefore could be trusted in the accuracy of his description, it would appear that he was well aware of the conundrum he was creating. The usual reaction, if the other stream of fluid which came from Christ's side is mentioned at all, and the matter is not always thought to be a proper subject for discussion, is to suggest that it was either sweat or seminal fluid. But both these suggestions are unlikely for obvious physiological reasons, so we are left with the problem. John's suggestion that it was water can also hardly be true: Christ's veins were not filled with water. Yet they contained two different, life-supporting fluids.

The only other clue to the identity of this mysterious fluid lies in the tradition that Joseph of Arimathea brought two cruets with him to Glastonbury, each containing one of the fluids which flowed from Christ's side. One of these contained red liquid and the other, a white fluid. In an expression of high magic rooted in earth, the two streams that flow from Glastonbury Tor and mingle in the orchard of the Chalice Well at its foot are also red and white. This entirely natural phenomenon, occurring at the very place in which it is said the young Christ once trod, has understandably supported a centre of religious and spiritual experience for many centuries.

Throughout this study we have noted the many descriptions of the white, shining appearance of those of the Faery race, as if the life-sustaining fluid within their bodies was white. The two streams of blood that flow from the living Christ are equally relevant to both the human and Faery races. It suggests that whatever was achieved by Christ's death and redeeming blood was as true for the Faery race as for the human race, and the relevance of Christ is equal both to humans and Faeries. Bearing this in mind, other enigmas within the Grail legends now begin to make more sense. Let us return to the image of the body of the dead King Garlon whose death, according to Chrétien de Troyes, was the cause of the Waste Land. We would have no difficulty at all in identifying the body as that of Christ were it not for the fact that the body is found within a Faery castle! The iconography of the scene bears close resemblance to that of the mediaeval carol *Corpus Christi* which describes a knight who lies upon a bed in a hall within an orchard, yet is neither dead nor alive. He is a knight, yet simultaneously he also is the body of Christ.

Lully, Lulley, Lully, Lulley,
The faucon hath born my make away.

He bare him up, he bare him down,
He bare him into an orchard brown.

In that orchard there was an halle,
That was hanged with purpill and pall.

And in that hall there was a bede,
It was hanged with gold so rede.

And in that bed there lithe a knight,
His woundes bleding day and night.

By that bede side kneleth a may,
And she wepeth both night and day.

And by that bede side there stondeth a stone,
Corpus Christi wreten there on.

Another variant, *Over Yonder's a Park,* contains similar imagery, but with the addition of a description of the two streams which run from the side of Christ, red and white.

Down in yon forest there stands a hall,
The bells of Paradise I heard them ring
It's covered all over with purple and pall
And I love my Lord Jesus above any thing.

In that hall there stands a bed,
It's covered all over with scarlet so red.

At the bedside there lies a stone
Which the sweet Virgin Mary knelt upon.

Under that bed there runs a flood
The one half runs water, the other runs blood.

At the foot of the bed there grows a thorn,
Which ever blows blossom since He was born.[8]

The words of these carols express a deep and complex Mystery with perfect simplicity. The words are that of the dove of the Holy Spirit who mourns the loss of her mate, or perhaps the words of Mary Magdalene for her beloved. The beloved's body has been taken by the falcon to a far distant orchard, where it now lies within a hall draped in purple, upon a bed hung with red and gold. This is not the Garden of Gethsemane but the apple orchards of the Faery kingdoms of Avalon, and the hall is the Grail Castle, reached by Gawain (and those who came later) at the end of his journey through the forest and along the causeway. It is the Grail Maiden who kneels beside the bed of the knight, whose body, still flowing with blood, is the Grail King, but also is Christ. The Grail King and Christ are brothers in spirit. The stone represents the stone which Joseph of Arimathea placed over the entrance to Christ's tomb in the Garden of Gethsemane, and is the paten which covers the chalice in the Holy Eucharist, and is also the sacred stone which cries out the name of the true King.

Here is the explanation for the mysterious brother of the Grail King. The Grail King's brother is Christ, as He is perceived by the Faeries.

Often one of the earliest signs experienced by those who venture into the Faery dimension is that of the mirroring of events between the worlds, not as if one is walking *through* a mirror and out the other side, but as if one is walking within an environment which continuously mirrors another. We have seen how this was experienced by Balin: as he approached the Grail Castle he found events became increasingly Faery in a pre-echo of what was to take place.

Gawain also experienced this phenomenon in the Chapel in the Forest, when the altar flame was extinguished by a disembodied hand. Within this strange temple between the worlds he was standing within the mirror, half way between human and Faery, unclear as to which world lay on which side. If the death which was causing such sorrow was Christ's within the human world, then this clearly has great significance and a healing effect within the Faery world because the storm outside the chapel is abated and the skies become clear and calm. If the death referred to is that of Garlon, within the Faery world, then his death similarly has significance and healing effect within the human world.

This is not to say that Garlon, or Pellehan, or any of the Grail Kings 'are' Christ. Nevertheless, they embody the Christ force within the Faery world, and the wounds caused to Christ are simultaneously suffered by them. Christ's wounding caused his death to the physical world, but within the Faery world an actual death in the physical sense cannot occur. The connection between the King of the Jews and the King of Faery is made manifest through the Sacred Hallows of the Cup, Spear, Sword and Stone which pass from the Faery world into the human world, and back into Faery. However, it is not the concern of the Grail chroniclers to describe such Mysteries in open terms to a general readership, which is why they are occulted through the veiled allusions to the Grail King's brother. After Christ's death to the physical world, his message and purpose, often so distorted by its human adherents, passed on into the Faery world. It may well be said that the Grail quest offers a fuller appreciation of the real nature of Christ than much that the exoteric Christian church has to offer.

Perhaps one of the most challenging problems to our acceptance of this is one of language. Does this mean that Christ is a "Faery"? When we remember that the Elven/Faery race are not tiny grotesque creatures lurking under toadstools but tall, shining beings of great beauty and grace who possess immense wisdom, knowledge and understanding and who inspire and bring light and love to all who come into contact with them, then we are halfway there, but the whole truth is that Christ was both human *and* Faery. He is of the original root race from which both human and Faery evolved, and it is this which makes him the avatar for the future of both races.

What, if anything, in Christ's recorded life would lead us to believe that there is any truth in this proposition? In so far as his life is recounted to us in the Bible, very little. The Bible offers scant clues as to the actual basis of the new religion that grew so rapidly after his death. Christ himself appears as a charismatic figure who possessed supernatural abilities and was obviously a gifted and challenging speaker, yet his words as recorded in the Gospels hardly offer a sound basis for an entirely new religion. Even more puzzling is Christ's connection with the Jewish faith. He was born a Jew and called 'Rabbi' yet was obviously at odds with the established voice of Judaism. The writers of the New Testament try hard to make the connection between the events of Christ's life and the prophecies of the Old Testament which he was said to fulfil, but convincing links between the Old and New Testaments are thin on the ground.

Yet the fact remains that by the very circumstances of his life in the Promised Land and his death in Jerusalem, for many people Christ somehow fulfilled a purpose which had been held within that land and within the beliefs of its Priesthood. It is less widely acknowledged that this Priesthood retained a close connection with the beings of what we now call the Faery race.

One of the most tantalising but often quoted statements concerning Christ's purpose is that he was a Priest after the order of Melchizedek. The author of the Letter to the Hebrews declares: "And no man taketh this honour unto himself (*i.e. the honour of becoming High Priest*), but he that is called of God, as was Aaron. So also Christ glorified not himself to be made an high priest; but he that said unto him, Thou art my Son, today have I begotten thee." [9] And again, "And being made perfect, he became the author of eternal salvation unto all them that obey him; Called of God an high priest after the order of Melchizedek." [10] Later, the writer makes a clearer distinction between the Levitical order of High Priests of which Aaron was the first, and those of the order of Melchizedek: "If therefore perfection were by the Levitical priesthood, (for under it the people received the law,) what further need was there that another priest should rise after the order of Melchizedek, and not be called after the order of Aaron? … for that after the similitude of Melchizedek there ariseth another priest, Who is made, not after the law of a carnal commandment, but after the power of an endless life." [11] The distinction could hardly be put more plainly.

In addition to the reference to the High Priest Melchizedek, it is also interesting to note that Christ is referred to as a High Priest. There was only one acknowledged High Priest within the Temple of Jerusalem, it being the sole office which permitted, once a year, entry into the innermost sanctum of the Temple: the Debir or Holy of Holies. We know that the High Priest of the Jerusalem Temple in Christ's time was Caiaphas, so of which Temple, then, was Christ the High Priest? The title implies that he was the head of a formal order of the Priesthood, an image at odds with that offered by the authors of the Gospels whose picture of Jesus is of one who informally preached his message as he walked amongst the hills of Judea and by the Sea of Galilee. It is hard to escape the implication that Christ was acknowledged amongst some of his contemporaries and followers as belonging to an order of the Priesthood, yet an order which was not acknowledged by the Jerusalem Temple.

This line of Priesthood, though rarely referred to and even more rarely recorded, can nonetheless be traced to its source. In order to do so we must turn to some of the many writings contemporaneous to those which were eventually chosen to make up the Bible but which were, for various reasons, excluded. One of the most interesting in this regard is the group of texts known as the *Books of Enoch*.[12] Enoch himself is mentioned in the Bible[13] as one who eventually "walked with God", but before the time when he was seen no more among men, he was a frequent visitor to a world slightly removed from the physical world, a world inhabited by tall, shining beings whom we would now recognise as Faeries. Enoch is such an eloquent witness of what he saw that it is hard to believe his account to be anything other than that of an eye-witness. He did not know the word

'Faery' but there can be little doubt that he encountered Faery beings and was able to freely communicate with them.

Among many fascinating visions and periods of instruction, of particular interest is his visit to the Garden of Eden. Accompanied by the Angel Michael, he is shown a range of seven mountains. The Tree of Life (i.e. the *second* tree as described in Genesis) is growing on one of these mountains, and Michael gives Enoch an explanation of this tree that adds considerably to what we are told in Genesis. Enoch describes what he saw: "And the seventh mountain was in the midst of these, and it excelled them in height, resembling the seat of a throne: and fragrant trees encircled the throne. And amongst them was a tree such as I had never yet smelt, neither was any amongst them nor were others like it: it had a fragrance beyond all fragrance, and its leaves and blooms and wood withered not for ever: and its fruit is beautiful, and its fruit resembles the dates of a palm." [14]

Enoch asks Michael what the significance of the tree is, and is told: "And as for this fragrant tree no mortal is permitted to touch it till the great judgement, when He shall take vengeance on all and bring (everything) to its consummation for ever. It shall then be given to the righteous and holy." [15] When the fruit has been eaten by the righteous, "…its fragrance shall be in their bones, And they shall live a long life on earth, Such as thy fathers lived: And in their days shall no sorrow or plague Or torment or calamity touch them." [16] This is clearly the second tree in the Garden of Eden, not the Tree of Knowledge but the Tree of Life, the White Tree of Immortality, the Faery Tree.

Later, Enoch sees another tree. "And I came to the Garden of Righteousness and saw … the tree of wisdom whereof they eat and know great wisdom." [17] This time it is the Angel Raphael who explains "This is the tree of wisdom, of which thy father old (in years) and thy aged mother, who were before thee, have eaten, and they learnt wisdom and their eyes were opened, and they knew they were naked …"

In accordance with Genesis, Adam and Eve have already eaten of the Tree of Knowledge and are now forbidden to eat from the Tree of Life. The reason why this Tree must not be touched is because it has been reserved for some of those amongst the human race who, in the far distant future, will be offered the ability to once again live for a very long time, and in a manner which is removed from the sorrows and restrictions of the physical world. In other words, those who can eat from this tree will become as Faeries or Elves, regaining the level of existence of the other half of the original, single root race that comprises those who inhabit the earth.

The Book of Enoch explains that the White Tree contains a substance which, when eaten, will bring about a change of state such that those who eat it will find their life-span on earth literally and substantially increased. The property of the Tree of Life that will confer this ability is likened to a fragrance that will have a physiological effect on the densest part of the human anatomy: the skeletal structure.

These strange and miraculous properties contained in the Tree of Life are also mentioned in other early texts. An early Gnostic sect, the so-called Ophite Gnostics, refer to it in one of their initiation rituals. Origen, a Christian theologian writing in c.250 AD describes how one of these rituals appears to have been based upon a diagrammatic representation of creation consisting of seven (or ten) circles circumscribed by one circle and divided by a thick black line. [18] Part of the ceremony connected with this representation of the universe involved the initiate receiving a 'seal' and saying: "I have been anointed with the *white chrism* which flows from the tree of life." [19] (My italics.) A later passage states: "Everywhere there is the Tree of Life and a resurrection of flesh from the tree." And "They are taught to say, after passing through the barrier of the Tree of Life … 'Let Grace be with me, Father, let it be with me.'" [20]

This suggests that the fruit of the Tree of Life is actually a substance excreted by the tree, perhaps a kind of sap which, when consumed, has an effect on the human body such that it does not age in the normal manner. The tree also seems to be representative of a barrier to be crossed, as if it acts as a veil or a gate between two planes of existence which are represented on the diagram by the black line which divides the spheres of the Cosmos. It would also of course be a diagrammatic representation of the division between the two races of Faery and human. Once this veil, or change of state, has successfully been passed through, the initiate no longer depends on physical food but asks that he or she should now receive the Grace that will be his or her sustenance from then on. Significantly, the colour of this mysterious substance, the chrism, is white.

Elsewhere the chrism is described as an oil, or resin. Clement, Bishop of Rome at the end of the first century AD describes how "The Son of God, the beginning of all things, became Man. Him first God anointed with oil which was taken from the wood of the Tree of Life." [21] By way of contrast, the author describes how Aaron, the first High Priest from the time of Moses, "was anointed with '*a composition*' of chrism, which was made after the pattern of the spiritual ointment …" [22] (My italics.) Clement asks, with good reason, that if this man-made substance was found to have contained some efficacy then it should be considered how much more potent would the real thing have been! We are not told why Aaron was anointed with a substitute chrism but the inference is clear: the line of Priesthood which descended from Aaron was not the original line and it did not have access to the unique and transformative properties of the chrism from the Tree of Life.

The knowledge and use of this mysterious white substance continued well into the Christian Era. *The Gospel of Philip*, probably compiled in the second half of the third century AD, testifies to a continued appreciation of the significance of the Tree of Life and of the use and meaning of chrism. [23] The author of this Gospel (who was probably not the apostle Philip) states that the terms 'Christ' and 'Christians' come from the word 'chrism'. We need not necessarily take this at face value, but there is no doubt that a close connection was made in the author's mind between Christ and the life-enhancing substance which issued from the Tree of Life.

The author of the Gospel of Philip is particularly concerned with the symbolism and meaning of the holy sacraments, of which several are listed that are not now recognised by the Church. "The lord [did] everything in a mystery, a baptism and a chrism and a eucharist and a redemption and a bridal chamber." [24] This list seems to indicate a natural progression from the first sacrament of baptism to the ultimate sacrament which took place within the bridal chamber or Holy of Holies, which latter is clearly something not recognised by the exoteric Church. Fascinating though this might be, it is the reference to the use of the chrism that is of particular interest here. It is described thus: "The fire is the chrism, the light is the fire. I am not referring to that fire which has no form, *but to the other fire whose form is white*, which is bright and beautiful, and which gives beauty." [25]

The author attempts to describe something almost beyond words, though he is as precise as possible. He draws a distinction between "fire which has no form," by which he presumably means the perceptible flames of an earthly fire; and another kind of fire which does possess form, and which is white, bright, beautiful and confers its property of beauty onto those who receive it. The similarity between the white fire called chrism, and the white fire which is the life-sustaining substance, the blood of the Faery race, is persuasive.

The ability to receive and be sustained by this white fire is one that characterised those of the line of Priesthood which, separate from that of Aaron was referred to as the Priesthood of Melchizedek. The Book of Enoch has more to say on this Priesthood, and describes how Enoch (whose name means "The Founder") was the first to be anointed by the true chrism from the White Tree. The Second Book of Enoch tells how, when Enoch was first taken into another (Faery) world he was made one of them. "And Michael extracted me from my clothes. He anointed me with the delightful oil; and the appearance of that oil is greater than the greatest light.... And I gazed at all of myself, and I had become like one of the glorious ones, and there was no observable difference." [26]

After Enoch, the continuing descent and lineage of this line of Priesthood is also described in the Books of Enoch. Enoch himself lived for 365 years. After his death, his son Methusalam became High Priest. Methusalam's son Lamekh had two sons, Noe (better known as Noah) and Nir. Methusalam invested Nir with the office of Priesthood, passing on all his wisdom.

Nir's wife Sopanim found herself to be pregnant, although Nir had not slept with her since he had become Priest, and she in any case had been barren for many years. She gave birth to a miraculous child at the very moment of her own death, and when Noe and Nir came to bury her they found what appeared to be a three year old child sitting upon the bed who spoke and blessed the Lord. They saw the recognised symbol of the priesthood upon his chest, so they bathed him and dressed him in the robes of the priesthood, and gave him some holy bread, and named him Melchizedek.

A great lawlessness was beginning to spread over the earth at this time and, worried as to the fate of the child, Nir asked the Lord what was to happen. The Lord explained that he was about to send the Flood, but that Melchizedek would not be affected by it as he would be taken up and placed within the paradise of Eden where he would remain safe until the waters receded. (This suggests that the area known as the Garden of Eden was an actual, not symbolic, location.) When the flood had abated, said the Lord, Melchizedek would become priest to all priests, the head of all future priests and also, in retrospect, would be recognised as the head of a line of 13 priests which had existed previously. Eventually there would be another Melchizedek who would be the first of a line of 12 priests, and the last of these would be the greatest of them all. This last would be both priest and king in a place called "Akhuzan", the centre of the earth and where Adam had buried his son Abel, a location which can perhaps be identified as Jerusalem. [27]

There is much of interest here. It would certainly appear that the last of this line of priesthood, the one who was to be the greatest of them all, was Christ. Also interesting is the statement that the Melchizedek born of Sopanim was one of a line of 13 priests, because so far as the Book of Enoch tells us there had only been four: Enoch, Methusalam, Lamekh and Nir. If Enoch was not the first of this line but it actually stretched far into the past, we are left with the suggestion that the priesthood Christ was heir to was of a more ancient origin even than Enoch.

Much has been written upon the archetypal significance of Adam and Eve's three sons, Abel, Cain and Seth. Most of this debate is extraneous to this study apart from interesting verses in Genesis which give two different lines of descent from Adam to Lamekh, grandfather of Melchizedek – one through Abel and one through Seth.

Genesis 4: 17–18 names six generations from Adam to Lamekh: Adam, *Cain*, Enoch, Irad, Mehujael, Methushael, Lamekh. This list is immediately followed by another, different list. Such an odd mistake gives the impression that the compilers of this part of Genesis knew that something of importance was hidden in these two lists of names such that they could not be omitted from the record, yet for some reason they were unable to make any elucidating comment. Genesis 5: 2–27 gives the line of descent as Adam, *Seth*, Enosh, Kenan, Mahalalel, Jared, Enoch, Methusalah, Lamekh. The first version names Lamekh's sons as Jabal, Jubal and Tubal-cain, while the second names his only son as Noah. Neither version makes mention of Lamekh's son Nir, nor of course is Nir's son Melchizedek mentioned at all as the Bible insists that Melchizedek had neither father nor mother.

Fortunately we have a third version of the line of descent in 2 Enoch,[28] which names Enoch's ancestors as Adam, Seth, Enos, Kainan, Maleleil and Ared his father, thus duplicating the second version in Genesis. As the Books of Enoch deal more openly than the Bible with the lineage of Melchizedek this tends to confirm that the line of Melchizedek Priesthood came through Seth, not Cain. It is no coincidence that the Gnostics favoured this line; Seth and his descendants were recognised by them as the bearers of the Gnostic tradition and of the hidden knowledge of Adam. (Masonic lore, on the other hand, gives more prominence to the line of descent from Cain through Jabal, Jubal and Tubal-cain.)

Although it is clear even in the Bible that the Melchizedekian line of priesthood was not the same as that initiated by Aaron and was probably far older, the Bible gives no clue as to the difference between them and the former is almost entirely ignored apart from the tantalising hints in the Letter to the Hebrews. Yet there must have been a persistent and significant difference, one that ran far deeper than superficial differences of opinion over matters of Temple etiquette. Abraham was probably not of the Melchizedek line. Although Melchizedek brought bread and wine to Abraham in acknowledgement and recognition of Abraham as *a* priest, he would not have done so if Abraham was himself the High Priest, nor is there any indication that this is the record of the making of a High Priest in the order of Melchizedek.

But whether or not the divergent lines of Priesthood existed happily side by side or, more likely, the Melchizedek line became increasingly withdrawn, the rift was literally set in stone when the Israelites emerged from exile in Egypt. Their leader, Moses, received a new set of instructions from Jahweh and a new religion was founded in tablets of stone. Based on the identification of Jahweh with the One God, this religion formed the substance of the set of writings which came to be called the Holy Bible and the basis of popular belief for several thousand years.

But at the heart of the Melchizedek Priesthood was guarded the knowledge of the two races of Faery and human, of their original unity, of their division into 'Elves and Men', and the knowledge of their ultimate task to find a way in which they could once more re-unite. We have traced the line of the Melchizedek Priesthood back to Seth, and forward to Christ, but what came next? If we look to the Christianity of the Church we will find no trace of the continuing work of this ancient Priesthood. Yet in John's description of Christ's death, in the two streams of the blood and the water, in the esoteric Christianity which also emphasises the red and the white, human and Faery, and in the many clues which are given to us in the Arthurian and Grail literature, we may discover the nature and practice of the Priesthood of the order of Melchizedek.

After Christ's death, the function of Melchizedek Priest was also released; not through the established Christian Church but through the esoteric Christian movement brought by Joseph of Arimathea to Britain and then, coming full circle, back into the Faery race.

The long line of Grail Guardians are Priests of the order of Melchizedek, and the Mysteries of this order are now in the safe keeping of the Guardians of the Grail. Christ, the greatest High Priest of them all, brought these Mysteries to their greatest manifesation within the human world but he marked the turning point of their evolution. After his death they passed from the outer world of men to the Inner world of Faery, as did the Faery weapons of Cup, Sword, Spear and Stone which had played their part so distinctively in the passion of Christ also return to the Inner Kingdoms of Faery from which they had originated.

The Grail legends are the liturgy of the Priesthood of Melchizedek. Their rituals are recorded in the stories of the quests of the Arthurian knights who sought the Faery Kingdom and the Grail Castle at its centre yet struggled to accept the reality of what they witnessed there.

The last two thousand years have witnessed a curious anomaly in which these ancient rituals of interaction between Faery and human have become increasingly externalised and made available to the population at large, yet the very process by which they have become common knowledge has simultaneously resulted in them becoming almost completely overlooked as a source of Inner Wisdom. Even when they were first committed to paper these rituals were occulted and their real significance was disguised. There is no doubt that many of the Arthurian and Grail chroniclers had access to this Inner wisdom. The enduring strength which underpins these stories and ensures their continuing attraction stems from the realities which lie hidden within them: they are memories of the rituals of an ancient order of the Priesthood which serves the combined Mysteries of Faery and human. The Priests of this order still call to their own, and the modern day seeker, just as the Arthurian knights of old, may hear their call and, spurred by faith and no little grace shall find their way to serve within the heart of the Grail Castle.

But while it is for the knights to seek out these Mysteries and ask their meaning, it is those such as Melusine, Étaín and above all Gwenevere, who leave behind their birthright of the Immortal Clan of Faery and enter into the human world, to cajole and inspire any who have heard the faint call of Faery to take the first step towards the most importance alliance our planet will witness.

1   A.E. Waite, *The Hidden Church of the Holy Grail* (London: Rebman Ltd, 1909)

2   As in the First Continuation to Chrétien discussed in Chapter 12

3   In the *Parzival* of Wolfram von Eschenbach, Percivale's father (here called Gahmuret) is buried in a magnificent tomb in a far distant land, but is worshipped as a God in a manner very similar to the veneration of the dead King Garlon. Wolfram von Eschenbach trans. T Hatto, *Parzival* (London: Penguin Classics, 1980)

4   One of the fullest versions is found in Robert de Boron's Trilogy, trans. Nigel Bryant, *Merlin and the Grail: Joseph of Arimathea* (Cambridge: D.S.Brewer, 2001)

5   ibid, page 31

6   The gift of the sword Excalibur is the best known example of this: a gift which, as we have seen, was precipitous of the events which led to the Dolorous Blow.

7   *King James Bible*, John 19, 34-36

8   Both carols appear in *Notes and Queries,* 10 S., IV, Sept. 2nd, 1905

9   *King James Bible*, Letter to the Hebrews 5.4-7

10 ibid, 9-10

11 ibid, 7.11, and 15-16

12 Several versions exist, the only complete one being that translated from the Ethiopian. Parts of these texts appear to have been written in the Maccabean period of c1750 BC.

13 Genesis 5, 18-24

14 Ed. R. H. Charles, *Translations of Early Documents Series 1: Palestinian Jewish Texts: The Book of Enoch* (London: Society for Promoting Christian Knowledge, 1925) page 50

15 ibid, page 51

16 ibid, page 51

17 ibid, page 54

18 Quoted in ed. Willis Barnstone, *The Other Bible,* from Origen, *Contra Celsum*, vi. 24-38. Quoted in Robert M. Grant, *Gnosticism* (New York: Harper & Brothers, 1961) pages 52-59

19 *The Other Bible,* page 665

20 ibid, page 666

21 from *The Clementine Recognitions,* cited by Margaret Barker, *The Great High Priest* (London: T & T Clark Ltd, 2003) page 133

22 ibid, page 133

23 Quoted in ed. James M Robertson, *The Nag Hammadi Library in English* (New York: E.J. Brill, 1977) pages 139 -160

24 ibid, page 150

25 ibid, page 150

26 Ed. James H. Charlesworth, *The Old Testament Pseudepigrapha* (London: Darton, Longman and Todd. 1983) page 139

27 ibid, *The Second Book of Enoch*

28 ibid, page 156

CHAPTER FOURTEEN
A Guided Journey to the Ship of Solomon

The following is a guided meditation based on the symbolism of the Ship of Solomon. It shows how the Inner Wisdom hidden within this story from Arthurian legend can be brought into reality through the individual involvement of the reader. Ideally it should be read by one person to another, or to a group, but the lone seeker will find that it works very well simply to read it through several times in order to commit it to memory, and then re-live it in the imagination.

First, enter into a state of meditation ...
We rise in vision until we can see below us the continent of Europe and, to the South, the Mediterranean Sea. And let us move in vision further south and towards the Middle East ... and below us now are the lands of the Fertile Crescent. We are looking at the landscape of three thousand years ago. To the North lie the restless mountainous regions of central Europe. To the East are the most ancient lands of Sumer, watered by the Tigris and Euphrates. And we see the Holy Land, and the rift valley of the Jordan running North-South. And still further south, the vast land-mass of Africa and the Nile running North until it spreads into the lotus of the delta.

Let us now slowly descend in vision to where the blue sea of the Mediterranean gives way to the rocky shore of the Holy Land. We see a small bay surrounded by cliffs, and moored upon the shore, a wooden ship. We descend further and find ourselves standing upon this shore, where the ship lies quietly before us. It appears to be deserted, yet a wooden plank has been made ready for us to board, should we so wish. The deck of the ship is bare of the usual accoutrements, and all that is visible is what seems to be a small chamber built of reeds, set at the centre. Across the entrance to the chamber hangs a heavy, embroidered curtain.

We pause for a moment, aware of the significance of our actions, and then slowly walk up the swaying plank onto the ship. Tentatively, we approach the curtained chamber. A rich odour of cedarwood incense hangs upon its folds. We draw the curtain aside, and step into the chamber. It is lit dimly by candles. We pause, and allow our eyes to become accustomed to the gloom.

We find that we are standing at the foot of what appears to be a large wooden bed made of great planks of cedarwood. It has no board at its head or foot, and is simply a raised platform. Before us, laid upon the floor at the foot of the bed, is a wondrous sword, sheathed in a great scabbard, and hung on a rough hempen belt. We reach towards it, but hesitate and draw back, content only to observe. The sword's hilt is made of two strange, fish-like shapes, of a substance we cannot identify. They seem to be far older than the golden blade. And the pommel of the hilt is also of a substance which cannot be metal, for it appears to contain every colour of the spectrum within its sphere. And these colours are fluid, as if what we are seeing is a vision of the sphere of the earth itself, in miniature.

We look at the head of the bed, and upon the floor stands a tall golden crown encrusted with many fabulous jewels. Again, we make no move to touch this hallowed object, but wonder at the mighty king who wore it, for its fabulous shape is unlike any which has graced a human head.

We know the significance of these objects, and of what may be the consequences if we choose to lie upon this bed. This is the Perilous Bed, and those who lie upon it take upon themselves the mantle of those who participate in service of the Western Mysteries. These Mysteries cannot be entered upon lightly, nor in a spirit of curiosity. Even now, we may withdraw with no blame.

We decide to continue. With reverence, we gently climb upon the bed and lie down upon its hard and unforgiving wood. We wonder if we should close our eyes, but find that even with this thought the chamber about us subtly begins to alter in appearance. The reed walls begin gently to shift and rustle, as if they were composed of living plants, and then expand so that we are no longer lying in a small chamber but in an orchard filled with many tall trees. We allow our senses to explore our surroundings. The trees are familiar, yet not so, for their form and substance is fluid and ever-moving. We see familiar shapes of trunk, leaf and branch, yet these forms are not fixed in colour or shape but appear to our vision as a moving kaleidoscope of living light. We see the upward surging of the sap, the inner life of the trees which takes life and sustenance to their every part, as if their outer form were translucent. And birds with radiant plumage of colours not of this world move about the trees, and their voices are liquid, and remind us of songs we once knew but had forgotten.

We become aware that at our right hand grows a tall tree whose trunk, branches and leaves are entirely red. Not a uniform red, but all shades of scarlet and crimson. We are able to see within the trunk of the tree, and perceive the sap. This red sap is like blood. We can sense the energy of this tree. It is strong and vigorous, yet also turbulent and restless, as if its life-energy still searched in discontent for a perfect form of expression. The shadow of this tree falls upon us. We know that we are of its root and stock. This is the tree of our ancestors, and every growth and movement of the human race is held within it. Here is every strength, every weakness, every war and every achievement of our human family.

And now we become aware that at our left hand grows a second tree. Its trunk, branches and leaves are entirely white. Not uniformly white, but all shades of silver, of milky opal, of the palest violet, and of many other pale and shining colours which lie beyond the visible spectrum. We are able to see within the trunk of this tree, and are aware of the energy which flows within it. We can sense its qualities: purity, harmony, serenity, and peace. We wonder how to make connection with this tree, and as we form the thought, a single leaf gently detaches and drifts downwards onto our open hand. We hold the leaf without grasping it, grateful for the gift.

Our inner vision is opened to this White Tree of Faery and we become aware of its intimate connection with the inner powers of the land, and of its effortless and harmonious expression of those powers. And we become aware that this tree grows so tall that it touches the stars, and draws down their substance into its leaves, so that a perfect synthesis is attained between stars and inner earth.

And we become aware of the power that this single leaf is working upon the red shadow which falls upon us. Its pure and harmonious energy flows into the red. The red becomes lighter and brighter, its turbulence giving way to serenity, until it shines with its own inner light. We are able to incorporate the blessings of the White Tree of Faery into our human bodies.

And now we become aware that a tall figure is standing at our feet. He is robed in shining white. His face is radiant; his head crowned with the wondrous crown which had been placed at the head of the bed. He holds before him the sword, now unsheathed. Its golden blade shines with a light which dazzles our eyes. We wonder what can be his name, and words drift into our mind ... Galahad, Gil-Galad ... he is both of these and more.

He raises the sword above his head, its point held high as if it would touch the highest star. Its light is reflected down upon us and unites all lights, all shadows, all colours, as One. And we are aware, above our heads, of the conjoining of the Two Trees in a perfect harmony, their mingled lights now shining with a deep and vibrant green.

The scenes about us begin to fade. The figure, the trees and the orchard disappear, giving way once more to the reed walls of the chamber of the Perilous Bed. Slowly we rise to our feet, and with a final glance at the chamber, draw aside the door-curtain and find ourselves in the sunlight upon the deck of the ship.

And we know that as we walk back along the plank to the shore so we will walk back to our own place and time, of here, and now.

BIBLIOGRAPHY

Adams, Alison, ed., *The Romance of Yder,* Cambridge: D.S. Brewer, 1983.

Baigent, Michael; Leigh, Richard and Lincoln, Henry, *The Holy Blood and the Holy Grail,* London: Jonathan Cape, 1982.

Barker, Margaret, *The Great High Priest: The Temple Roots of Christian Liturgy,* London: T&T Clark Ltd, 2003.

Barnstone, Willis, ed., *The Other Bible: Ancient Esoteric Texts,* San Francisco: Harper San Francisco, 1984 P.

Bartrum, P. C., *Welsh Genealogies AD 300–1400,* Cardiff: University of Wales Press, 1974.

Berg, Wendy and Harris, Mike, *Polarity Magic,* St Paul, Minnesota: Llewellyn Publications, 2003.

de Boron, Robert, trans. Nigel Bryant, *Merlin and the Grail,* Cambridge: D.S. Brewer, 2001.

de Boron, Robert, trans. Nigel Bryant, *Merlin and the Grail: Joseph of Arimathea,* Cambridge: D.S. Brewer, 2001.

Bromich, R., *Trioedd Ynys Prydein,* Cardiff: University of Wales Press, 1961.

Bryant, Nigel, *The High Book of the Holy Grail,* Cambridge: D.S. Brewer, 1996.

Charles, R.H., *Translations of Early Documents Series 1: Palestinian Jewish Texts: The Book of Enoch,* London: Society for Promoting Christian Knowledge, 1925.

Charlesworth, James, H., *The Old Testament Pseudepigrapha,* London: Darton, Longman and Todd, 1983.

Chrétien de Troyes, trans. D. D. R. Owen, *Arthurian Romances,* London: Everyman, 1986.

Chrétien de Troyes, trans. Nigel Bryant, *Perceval: The Story of the Grail,* Cambridge: D.S. Brewer, 1982.

Coghlan, Ronan, *The Illustrated Encycolopaedia of Arthurian Legends,* London: Vega, 2002.

John Darrah, *Paganism in Arthurian Romance,* Cambridge: D.S. Brewer, 1997.

Fletcher, R. H., *Arthurian Material in the Chronicles,* Boston: Ginn, 1906.

Fortune, Dion, *The Sea Priestess,* London: Aquarian Press, 1957.

Foster, Robert, *The Complete Guide to Middle Earth*, London: Unwin Paperbacks, 1978.

Geoffrey of Monmouth, *The History of the Kings of Britain*, trans. Lewis Thorpe, Middlesex: Penguin, 1966.

Guest, Lady Charlotte, trans., *The Mabinogion*, London: J.M. Dent and Sons, 1906.

Harris, Mike, *Awen: The Quest of the Celtic Mysteries*, Oceanside, California: Sun Chalice Books, 1999.

Harrison, Jane, *Prolegomena*, Cambridge: Cambridge University Press, 1903; reprinted by Princetown University Press, 1991.

Hartley, Christine, *The Western Mystery Tradition*, Wellingborough: Aquarian Press, 1986.

Heinrich von dem Türlin, *Diu Crône*, ed. G. H. F. Scholl, Suttgart: Bibliothek de Littevarischen Vereins, Vol XXVIII, 1852.

Hope, Murry, *The Sirius Connection*, Shaftesbury: Element Books, 1996.

Jung, Emma and von Franz, Marie-Louise, trans. Andrea Dykes, *The Grail Legend*, London: Coventure, 1986.

Knight, Gareth, *The Magical World of the Inklings*, Shaftesbury: Element Books, 1990; new edition by Skylight Press, 2010.

Knight, Gareth, *The Secret Tradition in Arthurian Legend*, York Beach: Weiser, 1996.

Lacy, Norris J., ed., *The Lancelot Grail Reader*, New York: Garland Publishing Inc., 2000.

Loomis, Roger Sherman, *Celtic Myth and Arthurian Romance*, London: Constable, 1993.

Macalister, R. A., trans. and ed., *Lebor Gabála Érenn: The Book of Invasions of Ireland*, Dublin: Irish Text Society, 5 vols, 1938-56 .

McCall, Alexander and McCall, William, *The Historic Artur, Gwenhwyvawr and Myrddin, Ancient Brythons of the North*, Durham: The Pentland Press Ltd, 1997.

Macleod, Fiona, arr. Mrs William Sharp, *The Collected Works of Fiona Macleod, 7 vols.*, London: William Heinemann, 1912.

Macleod, Fiona, arr. Mrs William Sharp, *Selected Writings of William Sharp, 5 vols.*, London: William Heinemann, 1912.

Malory, Thomas, ed. Janet Cowen, *Le Morte D'Arthur*, London: Penguin Books, 1961.

Matthews, Caitlín, *Arthur and the Sovereignty of Britain*, London: Arkana, 1979.

Matthews Caitlín, *Mabon and the Mysteries of Britain*, London: Arkana, 1987.

Matthews, John and Green, Marian, *The Grail Seekers' Companion,* Wellingborough: Aquarian Press, 1986.

Nash, D. W., trans., *Preiddeu Annwn (The Spoils of Annwn)* from *Taliesin and the Bards or Druids of Britain,* London: J. Russell, Smith, 1858.

O'Brien, Christian and O'Brien Barbara Joy, *The Shining Ones,* Cirencester: Dianthus Publishing Ltd, 1997.

Rees, Alwyn and Rees, Brinley, *Celtic Heritage: Ancient Tradition in Ireland and Wales,* London: Thames and Hudson, 1961.

Robinson, James, ed., *The Nag Hammadi Library,* Leiden: Brill, 1988.

Rolfe, Mona, *Initiation by the Nile,* London: Neville Spearman Ltd, 1976.

Santillana, Giorgio de, and von Dechend, Hertha, *Hamlet's Mill,* Boston: Godine, 1977.

Tolkien, J.R.R., *The Lord of the Rings,* London: George Allen and Unwin Ltd, 1954.

Tolkien, J.R.R., *The Silmarillion,* London: George Allen and Unwin Ltd, 1977.

Ulrich von Zazikhoven, ed. K. A. Hahn, *Der Lanzelet,* Frankfurt: 1845.

Vidler, Mark, *The Star Mirror,* London: Thorsons, 1998.

Wace and Lawman, *The Life of King Arthur,* trans. Judith Weiss and Rosamund Allen, London: J.M. Dent, Everyman Paperbacks, 1997.

Waite, A. E., *The Hidden Church of the Holy Grail,* London: Rebman Ltd. 1909.

Webster, G. T., *Guinevere: A Study of her Abductions,* Milton, Massachusetts: The Turtle Press, 1951.

West, John Anthony, *Serpent in the Sky,* Illinois: Quest Books, The Theosophical Publishing House, 1993.

Wolfram von Eschenbach, trans. T. Hatto, *Parzival,* London: Penguin Classics, 1980.

INDEX

abduction 67, 86, 94, 115, 117
Abel 42–3, 180–1
Adam 22–26, 29, 36, 42–3, 177, 180–1
Agravaine 10
Ambrosius Aurelianus 52–5, 78
Amlawdd Wledig 47, 49–50, 56–7, 61, 79, 129
Anoeth 47, 48, 53
Apocrypha 13, 176–80
Aragorn 36, 40, 140–1, 161
Archangels 32, 33, 177
archetypes 7, 10–11, 79, 107, 115
Arimathea, Joseph of 107, 166, 168–70, 172, 174, 182
Arthur, King 7–14, 38–39, 46–9, 52–3, 56, 58–61, 63–71, 73–97, 99–101, 106–111, 113, 115–125, 129–132, 134–35, 138–43, 145–154, 158, 161–163, 165, 168, 171
   attitude to Faery 12, 63, 90–91, 96, 129–132, 138, 143, 145
   destiny of 68, 71, 90–1, 138–9, 141
   marriage to Gwenevere 7, 11, 14, 66, 68, 74, 80, 86, 90, 123, 131, 134
   parentage 56, 66–7, 69, 122
Arwen 20, 29, 36, 161
Atalantë 31, 36
Atlantis 21–2, 31, 34–35, 46–47, 51, 58–59, 68–71, 75, 110, 122, 140–1
Avalon 38, 43–4, 48, 125, 142, 144, 148, 163, 171, 174
Avebury 49, 52
Bademagu 93, 97, 105, 109–11, 113, 139
Balan 148–9, 164
Balin 108, 122, 137–8, 143, 145–9, 151–5, 158, 160–5, 174

bed 41, 104, 163, 173, 186
Bendigran 75
Berenice 106
Bertelay 89, 92–3, 127
Bible 13, 23, 25–6, 31, 34, 38, 42, 45, 113, 169, 171, 175–6, 181–2
blood 14, 36, 41–43, 52, 60, 67, 69, 77, 109–10, 112–3, 123, 136, 140, 151–2, 157, 160–2, 166–9, 171–4, 179, 182, 187
Bors 119, 160
Bran 108
British Isles
   mystery tradition 43, 45–6, 56
   stellar alignments 48–9, 54
Caerdoel 119–20, 129, 135
Cain 42, 181
Camelot 8, 75, 87, 93–95, 100, 142
Carmelide (Cameliard) 10, 75, 88, 93, 140
Carohaise 75
Castle Meliot 160–1
Castle of Maidens 130–1
Castle Terrabil 149–50
Celeborn 35
Celidon, Forest of 58–9
Ceridwen 59
chakras 51
Chrétien de Troyes 66, 120–1, 172
chrism 178–80
Christ 45, 54, 71, 104, 126, 136, 157–9, 161, 166–9, 171–6, 179–82
Cilydd 47, 57–60
constellations 45, 49–50, 52, 61, 77
   Coma Berenice 106, 108
   Draco 48–9, 52, 54, 78
   Leo 77, 106
   Little Bear 52
Cornwall 9, 59, 65–7, 73, 75, 124, 148

Corpus Christi carol 172
Culhwch 47, 57–8, 60–5, 68, 76, 92
Custennin 56–7, 64
Cynwal Hundred-Hogs 56–8
Dalua 125–6
Dindrane 41, 106, 139, 160–1
Dolorous Blow 137–8, 142, 147, 149, 165
Dolorous River 107
dragon energy 48–9, 52–4, 76
Dweller on the Threshold 104
Egypt 52, 77–8, 106, 111, 128, 141, 182
Elves 13, 31–8, 40, 44, 56, 71, 78, 110, 139, 140–1, 146, 177, 182
Enoch 176–81
Eochaidh, King 126–7
Étaín 20, 28, 125–8, 183
Eve 22–6, 36, 42–3, 121, 177, 181
evolution 12, 21, 23, 34, 85, 135
Excalibur 39, 94, 107–8, 124, 139, 145, 152, 171, 183
Faery
  entrance to 54, 63–4, 92, 97, 99, 102–3, 117, 126, 138, 142, 153–6, 170
  kingdoms of 11, 75, 88–9, 93–4, 97, 99, 105, 108, 140, 142, 153–4, 156, 174, 183
  magical weapons 62–3, 104, 136, 138, 171, 174, 182
  marriage to humans 28, 58, 68–9, 74, 86, 91, 123, 125, 128, 135, 144
  nature of 16–22, 51, 82, 144, 161
Faery Priesthood 46, 48, 55, 58, 70–1, 73, 85, 94, 97, 123, 134, 142, 147, 171
Fall, the 20–1, 31, 70
ferryman 107–9
Fisher King 136
Fortune, Dion 68–70
France 54, 68
Gaheris 10

Galahad 38–9, 41, 44, 107, 143, 160, 187
Galathilion 35
Galehaut 87–9, 92–4
Gandalf 36
Garden of Eden 22, 25–6, 28–9, 31, 34, 39–42, 113–4, 121, 177, 180
Gareth 10
Garlin of Galore 117
Garlon 117, 153–4, 159, 161–2, 167, 172, 174, 183
Gasozein le Dragoz 117–9, 126, 134–5
Gawain 10, 86, 89, 92, 102–5, 107, 110, 118–20, 122, 131–2, 134–5, 150, 153–9, 164, 174
Genesis, Book of 13, 22–5, 29, 32, 36, 39, 41–3, 177, 181
Geoffrey of Monmouth 9, 52, 73, 82, 122, 124
Glastonbury 58, 76, 115, 140, 142, 172
Gnostics 13, 26, 178, 181
Gogfran 75–6
Goleuddydd 47, 56–60, 66
Gorlois 66–8, 81, 122
Gorre 93, 95–99, 105–8, 110–1, 120
Gorrun 109–13
Gotegrin 117–8, 120, 134–5, 137
Grail Castle 10, 91, 105, 122, 136–38, 140, 148, 151, 154, 157–62, 164, 165, 168, 170–1, 174, 183
Grail Hallows 5–6, 163, 166, 168, 170–1
Grail King 6, 44, 90–1, 113, 136–7, 140, 147, 153, 157, 159, 161–7, 174–5
Green Tree 14, 43
Guenloie, Queen 130–2
Gweir 56–7, 76
Gwen Alarch 56
Gwenevere 7–14, 20, 29, 38, 46–7, 66, 68, 73–102, 105–6, 108–32, 134–5, 154, 158, 183
  abduction of 8, 83–7, 93–95, 101, 115–20, 134

ancestry 9, 73–6, 116–7

as Faery 11, 14, 73–4, 82–3, 101, 113–5, 118, 125, 183

'false' Gwenevere 81–3, 85, 87–93, 127

lovers 8, 85, 88, 118, 120–22, 124, 128

marriage to Arthur 7, 11–2, 14, 74, 79–80, 83, 85, 88, 118–9, 123–4, 131, 134

Gwen PenDragon 47–50, 56, 67, 79, 129

Gwrfoddw Hen 56–58

Gwyar 56–7

Gwyn ap Nudd 57–8, 76, 129, 140

Gwythyr ap Greidawl 76

hair 106, 108

Hart Fell 58

Holy Grail 8, 10, 38, 46, 69, 90, 115, 135–7, 150, 157, 160, 164–6, 168–9, 171

Ilúvatar 31–3

imagination 13, 16, 39, 127

Immortal Hour, The 28, 125

Inner Planes 38, 41, 43, 56, 59, 64, 71, 100–1, 116, 137

Inner Priesthood 13, 56

Ireland 49, 54, 65, 74, 140

Isis 69–70, 77–78, 137

Jandree 116, 123

Jerusalem 38–40, 168, 170, 175–6, 180

Kay 64, 100–2, 105, 110–3, 122, 131–2, 154

Knights of the Round Table 8, 38, 46, 74, 80, 103, 115, 135

Kundrie 9

Lady of the Lake 9, 88, 94–7, 100–1, 107–8, 120, 125, 127, 141–2, 145–8, 150

Lake of Memory 27

Lancelot 8, 86–8, 94–5, 97, 99–114, 117, 120–2, 124, 149

Laurelin 34

Lebor Gabála Érenn 62

Lemuria 21–2, 31, 34–5, 46–7, 51, 71, 139, 160

Lenomie 117

Leodegrance 10, 75–81, 83, 139

Listenois 75, 140, 153–6, 161, 167, 169–70

Lludd 76

Llygadrudd Emys 56–58

Lord of the Rings, The 13–4, 31, 33, 140, 161

Lot, King 119–20, 149–50, 153

Luned 9

Lyonesse 10, 65, 75, 88

Mabinogion, The 46–48, 62–3

Macleod, Fiona 28

Madeglans of Oriande 116, 123

magical ritual 7, 79, 93, 99, 100–1, 107–8, 113, 121, 152, 156, 165, 170, 178, 183

Mary Magdalene 54, 173

Mary Queen of Scots 86

Melchizedek 125, 175–6, 179–82

Meleagant 93, 95–102, 105, 109–13, 116

Melkor 32–3, 35

Melusine 20, 29, 183

Melwas 115–6

Merlin 8, 46, 53–6, 59–60, 63, 66–71, 73, 79, 81–3, 90, 94, 122–3, 125, 127, 132, 134–5, 138–9, 141, 149–53

Middle Earth 31, 35–6, 38, 40, 44, 140, 161

Midlands 9

Milesians 13, 140

Mordred 8, 86, 93, 119, 122–5, 135, 151

Morgan le Fey 9, 67, 73, 117, 122–24, 127

Morgawse 10, 122, 150

music 18, 32

Narsil 40, 140–1

Nero 149–50

Newgrange 54, 140
Nimloth 35
Nuada, King 129, 166
Nudd 57, 128–9
Númenor 31, 35–6, 140–1
Oeth 47–8, 53
Olwen 47, 58, 60–1, 63–4, 76
orchard 172–4, 186, 188
Orphic tablets 27, 47
Pellam 153, 161, 163
Pellinore, King 138–40, 150, 153, 158, 161, 163
Percivale 10, 41, 106, 136–7, 139, 159, 160–1, 167
Peredhil 36
Perilous Bed 104, 186, 188
Persephone 87
Pole Star 52, 79
Procession of the Grail 10, 136, 162
Prose Lancelot 81, 87, 92–3, 96, 119
purple mantle 63, 173–4
Qabala 40, 111
Red Tree 14, 186
Rhienlwydd 56–7
root race 22, 31, 36, 42, 51, 175, 177
Round Table 10, 66, 73–4, 77–80, 116, 121, 150
Sauron 35, 140, 150
scabbard 40–1, 141–4, 151–2
Scilly, Isles of 75
Scotland 9, 49, 58, 65, 73
Sea Priestess, The 68–70
Secret Gate, The 29
Seth 181–2
Sharp, William 28, 47, 125, 127
Sheba, Queen 38–9, 41
Ship of Solomon 14, 38–9, 41–6, 104, 160, 185
Silbury Hill 49
Silmarillion, The 14, 31, 33, 40, 78, 140, 146
Sirius 52, 77–8
Solar Logos 34
Solomon, King 38–46, 106, 158, 170

song of creation 32
Sorelois 75, 88–9, 93, 120, 140
spear, as magical weapon 61, 104–5, 137, 139, 153–4, 157–9, 162–4, 169–71
spiritual impulse 8, 40, 52
Stonehenge 52, 54–5, 58, 78
Stone of Echymeint 47, 49, 53–5
swineherd 59, 64
sword, as magical weapon 39–41, 61, 138–9, 141, 143–6, 149, 156, 158, 162, 186–7
synaesthesia 18
Tarot 78, 138
Telperion 34–5
Temple of the Sea and the Stars 46, 51, 70–1
Temple of the Sun 46, 51, 70–1
Thomas the Rhymer 92
thorn tree 60–1, 117, 173
Tintagel 8, 58–9, 66–7, 69, 81, 83, 94
Tol Eressëa 35
Tolkien, J.R.R. 13–4, 26, 31–8, 43, 47, 78, 110, 140, 146, 150
tomb 107, 148–9, 153
Tree of Knowledge 22–5, 34, 177
Tree of Life/Immortality 25–6, 28, 31, 34, 42–3, 177–9
Tuatha dé Danaan 13, 54, 62, 74, 129, 140
Twrch Trwyth 64–5
Tywanwedd 56–7, 129
Urien, King 73, 117, 120, 132
Uther PenDragon 48, 52, 66, 68–9, 78, 106, 122, 129
Valar 32–3, 35
Valerin, King 116–7, 120
Venus 106, 125
vesica piscis 100
Vortigern 52–3
Vulgate Cycle 10, 38, 43–4, 75, 79, 120–1
Wales 9, 53, 65, 76
Waste Land 90–1, 164, 172

Well of Forgetfulness 27
Well of Memory 28, 31, 47
Western Mystery Tradition 7, 38, 104,
    135, 186
White Shadow 11, 74
White Tree 14, 31, 34–6, 38, 42–3,
    177–8, 180, 187
Wolfram von Eschenbach 66–7
Yder 128–32
Ygrainne 3, 56, 58, 60, 64, 66–69, 76,
    78, 81, 83, 110, 122–3, 128–9
Ysbaddaden 56, 60–1, 64